The Macintosh iLife

by Jim Heid

Peachpit Press

The Macintosh iLife
Jim Heid

Peachpit Press
1249 Eighth Street
Berkeley, CA 94710
510/524-2178
510/524-2221 (fax)
Find us on the World Wide Web at: www.peachpit.com
To report errors, please send a note to errata@peachpit.com

Peachpit Press is a division of Pearson Education

Editor: Barbara Assadi, BayCreative
Art Direction/Illustration: Arne Hurty, BayCreative
Compositor: Jonathan Woolson
Project Editor, Peachpit Press: Karen Reichstein
Production Coordinator: Lisa Brazieal
Technical Editor: Victor Gavenda
Indexer: Emily Glossbrenner, FireCrystal Communications
Cover design: Arne Hurty, BayCreative

ISBN 0-321-17011-3
9 8 7 6 5 4 3 2
Printed and bound in the United States of America.

For Maryellen,

for my mother,

and in loving memory

of George Heid, my dad.

A master of the analog

hub, he would have

loved this stuff.

George Heid (right), recording direct to disc on a moving train, in the early 1950s.

About the Author

Jim Heid has been working with and writing about personal computers since 1980, when he computerized his home-built ham radio station with a Radio Shack TRS-80 Model I. As Senior Technical Editor of one of the first computer magazines, *Kilobaud Microcomputing*, he began working with Macintosh prototypes in 1983. He began writing for *Macworld* magazine in 1984, and has been a Contributing Editor ever since. He has also written for *PC World, Internet World,* and *Newsweek* magazines, and until recently wrote a weekly, nationally syndicated Macintosh column for the *Los Angeles Times.*

Jim frequently teaches courses in digital video, DVD authoring, and related topics. He has taught at the Kodak Center for Creative Imaging in Camden, Maine, at the University of Hawaii, and at dozens of technology conferences in between. He's also the host and editorial director of iDay, a series of one-day seminars covering iLife and digital-media topics (www.avondalemedia.com).

Jim's interest in audio, photography, and movie-making preceded his passion for personal computers. He got his first reel-to-reel tape recorder—a hand-me-down from his father's recording studio—when he was 10, and his first camera when he was 12. He set up a basement darkroom at 14, and began making home movies at 16.

In the mid-1990s, Jim developed several interactive CD-ROMs, which included video that he edited on a Mac Quadra 840AV. In 1996, he was smitten by the World Wide Web. One year later, he dragged his wife and dog on a seven-week, 10,000-mile road trip to research and write about the Internet's impact on rural America, a trip that was covered by *USA Today,* the *New York Times,* and MSNBC.

Jim's interest in Web publishing led to a book, *HTML & Web Publishing Secrets,* and to a relationship with Thunder Lizard Productions, producers of technology conferences. In 2002, Jim and two Thunder Lizard colleagues co-founded Avondale Media, a video-production company that produces instructional DVDs. As editorial director, he oversees the editorial development and production of DVDs.

Jim lives with his wife and colleague, Maryellen Kelly, and their standard poodle and mascot, Sophie, on a windswept headland near Mendocino, California. On most Wednesday evenings, he co-hosts "Point & Click Radio," a weekly computer radio show, which you can listen to at www.kzyx.org.

Acknowledgements

The Macintosh iLife is the result of the heroic efforts of an exceptional group of people, all of whom have my thanks and admiration.

One of them also has my love. My deepest thanks go to Maryellen Kelly, my wife, colleague, and best friend. Few things are possible without you, and none are enjoyable. I love you!

Next up are the dream teams that helped produce the DVD and book. On the book front, there's the dynamic duo of Barbara Assadi and Arne Hurty, principals of San Francisco's BayCreative. Your design and editorial talent never ceases to amaze me. I'm so glad we're able to work together.

In the production trenches, Jonathan Woolson dug himself in and didn't leave until the layouts glittered, making insightful design and content recommendations all the while. This project would have been far more painful without your attention to detail.

Thanks also go to everyone at Peachpit Press: to Marjorie Baer and Nancy Ruenzel, for having the vision to recognize just how special this project could be; to Karen Reichstein, who deftly carried the second edition torch; and to Lisa Brazieal, Victor Gavenda, Scott Cowlin, Kim Lombardi, Mimi Heft, and indeed, to everyone who labors on Eighth Street. You make the others look like amateurs.

Then there's the other dream team. The DVD wouldn't have happened without Steve Broback and Toby Malina, my partners at Avondale Media and my good friends. Steve's support and savvy make all of my Avondale endeavors a pleasure. Toby directed the video shoot with astonishing skill, which, as it turns out, is something she exhibits frequently. You'll always be Ms. Moxie to me.

The video owes its look to lighting director Arthur Aravena; to B. T. Corwin, the artist behind the lens; to Tom Wolsky, production consultant and Final Cut Pro master; to video technician Tari Karkanen; and to Vicky Helstrom, makeup artist. To say "we couldn't have done it without you" is to overstate the obvious.

And speaking of which, my thanks and respect go to the Apple engineers and product managers who helped bring the iLife programs to life. Michael Uy and Fred Johnson answered innumerable technical questions despite crushing schedules, and somehow managed to make the process fun. Thanks also to Greg Scallon, Stan Ng, Xander Soren, Peter Lowe, and Steve Jobs. I love your products and am profoundly gratified that you liked mine.

And finally, the last-but-definitely-not-least department: thanks to Terry Oyama for the beautiful Once Upon a Dream; to my brothers, Bill and George Heid, for the ought-to-be-a-classic All Out Vota; to Laura Ingram; to Alicia Awbrey and Keri Walker; to Rennie and everyone at MCN; to Chuck Wilcher of To The Macs consulting in Fort Bragg, California; to my friend and radio partner Bob Laughton; and to Sophie, my silver lining.

Jim Heid

Table of

Contents

DVD
Table of Contents

Read Me First: Using the Book and DVD

Why combine a book and a DVD? Because each has its own strengths. The printed word conveys depth and detail, but many people learn best by watching over someone's shoulder. Video lets you see for yourself, and video on a DVD lets you watch in any order you want.

Print and video complement each other, and that's why you will find references to the DVD throughout this book. It's also why you will find references to the book throughout the DVD.

Where should you begin? You decide. If you're new to the iLife, you might want to break open a Mountain Dew and watch the DVD from start to finish. Or, watch the introduction, then use the DVD's main menu to jump to the segment you're most interested in. Or, keep the book near your Mac as a reference, and check out chapters of the DVD when you want to see something in action.

How you master iLife is up to you; just have fun doing it.

How the Book Works

This book devotes a separate section to each of the iLife programs: iTunes and iPod for music; iPhoto for photography; iMovie for video editing; and iDVD for creating DVD-Video discs. Each section is a series of two-page spreads, and each spread is a self-contained reference that covers one topic.

Most spreads begin with an introduction that sets the stage with an overview of the topic.

Most spreads refer you to relevant chapters on the DVD to help you locate video that relates to the current topic.

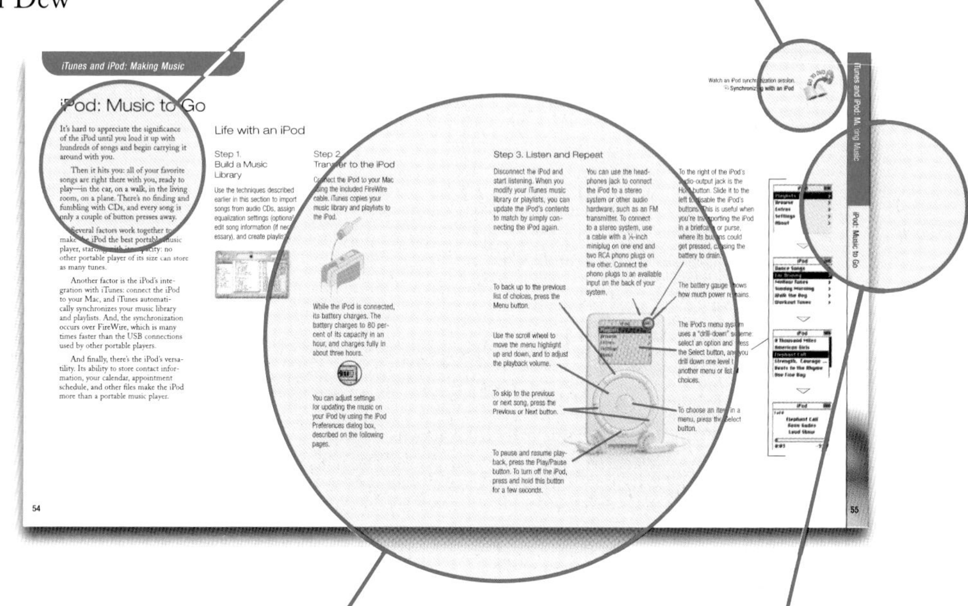

Here's the main course of each spread, where you'll find instructions, background information, and tips.

The section and spread names appear on the edges of the pages to allow you to quickly flip to specific topics.

How the DVD Works

The Macintosh iLife DVD plays on any standard DVD player, as well as on Macs (and PCs) equipped with DVD drives. Because of the nature of video, picture quality is a bit better if you play the DVD on a TV set instead of on your computer. Still, you may find it fun to have the DVD playing in a small window on your computer monitor as you learn about an iLife program.

To return to the Main Menu, press your DVD remote's Title key (which instead may be called Top Menu or Disc).

To watch a segment, choose its menu item. When that segment ends, playback continues on to the next segment. Use your DVD player's Menu button to return to the main menu.

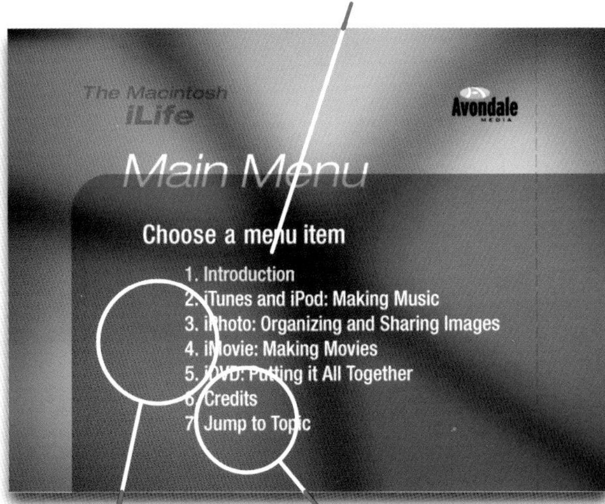

Most DVD player remote controls have number keypads. You can jump straight to a topic by pressing its number. See your DVD player's user manual for details on entering numbers using your remote control.

To browse the DVD by topic, choose Jump to Topic. To return to the topic menu, press your DVD remote's Menu key.

When you choose a segment from this menu, you see another menu that lists the topics within that segment.

When you choose a topic, you'll go straight to the portion of the DVD that covers that topic.

The Book, the DVD, the Web Site

There's just one thing this book and DVD don't cover: tomorrow. The iLife scene is always evolving as new programs and new developments change the way we work with digital media.

That's why this book and DVD also have a companion Web site: *www.macilife.com*. At this site, you'll find links to the products discussed in the book and on the DVD as well as occasional news items, updates, and reviews of iLife-related products.

Introducing iLife

The Macintosh
iLife

Personal Computers Get Personal

Music, photographs, and movies can inspire, amuse, persuade, and entertain. They're time machines that recall people and places. They're vehicles that carry messages into the future. They're ingrained in infancy and become intensely personal parts of our lives. And they've all gone digital.

It's now possible to carry a music library in your pocket, to take photos without film, and to edit video in your den—or on a cross-country flight. It's easier than ever to combine music, images, and video. And it's easy to share your finished product, whether with loved ones in the living room, clients in a conference room, or a global audience on the Internet.

Behind this digital age are breakthroughs in storage technologies, processor speed, chip design, and even in the types of connectors and interfaces used to attach external gear. In the past, personal computers weren't powerful enough to manage the billions of bits that make up digital media. Today, they are.

You might say that personal computers have finally become powerful enough to become truly personal.

Audio

1962	1972	1979	1982	1988
Bell System begins first digital phone transmissions.	Nippon Columbia Company begins digitally recording master tapes.	Sony's Walkman is the first portable music player.	Billy Joel's 52nd Street is the first album released on CD.	CDs outsell vinyl albums for the first time.

Imaging

1969	1986	1991	1992	1994
Bell Labs researchers invent the charge-coupled device (CCD).	Kodak develops first megapixel CCD.	Kodak adapts Nikon F-3 camera with 1.3-megapixel CCD.	Kodak's Photo-CD system puts scanned images on CDs.	Apple's QuickTake 100 camera debuts at $699.

Video

1956	1967	1975	1983	1985
First videotaped TV program is broadcast.	Sony delivers first portable videotape recorder.	Bell Labs demonstrates CCD TV camera. Sony Betamax debuts.	Sony's Betamovie is the first one-piece camcorder.	Small, 8 mm tape cassettes allow for compact camcorders.

Storage

1956	1973	1980	1984	1992
IBM disk system holds 5 megabytes and uses disks two feet wide.	First hard disk: 30MB on an 8-inch disk platter.	Philips and Sony develop the compact disc standard.	First Mac hard disks store 5MB and cost over $2500.	Apple includes CD-ROM drives with Macs.

Truly Personal Computing

1989 MP3 audio compression scheme is patented.

1990 Digital audio tape (DAT) recorders debut.

1991 Sony's Mini-Disc format debuts.

1996 Fraunhofer releases MP3 encoder and player for Windows PCs.

1999 Napster and other Internet services enable swapping of MP3 files.

2001 Apple introduces iPod. First copy-protected audio CDs appear amid controversy.

2002 Apple updates iTunes and the iPod family.

1997 The Associated Press switches to digital photography.

1998 1-megapixel cameras proliferate. Online photo sites offer prints and other services.

1999 2-megapixel cameras, led by Nikon's $999 Coolpix 950, are the rage.

2000 3-megapixel cameras add movie modes. Digital cameras represent 18 percent of camera sales.

2001 Consumer cameras hit 4 megapixels. Digital cameras comprise 21 percent of camera market.

2002 Apple introduces iPhoto. Consumer cameras reach 5 megapixels.

2003 Apple updates iPhoto.

1989 Hi-8 format brings improved image and sound quality.

1991 Apple's QuickTime 1.0 brings digital video to the Mac.

1994 miniDV format debuts: digital audio and video on 6.3 mm-wide tape.

1995 FireWire, invented by Apple in the early 90s, is adopted as industry standard.

1999 Apple builds FireWire into Macs and releases iMovie 1.0.

2001 Apple wins Primetime Emmy Engineering Award for FireWire.

2003 Apple releases iLife, incorporating iMovie 3.

1993 A 1.4GB hard drive costs $4559.

1995 DVD standard is announced.

1999 IBM MicroDrive puts 340MB on a coin-sized platter.

2001 5GB Toshiba hard drive uses 1.8-inch platter; Apple builds into iPod.

2001 Apple builds DVD burners into Macs.

2002 Apple delivers PowerBooks with DVD burners.

2003 Apple updates iDVD.

A Sampling of the Possibilities

This technological march of progress is exciting because it enables us to do new things with age-old media. I've already hinted at some of them: carrying a music library with you on a portable player, shooting photographs with a digital camera, and editing digital movies.

But the digital age isn't about simply replacing vinyl records, Instamatic cameras, and Super 8 movies. What makes digital technology significant is that it enables you to combine various media into messages that are uniquely yours. You can tell stories, sell products, educate, or entertain.

And when you combine these various elements, the whole becomes greater than the sum of its parts.

Sell a Product

Create a DVD whose video and images allow prospective customers to see your product in action.

Bring Back the Past

Relive a memorable vacation with digital images, video, and sounds.

Create for the Future

Produce a book of photographs that commemorates a baby's first year.

Tell a Story

Interview relatives and create a multimedia family history, complete with old photographs and oral histories.

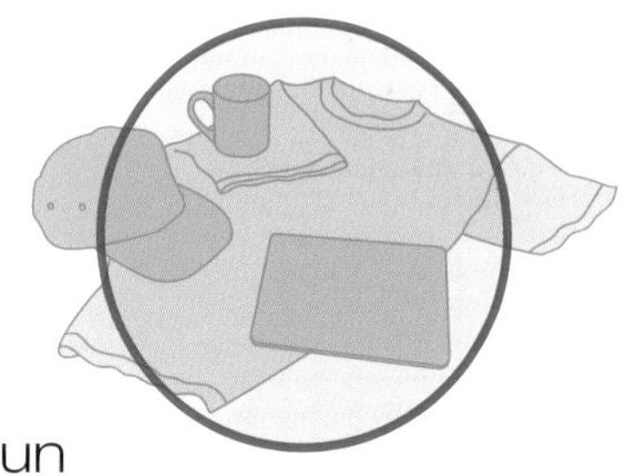

Have Fun

Put your favorite photo on a mousepad, a coffee mug, a T-shirt—or a dozen cookies.

Tunes on the Road

Carry your music with you, and plug your portable player into a stereo system when you get there. Or use an adapter to listen on your car radio.

Become a Digital DJ

Create playlists that play back your favorite tunes in any order you like.

Educate

Create a training video that teaches a new skill—or a new language.

Promote Yourself

Distribute a portfolio of your design work or photography on a DVD.

Where the Mac Fits In

All of today's personal computers have fast processors, fat hard drives, and the other trappings of power. But powerful hardware is only a foundation. Software is what turns that box of chips into a jukebox, a digital darkroom, and a movie studio.

Software is what really makes the Macintosh digital hub go around. Each of Apple's iLife programs—iTunes for music, iPhoto for photography, iMovie for video editing, and iDVD for creating DVDs—greatly simplifies working with and combining digital media.

Equivalent programs are available for PCs running Microsoft Windows. But they aren't included with every PC, and they lack the design elegance and simplicity of Apple's offerings. It's simple: Apple's iLife has made the Mac the best personal computer for digital media.

iMovie
- Capture video from camcorders
- Edit video and create titles and effects
- Add music soundtracks from iTunes
- Save finished video to tape or disk

iDVD
- Create slide shows from iPhoto images
- Add music soundtracks from iTunes
- Present video created in iMovie
- Distribute files in DVD-ROM format

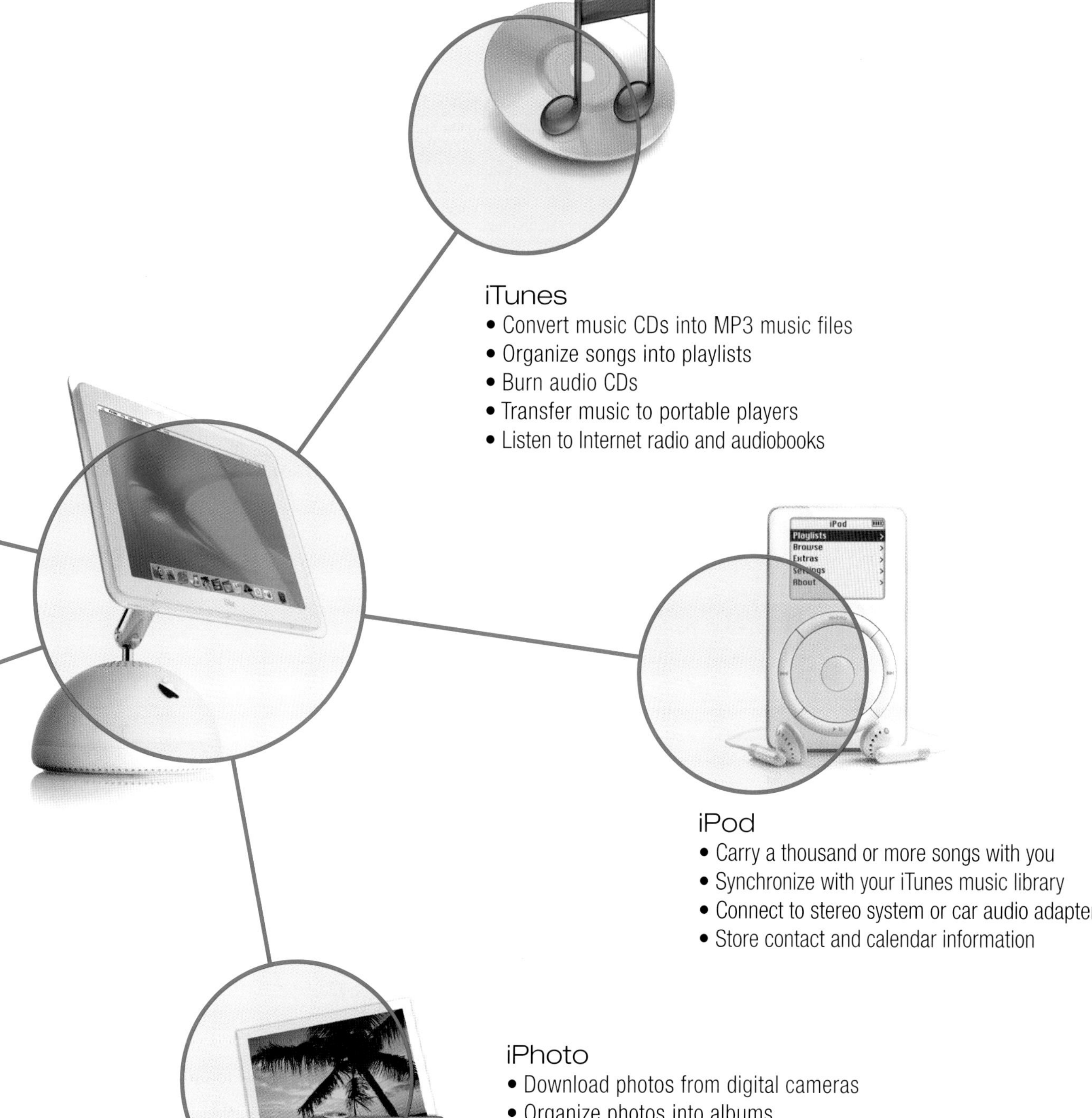

iTunes

- Convert music CDs into MP3 music files
- Organize songs into playlists
- Burn audio CDs
- Transfer music to portable players
- Listen to Internet radio and audiobooks

iPod

- Carry a thousand or more songs with you
- Synchronize with your iTunes music library
- Connect to stereo system or car audio adapter
- Store contact and calendar information

iPhoto

- Download photos from digital cameras
- Organize photos into albums
- Crop and modify photos
- Share photos via books and Web albums
- Order prints and enlargements

No Medium is an Island

Combining multiple media is a key part of audio-visual storytelling—even silent films had soundtracks played on mighty Wurlitzer theater organs.

Combining media is easy with the iLife programs. There's no need to plod through export and import chores to move, say, a photograph from iPhoto into iMovie. iPhoto, iMovie, and iDVD each have media browsers that put all your media just a few mouse clicks away, no matter which program you're using. Most of the media browsers also have Search boxes to help you find the music track, photo, or movie you want.

You can also move items between programs by simply dragging them. Drag a photo from iPhoto into iMovie or iDVD. Drag a music track from iTunes into iPhoto, iMovie, or iDVD.

The iLife programs work together in other ways, which I'll describe as we go. In the meantime, think about ways to marry your media and tell a stronger story.

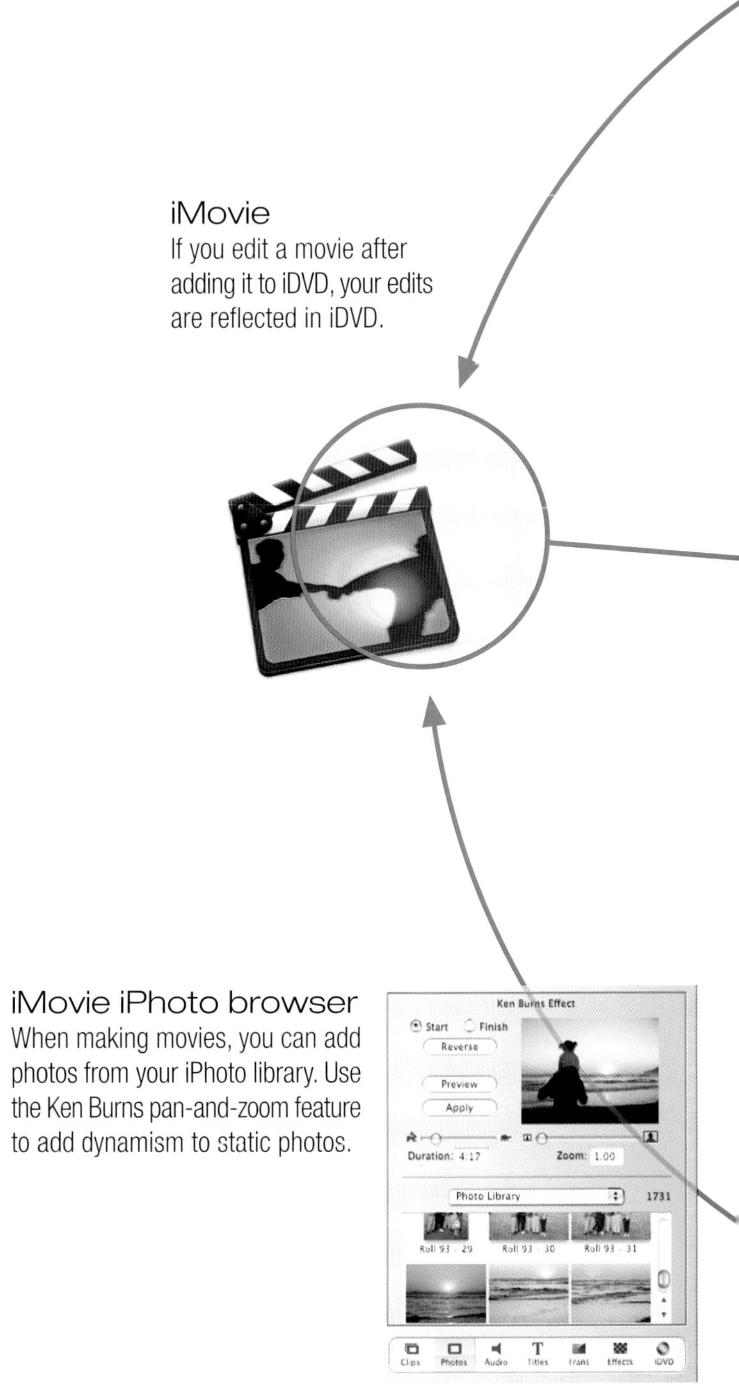

iMovie
If you edit a movie after adding it to iDVD, your edits are reflected in iDVD.

iMovie iPhoto browser
When making movies, you can add photos from your iPhoto library. Use the Ken Burns pan-and-zoom feature to add dynamism to static photos.

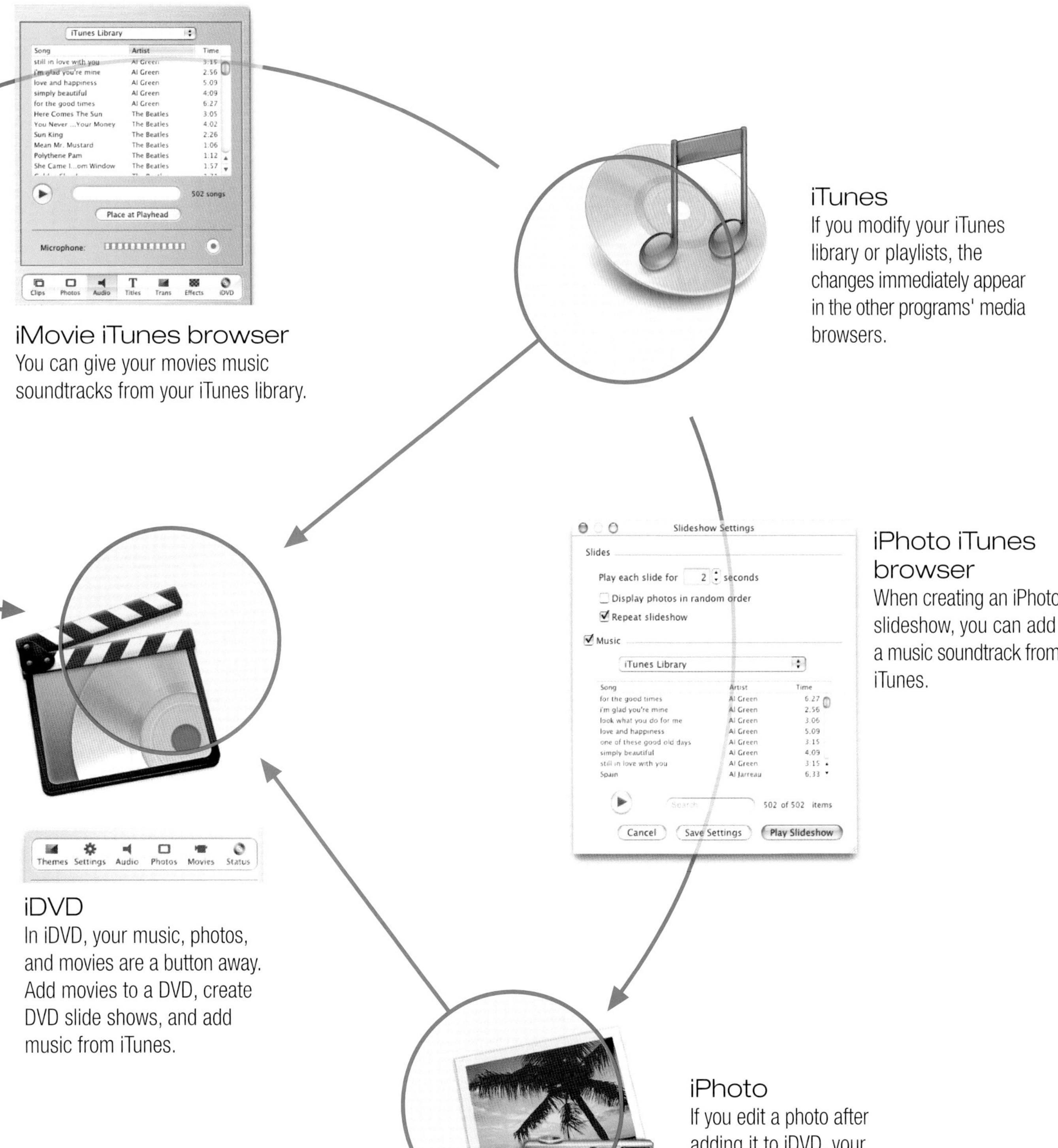

iMovie iTunes browser

You can give your movies music soundtracks from your iTunes library.

iTunes

If you modify your iTunes library or playlists, the changes immediately appear in the other programs' media browsers.

iPhoto iTunes browser

When creating an iPhoto slideshow, you can add a music soundtrack from iTunes.

iDVD

In iDVD, your music, photos, and movies are a button away. Add movies to a DVD, create DVD slide shows, and add music from iTunes.

iPhoto

If you edit a photo after adding it to iDVD, your modifications are reflected in iDVD.

Putting the Pieces Together

Software is important, but so is hardware. Several aspects of the Mac's hardware makes it ideally suited to digital media work. One is the speed of the PowerPC, the central processor at the heart of each Mac.

Converting audio CD tracks into MP3 music files, generating special video effects, preparing video for burning onto a DVD—these are demanding tasks, far more demanding than moving words around, calculating budget spreadsheets, or displaying Web pages. But the PowerPC G4 chip contained in most Macs has special circuitry—Apple calls it the Velocity Engine—which specializes in performing complex calculations.

Another factor in the hardware equation is ports: the connection schemes used to attach external devices, such as portable music players, digital cameras, camcorders, printers, and speakers. Every Mac contains all the ports necessary for connecting these and other add-ons.

And finally, the Mac's hardware and software work together smoothly and reliably. This lets you concentrate on your creations, not on your connections.

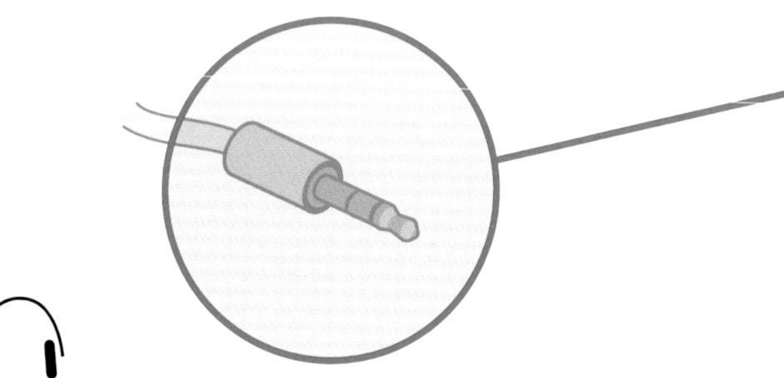

Audio Output

Standard 3.5 mm stereo minijack connects to headphones, amplifiers, and other audio equipment.

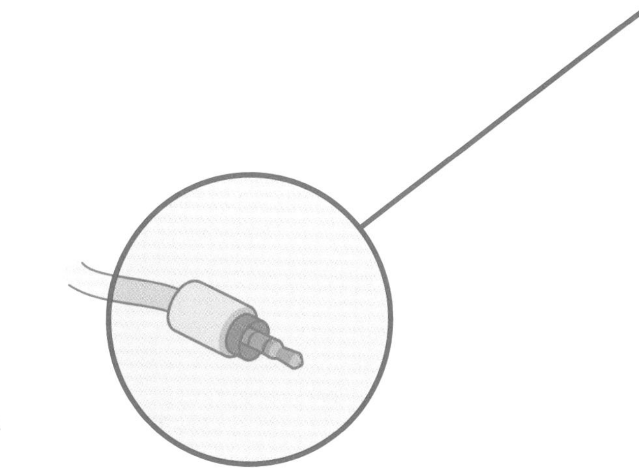

Apple Speaker Minijack

Connects to Apple Pro Speakers. This special jack has a smaller diameter (2.5 mm) than the headphone jack so that you can't inadvertently plug headphones into it.

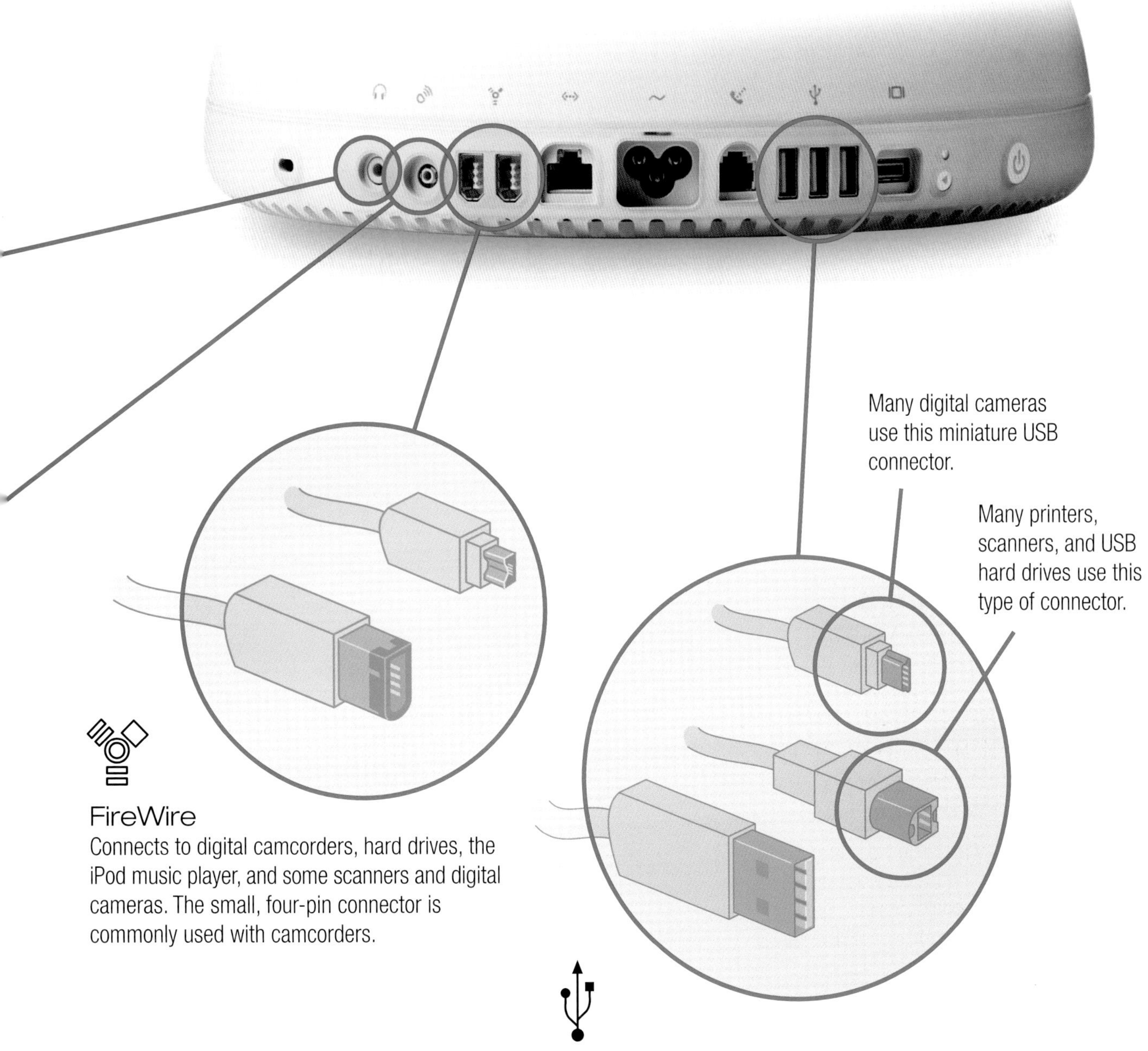

Many digital cameras use this miniature USB connector.
Many printers, scanners, and USB hard drives use this type of connector.

FireWire

Connects to digital camcorders, hard drives, the iPod music player, and some scanners and digital cameras. The small, four-pin connector is commonly used with camcorders.

Universal Serial Bus (USB)

Connects to digital cameras, scanners, some speaker systems, microphones, printers, and other add-ons.

Essential Add-Ons: Outfitting Your Mac for Digital Media

With their built-in USB and FireWire ports, today's Macs are well equipped to connect to cameras, portable music players, camcorders, and other digital devices.

But there's always room for improvement. To get the most out of iLife, consider upgrading several key components of your Mac. Here's a shopping list.

Memory

Adding memory is a great way to boost any Mac's overall performance. And with most Macs, you can install a memory upgrade yourself. (With older iMac models that have tray-loading CD-ROM drives, it's a good idea to have memory installed by a qualified technician.)

Add as much memory as you can afford. I consider 384 megabytes (MB) to be a bare minimum for the iLife programs; 512MB or more are better.

Hard Drive

All digital media eat up a lot of disk space—except for video, which utterly devours it. If you're serious about digital media, you'll want to expand your Mac's storage.

It's easy to do. If you have a tower-style Mac, you can install a second hard drive inside the Mac's case. For iMacs and PowerBooks, you can connect an external FireWire hard drive—or several of them, if you like.

External FireWire hard drives are available in a wide range of capacities and case sizes. Portable drives are particularly convenient: they fit in a shirt pocket and can draw power from a Mac's FireWire jack—no separate power supply needed. On the downside, though, portable drives cost more than conventional external drives.

Speakers

Some Mac models include the Apple Pro Speakers, lovely transparent orbs that sound surprisingly rich for their small size.

You can also buy the Apple Pro Speakers separately, but note that they require a Mac containing a special jack. They work with flat-panel iMacs and newer Power Mac models, but not with Power Macs introduced prior to 2001.

The small size of the Apple Pro Speakers means their bass response is a bit anemic. To beef up your bass, consider adding Harmon Kardon's iSub. This subwoofer connects via USB and sits under your desk, although its exotic, jellyfish-like design will tempt you to keep it out where everyone can see it. And its deep, gut-punching bass will amaze everyone who hears it.

If you don't yet have a speaker system, Harmon Kardon's SoundSticks system is a great choice. It includes an iSub-like subwoofer and two see-through acrylic satellite speakers that sit on either side of the Mac.

One drawback to all the speakers I've discussed here is that they can't connect to an iPod or other device that uses a standard stereo miniplug. The Apple Pro Speakers use an oddball connector, and the iSub and SoundSticks connect via USB.

If you'd like a more versatile set of speakers—ones that will connect to virtually any audio device—go for a system such as JBL's Creature, which looks like a futuristic spaceship and provides a standard stereo miniplug and includes a subwoofer and two satellite speakers. Or connect your Mac or iPod to a stereo system, either directly or through an FM transmitter.

A FireWire Hub

The Mac's FireWire connectors are durable, but they aren't indestructible. All that plugging and unplugging of camcorders, hard drives, iPods, and other doodads can take its toll. What's more, many Macs have just one FireWire connector, limiting the number of devices you can connect directly to the Mac.

A FireWire hub is an inexpensive add-on that addresses both issues. A hub is to FireWire what a power strip is to a wall outlet: it provides more jacks for your devices. After connecting the hub to your Mac, you can connect several devices to the hub.

You can also buy USB hubs that provide the same expansion benefits for USB devices.

A .Mac Account

Okay, so this isn't an add-on per se, but it is something you may want. If you sign up for a subscription to Apple's .Mac service, you can create your own Web page and Web photo albums using iPhoto. You'll also be able to access Apple's iDisk remote storage service, where you'll find lots of software downloads as well as a library of royalty-free music that you can use in your digital hub endeavors.

To sign up for .Mac, go to www.mac.com. If you aren't sure whether .Mac is for you, sign up for a free trial membership.

More Accessories You Might Want

While you're filling your shopping cart, you might also want to consider some accessories that will help you get more out of your digital devices.

Memory Cards

Many digital cameras come with an 8MB memory card, which doesn't hold all that many photos. You can get memory cards in much higher capacities—128MB, 256MB, and more.

Buy at least one additional memory card for your camera. Memory cards are inexpensive, and they're the best way to boost your shooting capacity.

Memory Media Reader

Speaking of memory, another accessory you might consider is a memory reader. You can transfer images by inserting your memory card into the reader, and then using the Mac's Finder to drag the photos on the card into iPhoto. If you get a reader that supports the Mac's FireWire interface, you can transfer images much faster than when using a USB connection.

FM Transmitter

With an FM transmitter, you can broadcast the audio from your iPod or your Mac throughout your house—or your car. In my house, we use an FM transmitter to broadcast streaming Internet audio throughout the house.

A number of FM transmitters are available, and in my experience, most of them work poorly. I have found one exception, though—C. Crane Company makes an FM transmitter that delivers excellent sound quality and very good range. Check it out at www.ccradio.com.

And from the "something completely different" category, there's Griffin Technology's iTrip, an FM transmitter that plugs into the top of an iPod music player. The iTrip gets power from the iPod's FireWire jack, so it doesn't require its own batteries.

Cassette Adapter

Here's another alternative for listening to your iPod in the car. Plug the cassette adapter into the iPod, and insert its cassette assembly into your car's tape deck. The sound quality won't do justice to the iPod's capabilities, but it's an inexpensive and easy way to hear your tunes in the car.

iPod Car Charger and More

If you're listening to the iPod in the car, why not charge it at the same time? Xtreme Mac sells a charging cable that enables you to charge an iPod on the road. One end of the coiled cable plugs into the cigarette lighter, while the other end plugs into the iPod's FireWire jack.

(Note that because the car charger and Griffin's iTrip each connect to the iPod's FireWire jack, you can't use them both at the same time.)

Xtreme Mac's other iPod accessories include the iWallet, an iPod carrying case that also has room for credit cards and cash; and an array of cable kits that enable you to connect an iPod to any audio system.

iTunes and iPod: Making Music

The Macintosh
iLife

iTunes at a Glance

All media may have gone digital, but music was there first. In the 1980s, the compact disc format turned the clicks and pops of vinyl into relics of the past—at least until hip-hop music brought them back.

More recently, the grassroots groundswell behind the MP3 format led to a frenzy of Internet music swapping and CD burning. And the trend continues to keep recording industry executives awake at night and put food on the table for more than a few lawyers.

MP3 and other digital audio formats have created a new era of musical freedom. Not freedom to steal—copying an artist's efforts without paying for them is just plain wrong—but freedom to arrange songs in whatever order you like and to play those songs on a variety of devices.

iTunes is the program that brings this freedom of music to the Mac. With iTunes, you can create MP3 files from your favorite audio CDs, and then organize those MP3 files into playlists. You can listen to your playlists on a Mac, burn them onto CDs, or transfer them to an iPod portable music player.

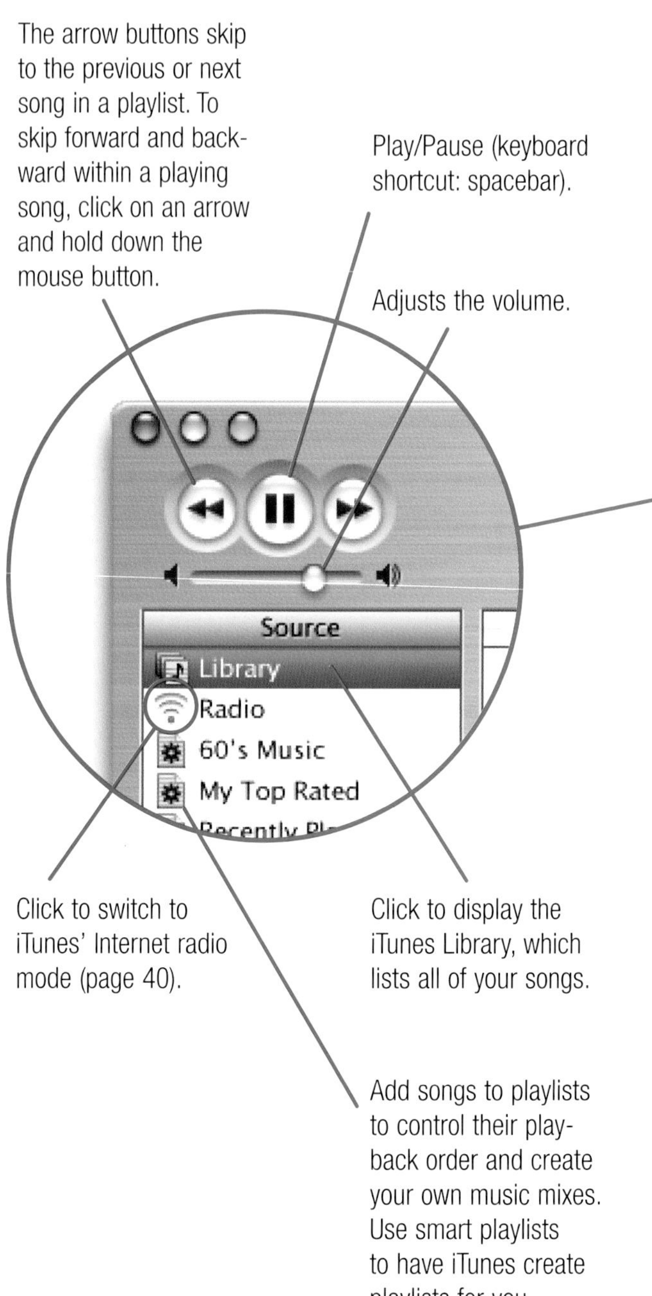

The arrow buttons skip to the previous or next song in a playlist. To skip forward and backward within a playing song, click on an arrow and hold down the mouse button.
Play/Pause (keyboard shortcut: spacebar).
Adjusts the volume.
Source
Library
Radio
60's Music
My Top Rated
Click to switch to iTunes' Internet radio mode (page 40).
Click to display the iTunes Library, which lists all of your songs.
Add songs to playlists to control their playback order and create your own music mixes. Use smart playlists to have iTunes create playlists for you.

See iTunes and the iPod in action.
iTunes and iPod: Making Music

Click this tiny button to switch between song information and iTunes' animated spectrum display.

Click the time display and artist name to view other time options and album information.

Drag the diamond left or right to scan through a song.

To sort a list by a specific column, click that column's heading. To reverse the sort order, click the heading again. To resize columns, drag their left and right boundaries.

Use the Browse button to view your music by artist and album (page 34).

Use the Search box to quickly locate songs (page 34).

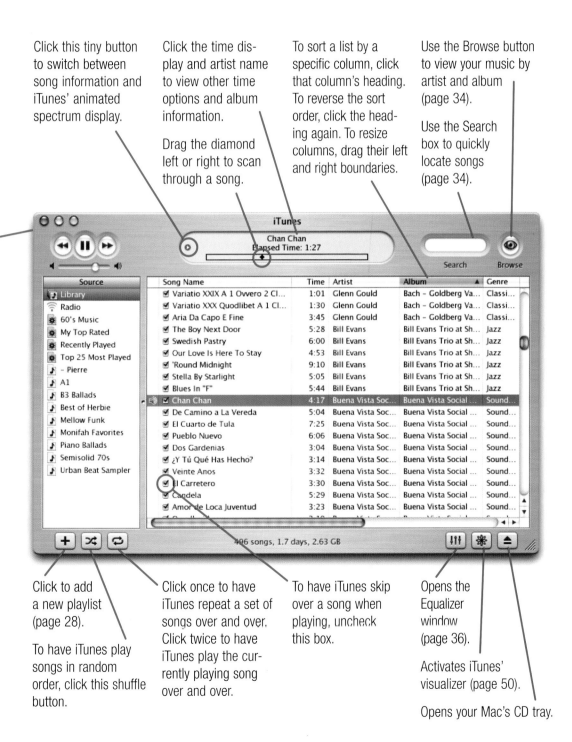

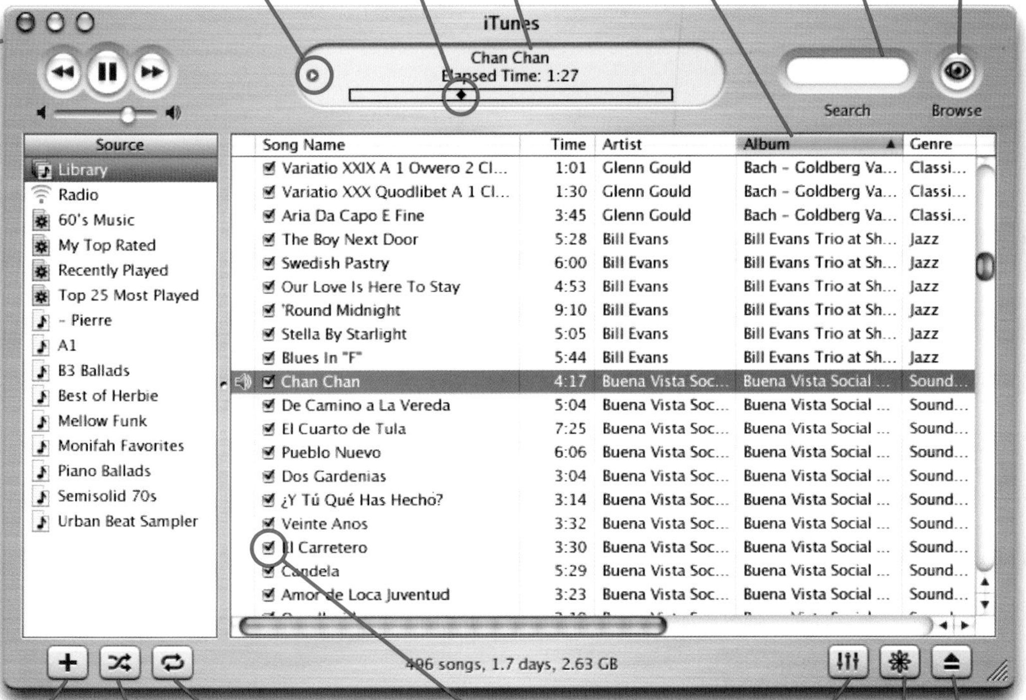

iTunes

Chan Chan
Elapsed Time: 1:27

Search
Browse

Source
Library
Radio
60's Music
My Top Rated
Recently Played
Top 25 Most Played
- Pierre
A1
B3 Ballads
Best of Herbie
Mellow Funk
Monifah Favorites
Piano Ballads
Semisolid 70s
Urban Beat Sampler

Song Name	Time	Artist	Album	Genre
Variatio XXIX A 1 Ovvero 2 Cl...	1:01	Glenn Gould	Bach - Goldberg Va...	Classi...
Variatio XXX Quodlibet A 1 Cl...	1:30	Glenn Gould	Bach - Goldberg Va...	Classi...
Aria Da Capo E Fine	3:45	Glenn Gould	Bach - Goldberg Va...	Classi...
The Boy Next Door	5:28	Bill Evans	Bill Evans Trio at Sh...	Jazz
Swedish Pastry	6:00	Bill Evans	Bill Evans Trio at Sh...	Jazz
Our Love Is Here To Stay	4:53	Bill Evans	Bill Evans Trio at Sh...	Jazz
'Round Midnight	9:10	Bill Evans	Bill Evans Trio at Sh...	Jazz
Stella By Starlight	5:05	Bill Evans	Bill Evans Trio at Sh...	Jazz
Blues In "F"	5:44	Bill Evans	Bill Evans Trio at Sh...	Jazz
Chan Chan	4:17	Buena Vista Soc...	Buena Vista Social ...	Sound...
De Camino a La Vereda	5:04	Buena Vista Soc...	Buena Vista Social ...	Sound...
El Cuarto de Tula	7:25	Buena Vista Soc...	Buena Vista Social ...	Sound...
Pueblo Nuevo	6:06	Buena Vista Soc...	Buena Vista Social ...	Sound...
Dos Gardenias	3:04	Buena Vista Soc...	Buena Vista Social ...	Sound...
¿Y Tú Qué Has Hecho?	3:14	Buena Vista Soc...	Buena Vista Social ...	Sound...
Veinte Anos	3:32	Buena Vista Soc...	Buena Vista Social ...	Sound...
El Carretero	3:30	Buena Vista Soc...	Buena Vista Social ...	Sound...
Candela	5:29	Buena Vista Soc...	Buena Vista Social ...	Sound...
Amor de Loca Juventud	3:23	Buena Vista Soc...	Buena Vista Social ...	Sound...

496 songs, 1.7 days, 2.63 GB

Click to add a new playlist (page 28).

To have iTunes play songs in random order, click this shuffle button.

Click once to have iTunes repeat a set of songs over and over. Click twice to have iTunes play the currently playing song over and over.

To have iTunes skip over a song when playing, uncheck this box.

Opens the Equalizer window (page 36).

Activates iTunes' visualizer (page 50).

Opens your Mac's CD tray.

Importing Music from CDs

The first step in stocking your digital jukebox involves bringing in music from your audio CDs. Apple calls this process *importing*, but most MP3 fans refer to it as *ripping* (from the Latin, meaning "to rip off").

Whatever you call it, iTunes is good at it. Insert a compact disc into your Mac's CD drive, and iTunes launches, connects to the Internet, and retrieves the name of the CD and its tracks. Click iTunes' Import button, and the program converts the CD's contents into MP3 files that are stored on your Mac's hard drive.

That's the big picture. You can create a vast digital music library with iTunes without having to know any more than that. But iTunes has several features that give you more control over the ripping process. You can, for example, specify that iTunes import only certain songs. And as described in later sections, you can customize the MP3 compression settings that iTunes applies to the music it imports.

Just want to play a CD instead of ripping it? Click the play button or double-click on any track.

Indicates which songs to rip. Don't like some songs? Uncheck their boxes, and iTunes will not import them.

Tip: To uncheck all tracks, press ⌘ while clicking on a track's check box.

Rips all tracks with check marks before their names.

Shows the currently inserted CD.

Ejects the CD.

Joining Tracks to Eliminate Gaps

In some cases, you might not want a gap of silence between songs. For example, the songs on a CD might be composed so that one flows seamlessly into the next.

iTunes indicates joined tracks with a bracket.

You can prevent a gap between two or more songs by importing them as joined tracks. Select the tracks, then choose Join CD Tracks from the Advanced menu. iTunes will import the tracks as one MP3 file. If you decide to not join the tracks after all, choose Unjoin CD Tracks from the Advanced menu.

Note that you can't join tracks that you've already imported.

See an iTunes importing session.
Importing a CD
GO TO DVD

How iTunes Retrieves Track Names

Back in the late 1970s, when the compact disc standard was being developed, no one foresaw the iLife era. As a result, the developers of the CD standard didn't create a way for CDs to store artist, album, and track names.

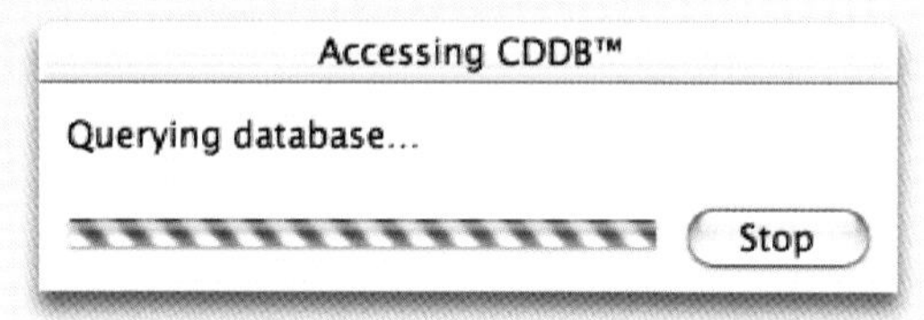

So how can iTunes retrieve this information? The answer lies in the fact that no two audio CDs are the exact same length. A CD is comprised of a specific number of blocks, each of which is one seventy-fifth of a second long. You might say that every CD has its own unique digital fingerprint.

In 1996, some clever programmers in Berkeley, California, realized they could create a database that would link these fingerprints to specific information. The compact disc database, or CDDB, was born. Soon, CDDB spawned a company, Gracenote, which provides disc-lookup features to Apple and other companies that have MP3- and music-related products.

When you insert a CD, iTunes calculates its digital fingerprint and then sends it over the Internet to Gracenote's server. If Gracenote finds a match, it transmits the corresponding information back to iTunes, which displays it.

Power Ripping: Changing CD Insert Preferences

Doing some binge ripping? Save yourself time and set up iTunes to automatically begin importing as soon as you insert a CD. Choose Preferences from the iTunes menu, then check the setting of the On CD Insert pop-up menu. Choose Import Songs or, better yet, Import Songs and Eject.

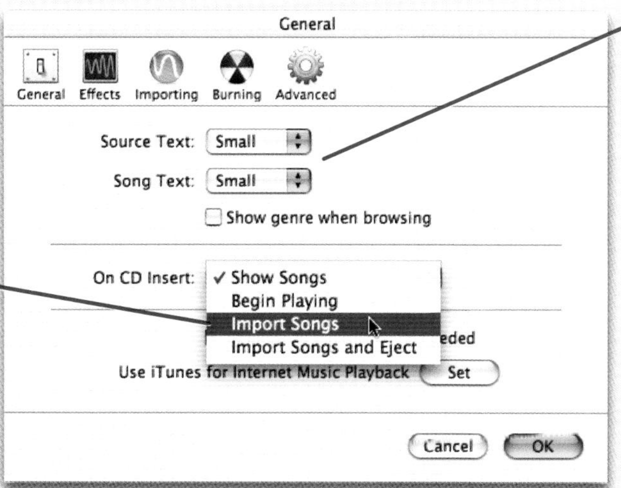

Aging eyes? Use these pop-up menus to have iTunes display large text.

Customizing Importing Settings

CD-quality stereo sound requires about 10MB of disk space per minute. By using *compression*, MP3 can lower audio's appetite for storage by a factor of 10 or more. (To understand how this loss of appetite occurs, see "A Matter of Perception: How MP3 Works" on page 24.)

MP3 sound quality depends in large part on how much the audio has been compressed. Compression is measured in terms of *bit rate*—the average number of bits required for one second of sound. To obtain near CD-quality audio, MP3 requires a bit rate in the range of 128 to 192 kbps (kilobits) per second. Higher bit rates mean less compression and better sound quality.

But the higher the bit rate, the larger the file. In this era of huge hard drives, file size may not be as important to you as sound quality. But if you're trying to shoehorn a vast music library onto a portable player—or if your hard drive is nearly full—you may need to assess how much space your MP3s are using.

iTunes is set up to encode at 160 kbps, striking a good balance between file size and sound quality. You can change those settings by choosing Preferences from the iTunes menu, and then clicking the Importing tab.

You don't have to fuss with iTunes' encoding settings at all, but if you're an audiophile or you're just curious, go ahead and experiment: rip a few songs using various settings, and then compare their file sizes and audio quality.

If you don't want to compress your music at all, choose the AIFF or WAV encoders, and iTunes will make exact copies of the tracks on the CD. But note that those tracks will require 10MB of disk space per minute. (AIFF, which stands for *Audio Interchange File Format,* is a standard audio format on the Mac; WAV is its equivalent on Windows. Both formats are broadly supported on Macs and Windows.)

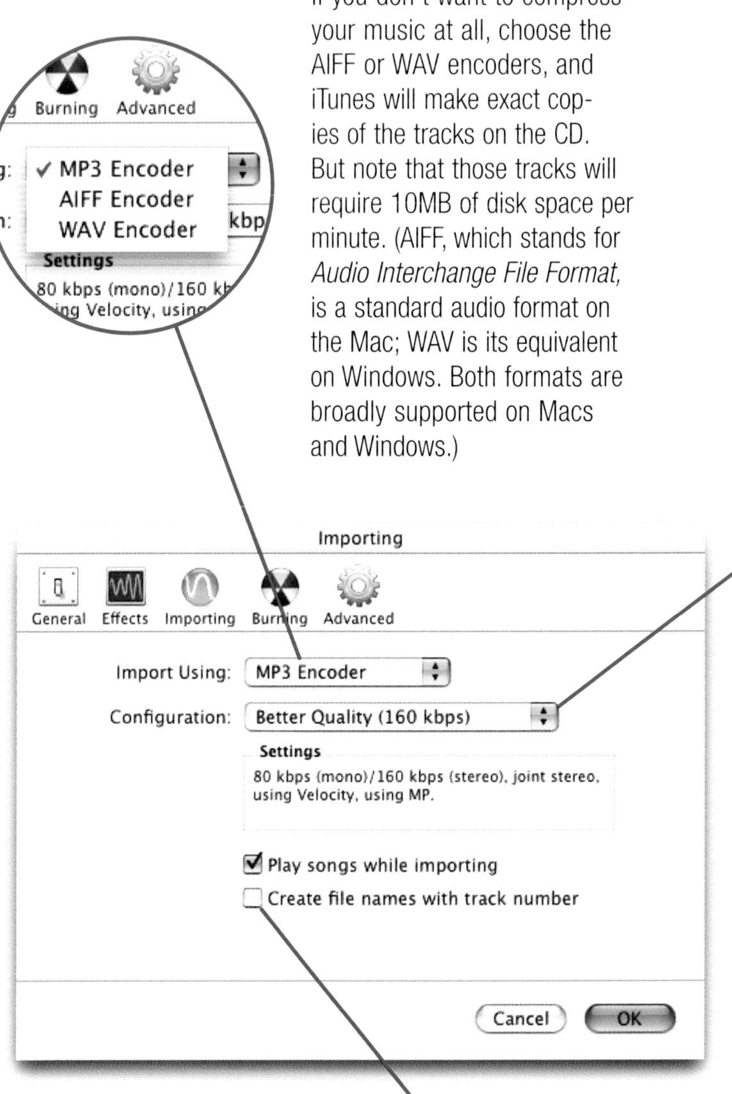

When checked, iTunes adds a number to the beginning of each imported MP3 file. This can be useful if you burn MP3-format CDs (see page 39).

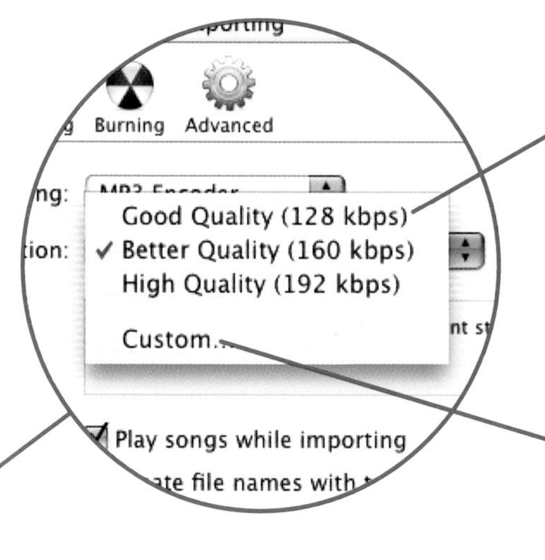

128 kbps is closer to FM-radio quality than to CD quality—you may notice a swirling quality to instruments that produce high frequencies, such as strings and cymbals. 192 kbps delivers better quality than 160 kbps, though my ears have trouble detecting it.

To explore the kinds of adjustments MP3 allows for, choose Custom to display the dialog box shown below. See below for custom setting choices.

Tweaks your encoding settings for the best quality given the bit rate settings you've specified. You can usually leave this box checked, but if you're a control freak who doesn't want iTunes making adjustments for you, uncheck it.

Specify the desired bit rate here. Monophonic audio requires a lower bit rate than does stereo, since there's only one channel to encode.

Variable bit rate (VBR) encoding varies a song's bit rate according to the complexity of the sound. For example, a quiet passage with a narrow range of frequencies is less "demanding" than a loud passage with a broad range of frequencies. VBR uses disk space more efficiently and, according to many MP3 fans, sounds better, too. Many iTunes users turn on VBR and then lower the bit rate—for example, encoding at 128 kbps with VBR instead of at 160 kbps without VBR.

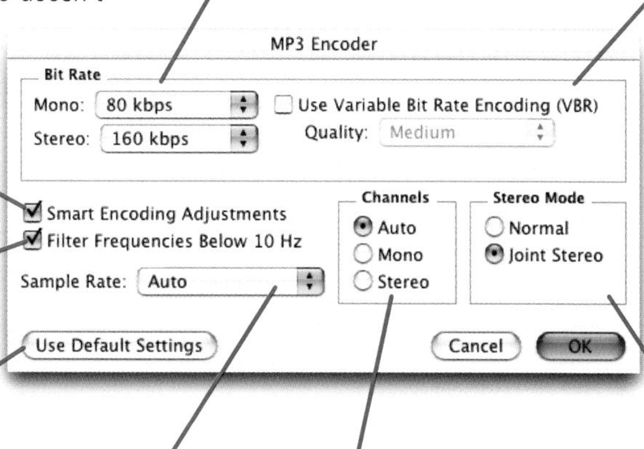

iTunes will filter out inaudible, low frequencies. Leave this one checked.

Click to restore iTunes' original settings.

Leave this pop-up menu set to Auto for most uses. If you're encoding a voice recording, however, you can save disk space by lowering the sample rate to 22.050 KHz or even 11.025 KHz.

In the Auto setting, iTunes detects whether the original recording is in stereo or mono. To force iTunes to encode in mono—for example, to save disk space—click Mono.

Our ears have trouble discerning where high frequencies are coming from. Joint Stereo encoding exploits this phenomenon by combining high frequencies into a single channel, saving disk space. Careful listeners say they can sometimes hear a difference in the spatial qualities of a recording.

A Matter of Perception: How MP3 Works

You don't have to understand how MP3 works in order to use iTunes, but you might wonder how an MP3 file can be roughly one-tenth the size of an uncompressed audio file and still sound nearly the same.

MP3's origins go back to the 1980s, when researchers began exploring ways to reduce the storage requirements of digital audio. One of the standards that came from these efforts was MPEG (Moving Picture Experts Group) Audio Layer III—MP3 for short.

Like many audio compression schemes, MP3 relies heavily on *perceptual encoding*, which eliminates those portions of an audio signal our ears don't hear well anyway. It's similar to how the JPEG image format works, compressing images by throwing away image data our eyes don't detect easily. Because some information is lost in the process, MP3 and JPEG are called *lossy* compression schemes.

MP3 is not the only audio compression scheme, nor is it the best. Compression technologies developed for streaming Internet audio are much more efficient than MP3—they require lower bit rates to achieve the same levels of quality.

MP3's dominance, then, comes not from technical superiority, but from its grassroots popularity and the wide availability of MP3 software and music files.

The uncompressed audio on a CD contains more information than our ears can detect. For example, if a loud sound and a quiet one reach your ears simultaneously, you may not even detect the quiet one.

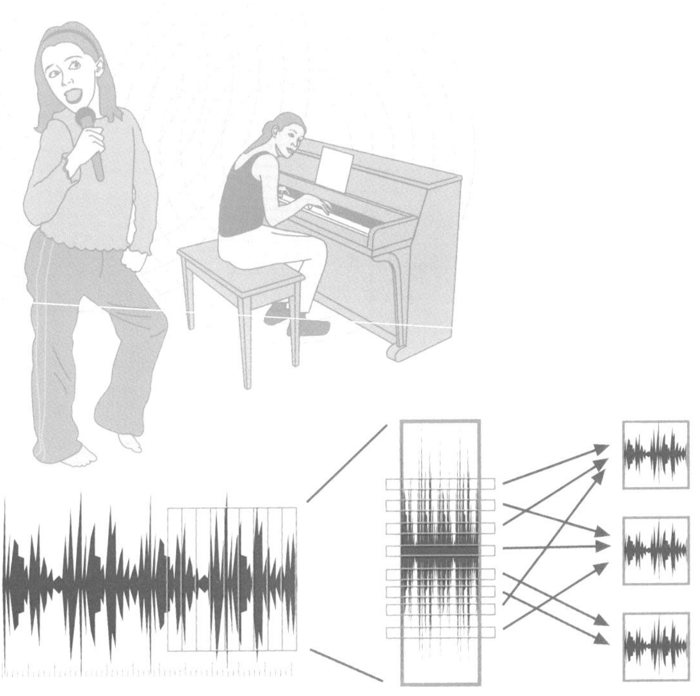

An MP3 encoder's first step is to break the original audio into a series of *frames*, each a fraction of a second in length.

The encoder further breaks down each frame into *sub-bands* in order to determine how bits will need to be allocated to best represent the audio signal.

The encoder compares the sub-bands to *psychoacoustics tables*, which mathematically describe the characteristics of human hearing. This comparison process, along with the bit rate that you've chosen for encoding, determines what portion of the original audio signal will be cut and what portion will survive.

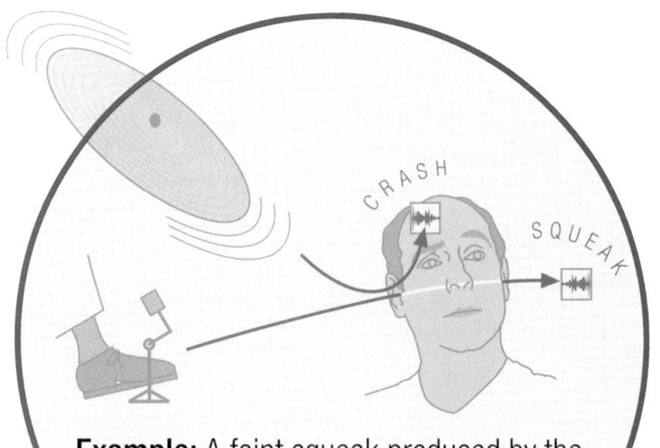

Example: A faint squeak produced by the foot pedal of a drum is cut because it happens at the same instant that a cymbal is struck.

Finally, the encoded data is further compressed by about 20 percent using *Huffman* compression, which replaces redundant pieces of data with shorter codes. You do the same thing every time you say "a dozen eggs" instead of saying "egg" twelve times.

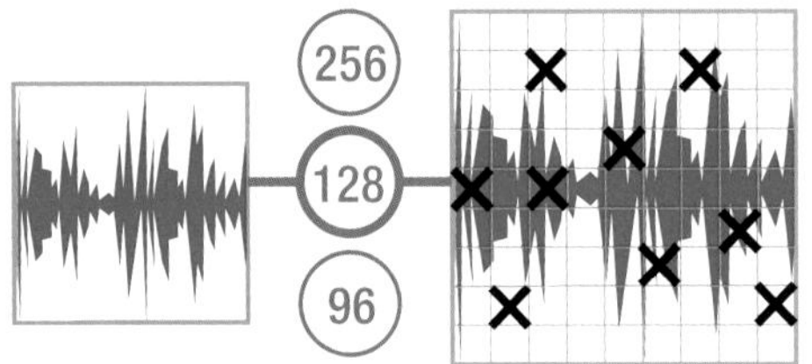

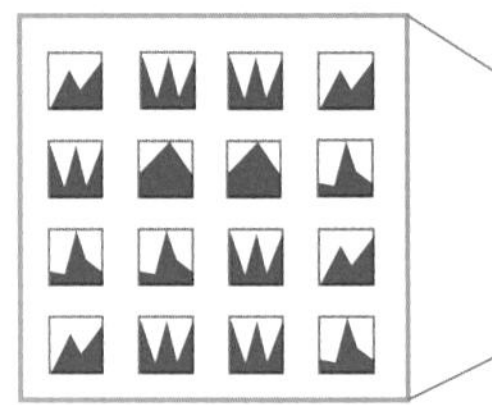

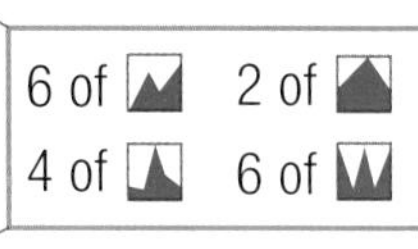

Where iTunes Stores Your Tunes

You'll want to back up your music library now and then to avoid losing it to a hard drive failure or other problem.

iTunes stores your music library in your Music folder. The fastest way to locate the Music folder is to choose Home from the Finder's Go menu.

You don't have to venture inside the Music folder—indeed, you should always add and remove songs to and from your music library by using iTunes itself, not by dragging files into and out of the Music folder.

iTunes 3 Music Library

If you're curious, here's how the Music folder is organized. The Music folder contains another folder named iTunes, and inside *this* folder is a file named iTunes 3 Music Library. This file contains a database of all the songs you've added to iTunes, as well as all the playlists you've created. But it doesn't contain the MP3 files themselves. Those files live in the folder named iTunes Music.

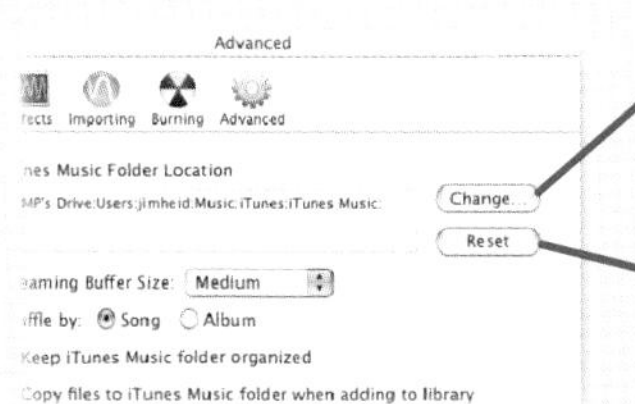

To tell iTunes where to store your music, click Change.

To restore the default location, click Reset.

Note that you don't have to store MP3s that you rip in the Music folder. You might want to store them elsewhere—on a portable FireWire hard drive, for example. To specify a different location for your music library, choose Preferences from the Advanced menu, click the Advanced button, and then specify the desired location.

It's worth noting that you can have MP3 files scattered all over your hard drive if you like—or even on multiple hard drives. For details, see "Adding MP3s from Other Sources" on page 47.

Tags and More: MP3 Nuts and Bolts

Here's another section you're welcome to skip if you're just getting started with MP3 and iTunes. But if you do skip it, I guarantee you'll be back. Why? Because there will be times when you'll want to edit the information for a song that iTunes displays.

Maybe the song is from an obscure CD that isn't in Gracenote's CDDB, and iTunes has given its tracks generic names like *Track 5*. (This will also happen if you rip a CD when not connected to the Internet.) Or maybe CDDB stored the song names in all-lowercase or all-capital letters, and you'd like to correct that.

Or maybe you've encountered a problem similar to the one illustrated at right. I ripped two CDs from jazz piano giant, Bill Evans. For one of the CDs, CDDB retrieved the artist name as *Bill Evans*, but for the other CD, it retrieved the name as *Bill Evans Trio*. When I transfer those songs to my iPod, I have two separate listings in the Artist view—even though both listings refer to the same artist.

For situations like these, you can use iTunes' Get Info command to edit the information of one or more songs. First, select the song whose attributes you want to edit, and then choose Get Info from the File menu, or press ⌘-I.

You can also edit common tags, such as artist, album, and song name, within the iTunes window: simply click on the item you want to edit.

Specify the song's name as you'd like it to appear in iTunes and on a portable player.

iTunes displays size, date, format, and location information here.

Change equalization, volume, and other playback settings here (see page 46).

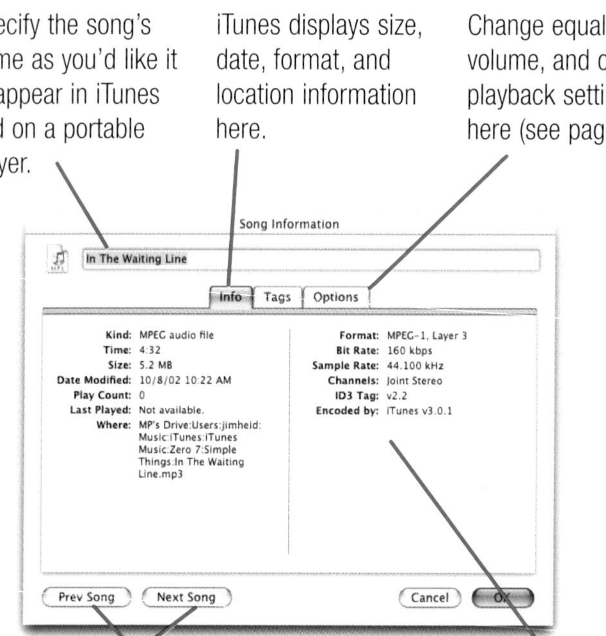

Need to edit information for multiple songs? Rather than repeatedly choosing Get Info, just click Prev Song to display information for the previous song (the one located above the current song in iTunes' window) or Next Song to get info for the next song.

Get the lowdown on a song's encoding format here.

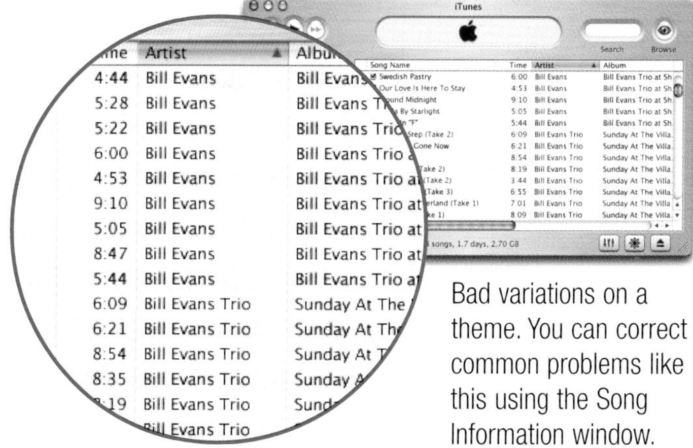

Bad variations on a theme. You can correct common problems like this using the Song Information window.

See links to useful MP3 utilities.
www.macilife.com/itunes

How MP3 Files Store Song Information

MP3 files can store more than music. They can also hold *ID3 tags*, which can hold artist, song, and album names as well as release dates, track numbers, genres, and even comments and lyrics. iTunes doesn't provide access to every tidbit that an ID3 tag can hold, but it does let you view and edit the most important ones, as shown here.

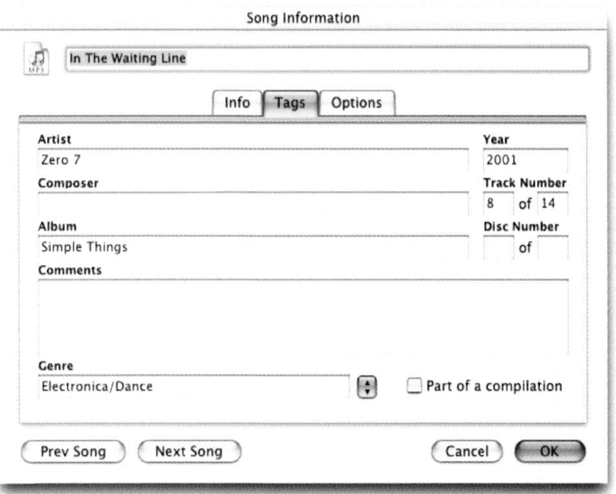

A Power Tool for ID3 Tag Editing

If you do a lot of tag editing or are just curious to see what other kinds of information an ID3 tag can hold, get a copy of Jörg Pressel's ID3X. This Mac OS X program lets you apply tag changes to an entire series of files in one fell swoop. It also supports tags that iTunes doesn't, including those that store lyrics and even scanned images of a CD's cover.

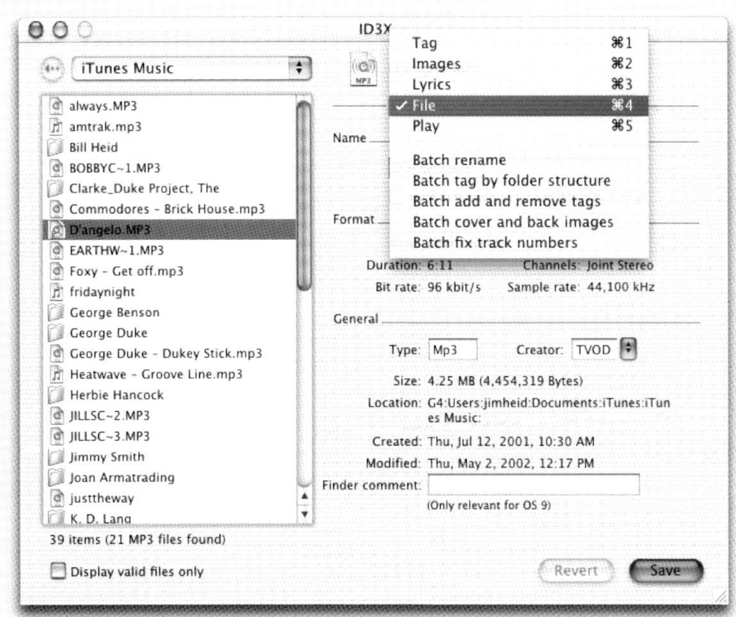

Sequencing Songs with Playlists

Once you've created a library of MP3s, you'll want to create playlists: collections of songs sequenced in whatever order you like.

You might create playlists whose songs set a mood: Workout Tunes, Road Trip Songs, Romantic Getaway Music.

You might create playlists that play all your favorite tunes from specific artists: The Best of U2, John Coltrane Favorites, The Artistry of Britney Spears. (That last one is pretty small.)

With playlists, you can mix and match songs in any way you see fit. You can add a song to as many playlists as you like, or even create a playlist that plays one song five times in a row.

Once you've created playlists, you can, of course, play them. But you can also transfer them to an iPod portable player (see page 54) and burn them to create your own compilation CDs (see page 38).

This section describes how to create playlists "by hand." You can also use iTunes' smart playlists feature to have the program create playlists for you. For details on smart playlists, see page 32.

Step 1. Create a New Playlist

To create a new playlist, click the plus sign or choose New Playlist from the File menu.

Step 2. Rename the New Playlist

Type a name for the new playlist.

Step 3. Drag Songs to the Playlist

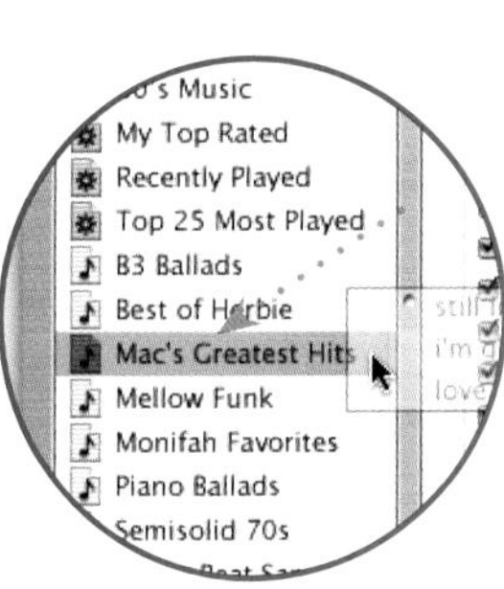

You can drag songs into the playlist one at a time or select a series of songs and drag them all at once. To select a range of songs that are adjacent to each other, use the Shift key: click on the first song, then Shift-click on the last one. To select songs that aren't adjacent to one another, press ⌘ while clicking on each song.

See how to create a playlist.
Creating a Playlist

Viewing and Fine-Tuning a Playlist

To view a playlist's contents, simply click on its name. To change the playlist's name, click again and then edit the name. To delete a playlist, select it and press Delete. (Deleting a playlist *doesn't* delete its songs from your Library.)

To change the playback order of the songs in the playlist, drag songs up or down. Here, the last song in the playlist is being moved to between songs 2 and 3.

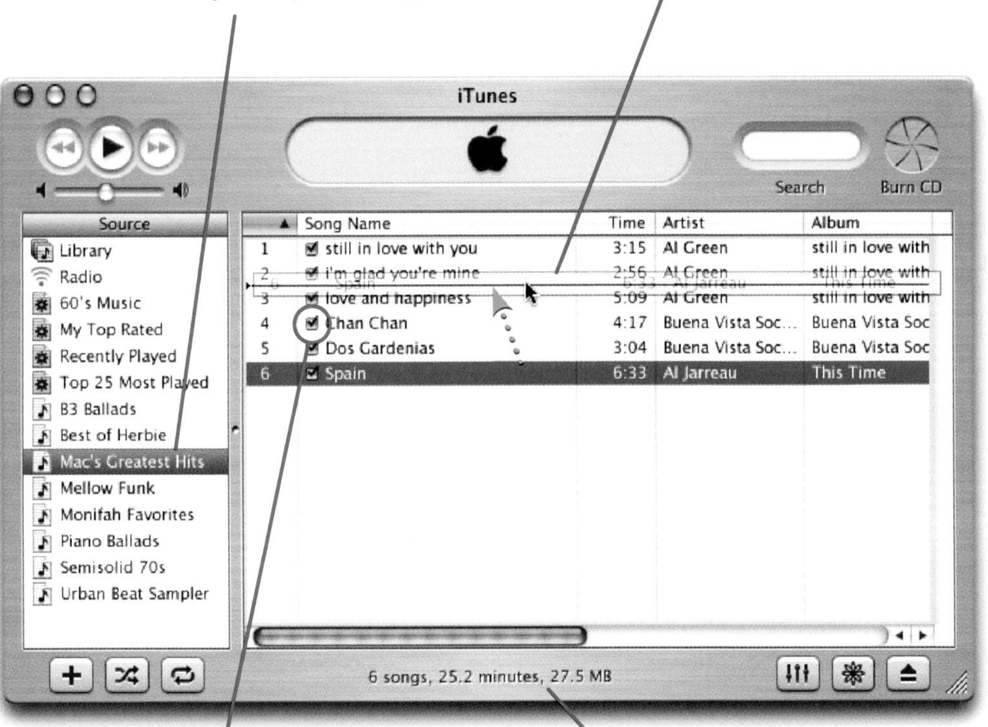

To omit a song from a playlist, select the song and press the Delete key. To omit the song without deleting it—for example, if you want to keep it in the playlist but not burn it or play it back this time—uncheck the box next to the song's name.

iTunes displays the playlist's statistics, including its duration, here.

Important: If you're burning an audio CD, keep the playlist's duration under 74 minutes.

Playlist Tips

Opening a Playlist in a Separate Window

To open a playlist in its own window, double-click the playlist's name. iTunes opens the playlist in a new window, and switches its main window to the Library view.

You can open as many playlist windows as you like, and drag songs between them, as shown here. It's a handy way to work, since it lets you see the contents of your Library and your playlist at the same time.

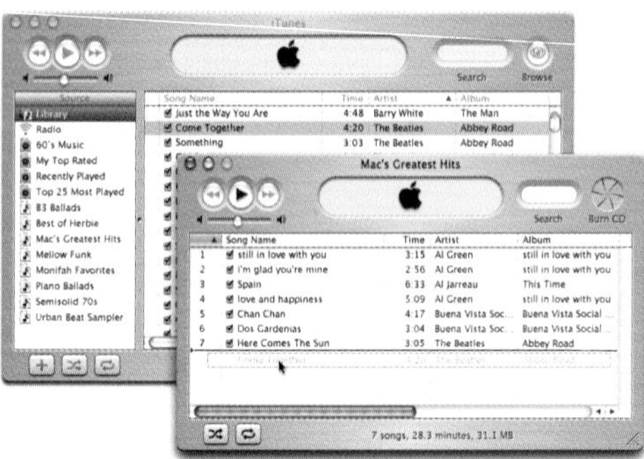

Creating a Playlist From a Selection

Here's a shortcut for creating a playlist: in the Library view, select the songs you want to include in a playlist, and then choose New Playlist From Selection from the File menu. iTunes will add the songs to a new playlist, which you can then rename.

Naming Playlists with iPod in Mind

If you plan to transfer your playlists to an iPod, there's a trick you can use to ensure that a given playlist will appear at the top of the iPod's Playlist menu. This cuts down on the time and scrolling required to find a specific playlist.

To have a playlist appear at the top of the iPod's Playlist menu, precede the playlist's name with a hyphen (-) character, as in *- Mac's Greatest Hits.*

A few other punctuation characters, including period (.), will also send a playlist to the top of the heap.

Exporting Playlists

In iTunes' File menu, there lurks a command called Export Song List. Select a playlist and choose this command, and iTunes will create a text file containing all the information about each song, from its name to its bit rate. You can open this text file using a word processor, or you can import it into a spreadsheet or database program.

The items—artist, song name, album name, and so on—in an exported playlist are separated by tab characters. (In geek speak, this command creates a tab-delimited text file.) Most spreadsheet and database programs can read these tabs and use them to put each piece of information in its own spreadsheet cell or database field.

See tips for working with playlists.
Playlist Tips

GO TO DVD

Better Ways to Export Playlists

Too much information! That's what you're likely to say when you open a file created with iTunes' Export Song List command. Maybe you've exported the playlist because you want to create a custom CD label or jewel case card. In such a case, you don't need the bit rate and format of every song, not to mention all the other stuff iTunes includes in the exported file.

Some programmers have created free AppleScripts that provide improved playlist-exporting features. (To learn about expanding iTunes with AppleScripts, see page 50.) The Doug's AppleScripts for iTunes Web site (www.malcolmadams.com/itunes/) contains a great selection, including an AppleScript that will create a Web page showing a playlist's contents.

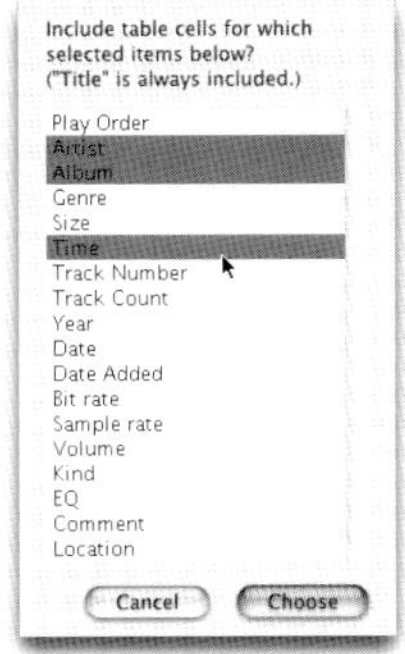

Playlist: **Mellow Funk** 11 songs, 58:13 total time, 65.4 MB

Title	Artist	Album	Time
C-Smooth	George Benson	Standing Together	5:56
The Touch	George Duke	After Hours	5:30
Keep Rollin'	George Benson	Standing Together	5:03
Butterfly	Herbie Hancock	Dis Is Da Drum	6:10
When Sly Calls	Michael Franks	Passion Fruit	5:51
Summer Breezin'	George Duke	A Brazilian Love Affair	4:50
Black Gravity	Herbie Hancock	Future 2 Future	5:29
Love Ballad	George Duke	Night After Night	4:39
Whatever Happened To...	George Duke	Is Love Enough?	4:43
Speak Low	George Duke	Snapshot	4:08
Until Sunrise	George Duke	Snapshot	5:54

Choose the information you want to export (right), and the AppleScript creates the Web page (far right).

Importing Playlists and Exporting in XML Format

You can also *import* playlists. Choose Import from the File menu and choose a previously exported playlist. This is a handy way to share playlists with friends or move them from one Mac to another. Note, however, that iTunes exports and imports only *information* about the songs in a playlist—it doesn't export and import the songs' MP3 files themselves.

Finally, it's worth nothing that your export options aren't just limited to tab-delimited text files. Using the pop-up menu in the Export Song List dialog box, you can also export a playlist in *XML* format.

When you export a playlist as XML, iTunes adds special codes to the file that identify each tidbit of information in the file. If you're curious to see what these codes look like, try exporting a playlist in XML format, then opening the resulting file with your word processor or any other program that can edit text.

Tech trivia: XML figures prominently in the iLife programs—it's how they exchange data. For example, iTunes and iPhoto use XML to enable your music and playlists to appear in iPhoto's slide show window. XML stands for *extensible markup language*, a phrase sure to earn you a wide berth at your next cocktail party.

Smart Playlists: iTunes as DJ

iTunes can create playlists for you based on criteria that you specify. When you're in a hurry—or if you're just curious to see what iTunes comes up with—use iTunes' *smart playlists* feature to quickly assemble playlists.

Creating a smart playlist involves specifying the criteria for the songs you want included in the playlist—for example, songs whose genre is jazz and whose year is in the range of 1960 to 1969. You can choose to limit the size of the playlist using various criteria, including playing time (don't create a playlist longer than 74 minutes); disk space (don't create a playlist larger than 2GB); number of songs (limit this playlist to 20 songs); and much more. You'll find some smart playlist ideas on the next page.

The smart playlists feature is really just a sophisticated search command: you tell iTunes to find songs that meet various criteria, and iTunes assembles them into a playlist. But a good playlist is more than just a series of songs that meet certain rules—it also presents those songs in a musically and emotionally pleasing way. A ballad may segue into an up-tempo tune, for example, or a laid-back instrumental may follow a dramatic vocal.

So go ahead and use iTunes' smart playlist feature to quickly throw together playlists. But to really do justice to your music, build your playlists by hand.

Creating a Simple Smart Playlist

To create a smart playlist, choose New Smart Playlist from the File menu or press the Option key while clicking the playlist button (⚙) in the lower-left corner of the iTunes window.

Choose an artist, composer, or genre from this pop-up menu, then type text in the adjacent box. (If you want to search on other items, such as song name, use the Advanced tab.)

The Simple tab lets you specify just one criterion. To specify multiple criteria, click the Advanced tab.

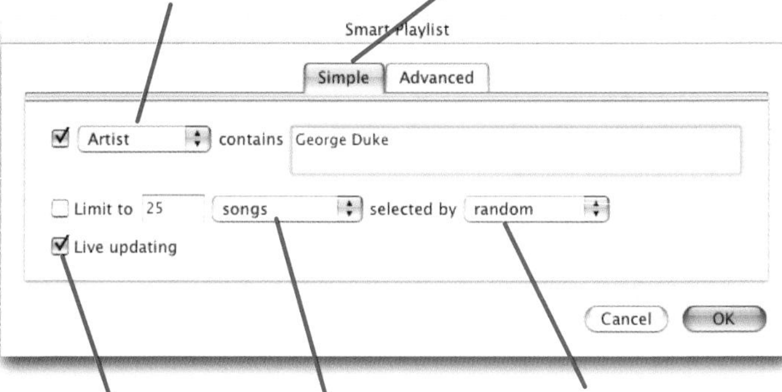

iTunes updates a smart playlist's contents as you add songs to (or remove them from) your music library. To turn a smart playlist into a static one, uncheck Live Updating.

iTunes normally organizes the songs in a smart playlist in random order, but you can choose to organize them by artist name, song name, and other criteria.

You can limit the size of the smart playlist to a maximum number of songs, minutes, hours, megabytes (MB), or gigabytes (GB).

Changing a Smart Playlist

To modify a smart playlist's criteria or update settings, select the smart playlist and choose Get Info from the File menu (or press ⌘-I).

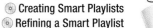

See how to create and modify smart playlists.
Creating Smart Playlists
Refining a Smart Playlist

Be More Specific: The Advanced Tab

The options in the Advanced tab enable you to be extremely specific about which songs iTunes includes in a smart playlist.

The criteria pop-up menus give you far more choices than their counterparts in the Simple tab.

To have iTunes apply all of your criteria as it searches and compiles the playlist, choose All. If you choose Any, iTunes adds a song if it matches any of your criteria.

To add another criterion, click the ⊕ button. To remove a criterion, click the ⊖ button.

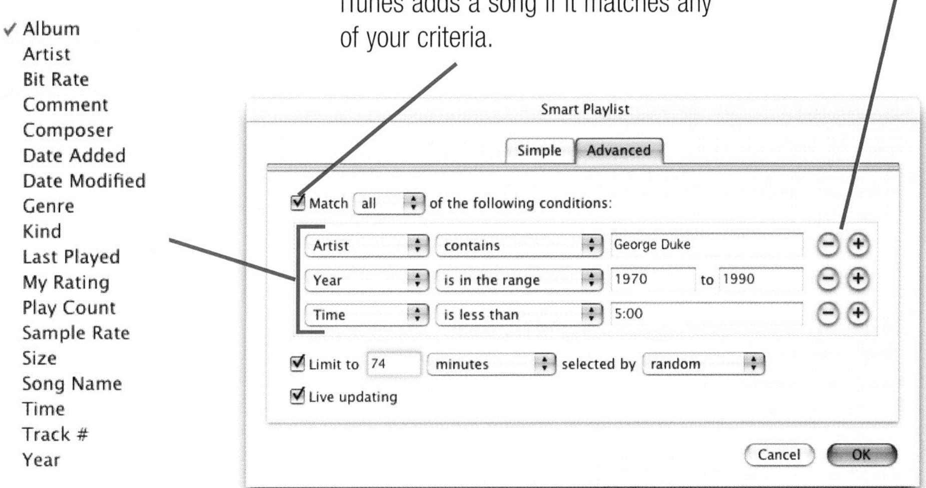

A Cookbook of Smart Playlist Ideas

Some smart playlist ideas are obvious: a playlist containing songs from your favorite artists, a playlist of dance tunes, and so on. But don't restrict yourself to the obvious—use the options in the Advanced tab to create smart playlists that present your music in new ways.

Here are a few ideas to get your creative juices flowing.

Smart Playlist Suggestions

For a Compilation of	Specify These Criteria
Short dance tunes	Genre is dance and Time is less than 5:00
The same song performed by various artists	Song Name is equal to *name*
Songs added to your library recently	Date Added is in the last 1 week (adjust date value as desired)
Songs from a particular artist and era	Artist Name is *name* and Year is in the range *years here*
Songs you haven't listened to recently	Last Played is not in the last *x* days (adjust date value as desired)
Songs or audio files that are not in MP3 format	Kind is not "MPEG audio file" (don't type the quotes)

Find that Tune: Searching and Browsing

As your music library grows, you'll want to take advantage of the features iTunes provides for locating songs, artists, and albums.

With the iTunes Search box, you can quickly narrow down the list of songs displayed to only those songs that match the criterion you typed.

With the Browse button, you can quickly scan your music library by artist, album name, or genre.

And with the Show Song File command in the File menu, you can quickly display the actual MP3 file that corresponds to a given song in your library or in a playlist.

Searching

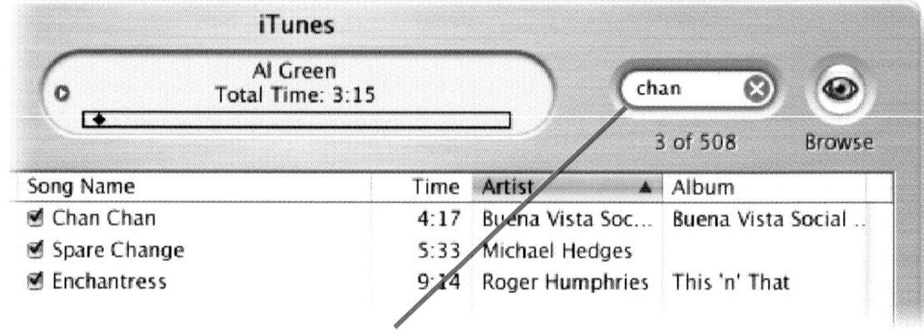

As you type in the Search box, iTunes narrows down the list of songs displayed. iTunes searches the album title, artist, genre, and song title items. To see all the songs in your library or playlist, select the text in the Search box and press Delete, or simply click the ⊗ in the Search box.

Browsing

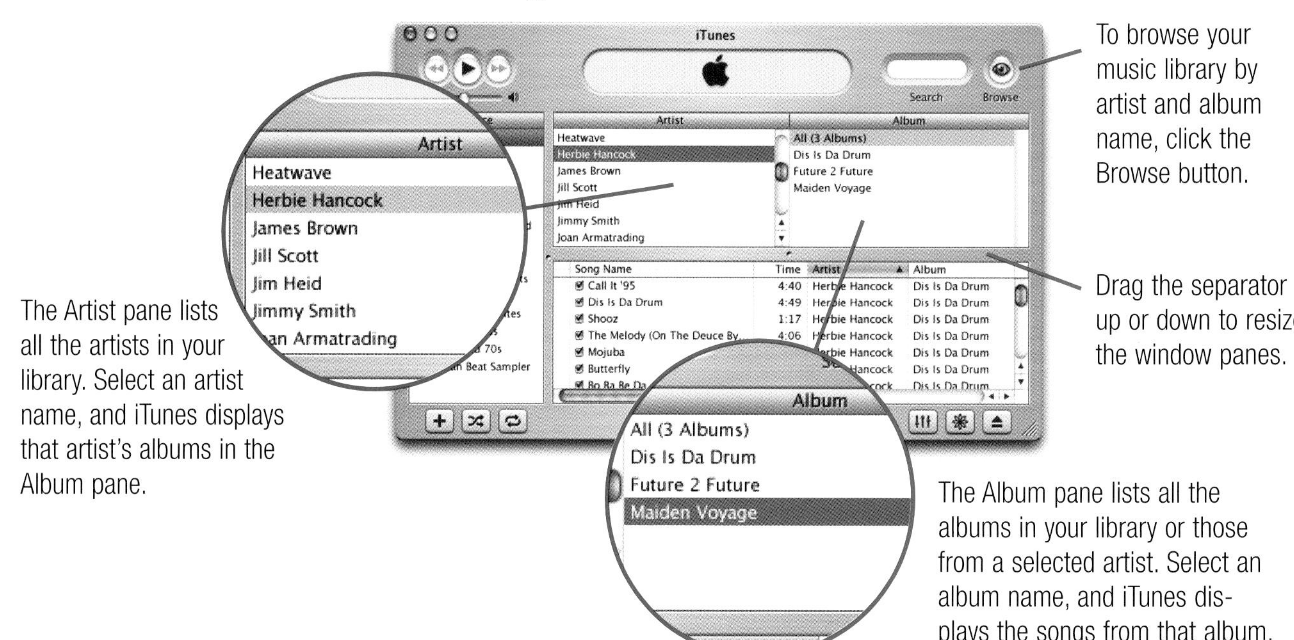

To browse your music library by artist and album name, click the Browse button.

Drag the separator up or down to resize the window panes.

The Artist pane lists all the artists in your library. Select an artist name, and iTunes displays that artist's albums in the Album pane.

The Album pane lists all the albums in your library or those from a selected artist. Select an album name, and iTunes displays the songs from that album.

See iTunes' searching and browsing features in action.
Searching for Songs
Browsing Your Song Library

Browsing by Genre

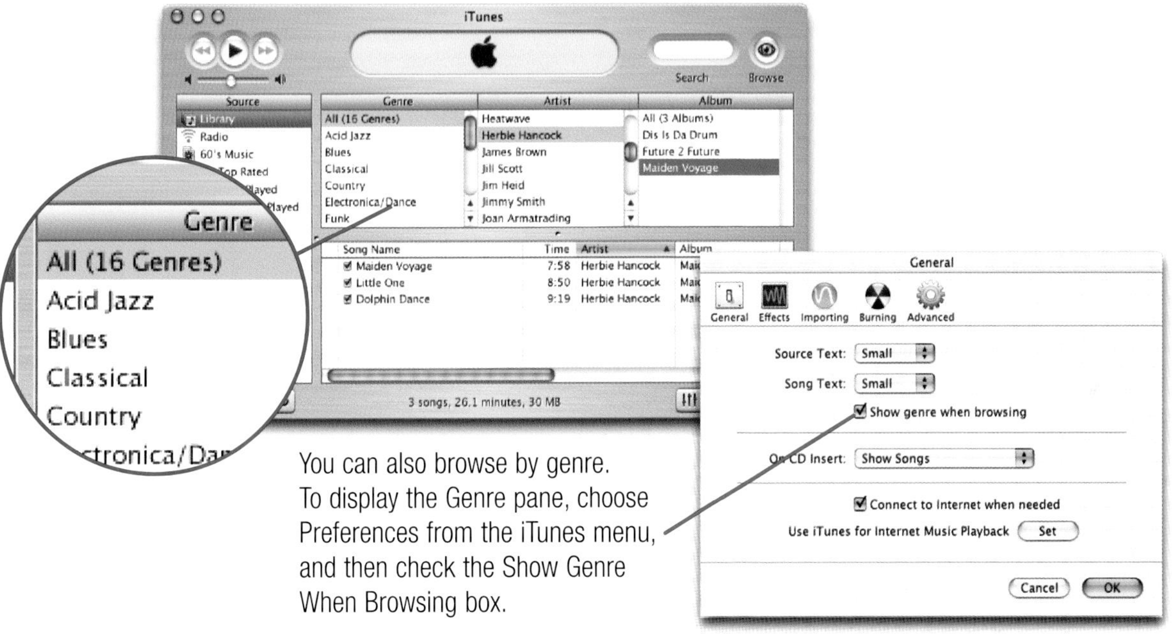

You can also browse by genre. To display the Genre pane, choose Preferences from the iTunes menu, and then check the Show Genre When Browsing box.

Finding a Song's MP3 File

There may be times when you want to locate a song's MP3 file on your hard drive—to back it up, for example, to move it to another drive, or to simply determine where it's stored.

To locate a song's disk file, select the song and choose Show Song File from the File menu (or press ⌘-R). iTunes switches you to the Finder, opens the folder containing the song, and highlights the song file.

Improving Sound Quality with the Equalizer

The iTunes *equalizer* lets you boost and attenuate various frequency ranges; think of it as a very sophisticated set of bass and treble controls. You might pump up the bass to make up for small speakers. You might boost the high frequencies to make up for aging ears. Or you might increase the mid-range frequencies to improve the clarity of a spoken recording.

The iTunes equalizer (EQ) divides the audio spectrum into ten *bands*, and provides a slider that lets you boost or attenuate frequencies in each band. The bands start at 32 hertz (Hz), a deeper bass than most of us can hear, and go all the way up to 16 kilohertz (kHz), which, while short of dog-whistle territory, approaches the upper limits of human hearing. (If you've been around for more than several decades or have listened to a lot of loud music, 16 kHz is probably out of your hearing range.)

iTunes provides more than 20 equalization presets from which to choose. You can listen to all your music with one setting applied, or you can assign separate settings to individual songs. You can also adjust EQ settings by hand and create your own presets.

To display the equalizer, click the Equalizer button (⊞) near the lower-right corner of the iTunes window, or choose Equalizer from the Window menu (⌘-2).

Finding Your Way Around the Equalizer

Click to turn on the equalizer.

Drag a slider up to boost the frequencies in that range; drag it down to attenuate them.

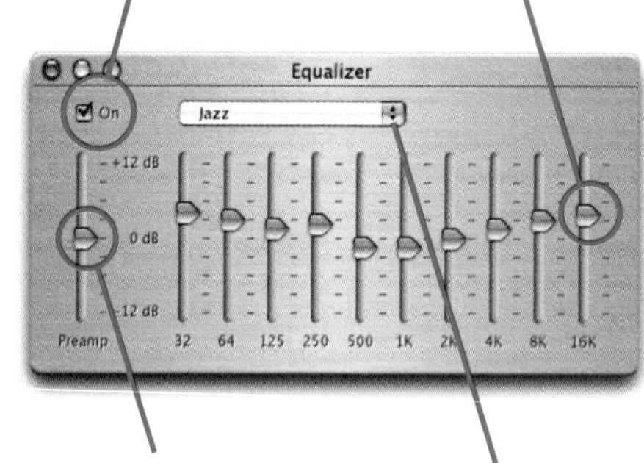

The preamp boosts or attenuates the volume for all frequencies equally.

Acoustic
Bass Booster
Bass Reducer
Classical
Dance
Deep
Electronic
Flat
Hip-Hop
✓ Jazz
Latin
Loudness
Lounge
Piano
Pop
R&B
Rock
Small Speakers
Spoken Word
Treble Booster

Choose a preset, create a new preset, or manage your list of presets.

Creating Your Own Preset

1. To save a customized preset, choose Make Preset from the preset pop-up menu.

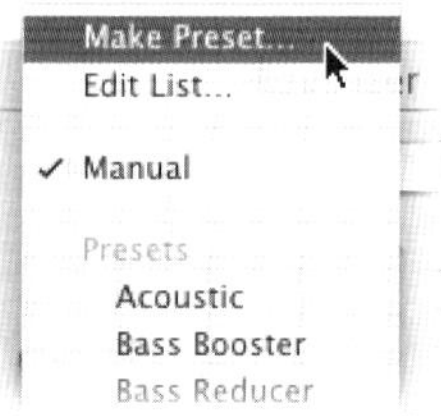

2. Type a name for the preset and click OK.

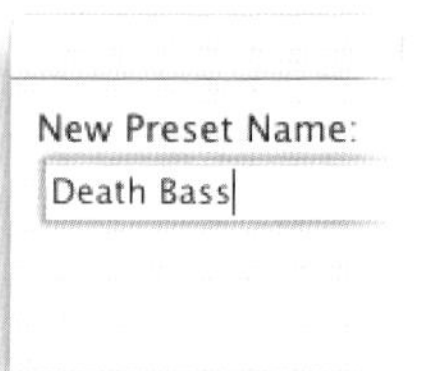

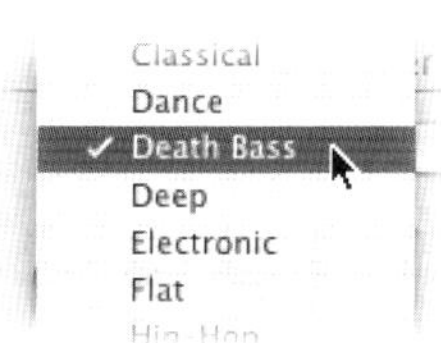

The new preset appears in the pop-up menu.

See the iTunes equalizer in action, and see how to apply EQ settings to individual songs.
Using the Equalizer
Assigning EQ Settings

Assigning Presets to Individual Songs

If you've turned on the equalizer, iTunes applies the current EQ setting to any song you play back. However, you can also assign EQ settings on a song-by-song basis.

First, choose View Options from the Edit menu and verify the Equalizer box is checked.

Next, choose the desired preset from the pop-up menu in the Equalizer column.

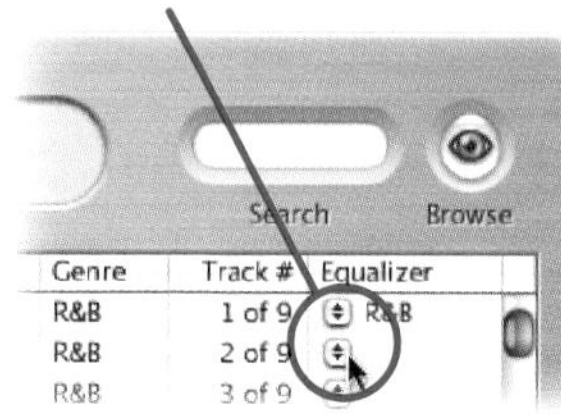

To change the EQ settings for several songs at once, select the songs and choose Get Info from the File menu. Then choose the desired EQ setting.

Presets that Make You Smile

You may have noticed that many of iTunes' presets have a smile-like appearance: the low- and high-frequency ranges are boosted to a greater degree than the mid-range frequencies.

Audio gurus call this shape the Fletcher-Munson curve. It reflects the fact that, at most listening levels, our ears are less sensitive to low and high frequencies than they are to mid-range frequencies.

Chances are your stereo system has a Loudness button. When you turn it on, the stereo applies a similar curve to make the music sound more natural at lower volume levels.

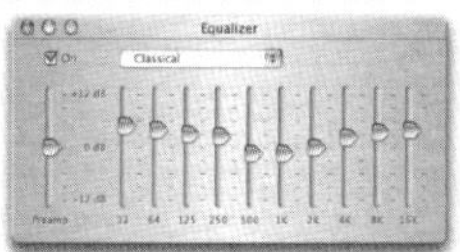
Classical

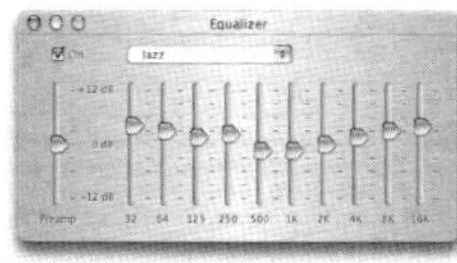
Jazz

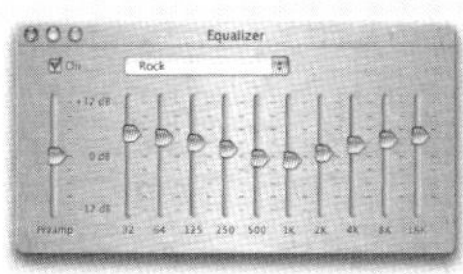
Rock

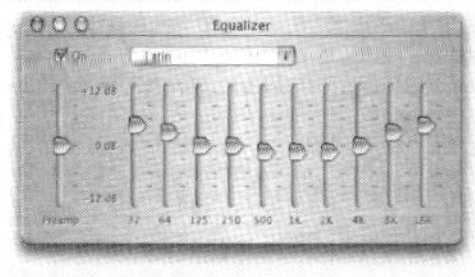
Latin

"That Song Needs a Bit More 250"

Being able to control the volume of 10 different frequency ranges is great, but how do you know which ranges to adjust? Here's a guide to how frequency ranges correlate with those of some common musical instruments and the human voice. Note that these ranges don't take into account harmonics, which are the tonal complexities that help us discern between instruments. Harmonics can easily exceed 20 kHz.

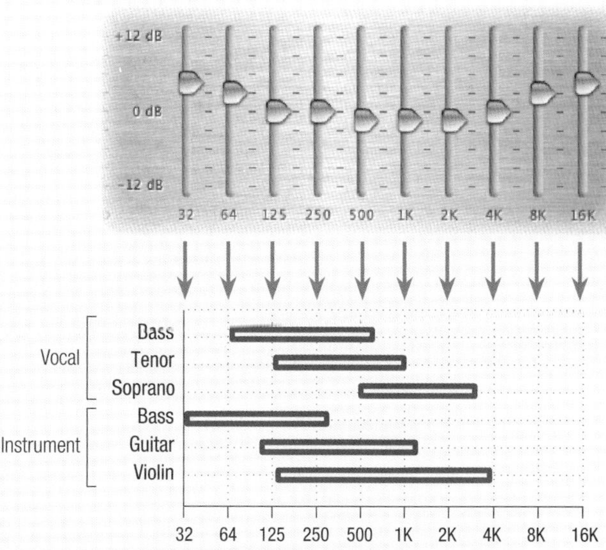

Burning CDs

After you've created some playlists, you can burn their songs onto audio CDs that will play in just about any CD player. (Some older CD and DVD players have trouble reading discs created using a CD burner.)

Burning a CD using iTunes is a two-click proposition. But there are some subtleties behind CD burning that you may want to explore.

Step 1. Select the Playlist You Want to Burn

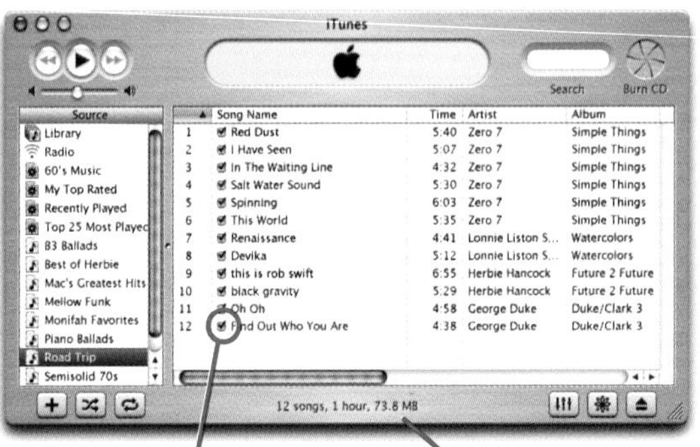

If the playlist contains a song that you don't want to burn, uncheck the box next to the song's name.

iTunes displays the playlist's total duration here.

Important: If you're burning an audio CD, keep the playlist's duration under 74 minutes.

Step 2. Click the Burn CD button

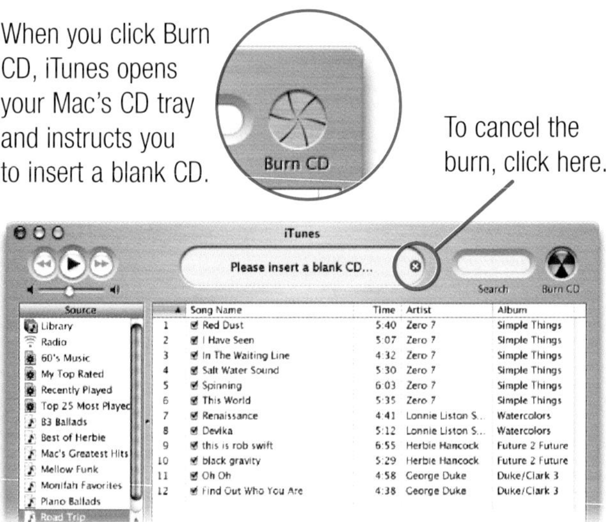

When you click Burn CD, iTunes opens your Mac's CD tray and instructs you to insert a blank CD.

To cancel the burn, click here.

Step 3. Begin the Burn

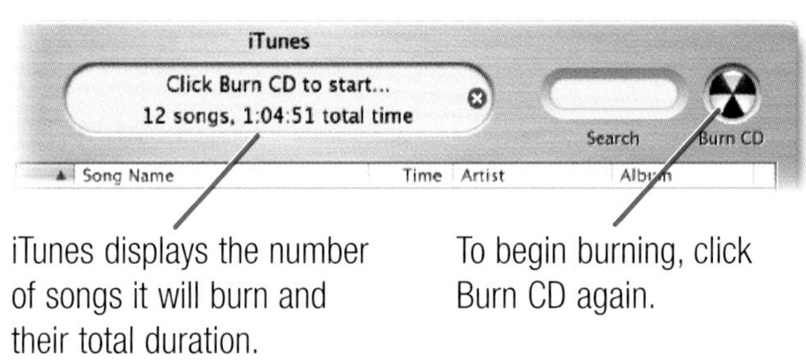

iTunes displays the number of songs it will burn and their total duration.

To begin burning, click Burn CD again.

As the CD burns, iTunes displays a status message. You can cancel a burn in progress by clicking the ⊗ button, but you'll end up with a *coaster*—a damaged CD blank whose only useful purpose is to sit beneath a cold drink.

Watch the CD-burning process.
Burning an Audio CD
GO TO DVD

Tips for Your Burning Endeavors

CD-R Details

Many brands of CD-R media are available, and some people swear by a given brand. Some users even claim that certain colors of CD-R blanks are better than others.

My advice: Don't sweat it—just buy name-brand CD-R blanks. And don't fret about their colors. Color varies depending on the organic dyes used by the CD-R's manufacturer, and different manufacturers use different dye formulations. Color isn't a useful indicator of CD-R quality anyway.

How long will your burned CDs last? Manufacturers toss out figures ranging from 75 to 200 years, but these are only estimates based on accelerated aging tests that attempt to simulate the effects of time.

One thing is certain: a CD-R will last longer when kept away from heat and bright light. Avoid scratching *either side* of a CD-R—use a felt-tipped pen to label it, and don't write any more than you need to. (The solvents in the ink can damage the CD over time.)

To learn more about CD-R media, visit the CD-Recordable FAQ at www.cdrfaq.org.

Burning MP3 CDs

Normally, iTunes burns CDs in standard audio CD format. But you can also burn tracks as MP3 files; this lets you take advantage of MP3's compression so you can squeeze more music onto a CD—roughly ten times the number of songs that an audio CD will hold.

But there's a catch: Most audio CD players can't play MP3-format CDs. If you're shopping for a CD or DVD player, you may want to look for one that supports MP3 playback.

To have iTunes burn in MP3 format, first choose Preferences from the iTunes menu, and choose the Burning button. Click the MP3 CD button, and then click OK.

When ripping CDs that you'll subsequently be burning in MP3 format, you might find it useful to activate iTunes' track-numbering option, described on page 22. That's because many players play the songs on MP3 CDs in alphabetical order—activating track numbering will enable the tracks to play back in the correct order.

Setting the Gap Between Tracks

Normally, iTunes uses two-second gaps to separate songs on an audio CD. But there may be times when you want to change that gap or remove it entirely—for example, many contemporary artists sequence the songs on their CDs so that one seamlessly flows into the next; a two-second gap would ruin that mood.

To change the gap, choose the desired setting from the Gap Between Songs pop-up menu in the Burning section of the iTunes Preferences dialog box.

Burning to CD-RW Media

For broadest compatibility with CD players, you'll want to burn using CD-R blanks, which can't be erased and reused. But the CD burners in all current Macs can also use CD-RW media—*rewritable* media—which costs more but can be erased and reused again and again.

A growing number of CD players can play back rewritable media, and if yours is among them, you might consider using rewritable media for some burning jobs. Maybe you've recorded some streaming Internet radio for a long car trip, programs you'll only want to hear once. Or perhaps you're creating a one-time playlist for a party. CD-RW is ideal for tasks like these.

Note that iTunes can't erase a CD-RW disc. To do that, use Mac OS X's Disk Utility program; it's located in the Utilities folder, inside the Applications folder.

Tuning In to Internet Radio

The Internet is transforming a lot of things, and broadcasting is one of them. You can tune into thousands of streaming Internet radio stations using iTunes and other programs.

Many of these stations are commercial or public broadcasters that are also making their audio available on the 'net. But most stations are Internet-only affairs, often set up by music lovers who simply want to share their tastes with the rest of us. You can join them, as described on page 42.

If part of streaming audio's appeal is its diversity, the other part is its immediacy. Streaming playback begins just a few seconds after you click on a link—there's no waiting for huge sound files to download before you hear a single note.

Several formats for streaming audio exist, and MP3 is one of them. Using the iTunes Radio tuner, you can listen to Internet radio stations that stream in MP3 format.

You can't use iTunes to listen to Internet radio stations that use formats other than MP3. To tune in the full range of Internet streaming media, use Apple's QuickTime Player (www.apple.com/quicktime), Microsoft's Windows Media Player (www.windowsmedia.com), and RealNetworks' RealOne (www.real.com).

Turn on the Tuner

The first step in using iTunes to listen to Internet radio is to activate the iTunes radio tuner.

Click Radio Tuner to switch the iTunes view to the radio tuner. To display the tuner in its own window, double-click.

iTunes retrieves its list of Internet radio categories and stations from the Internet. Click Refresh to have iTunes contact the tuning service and update its list of categories and stations.

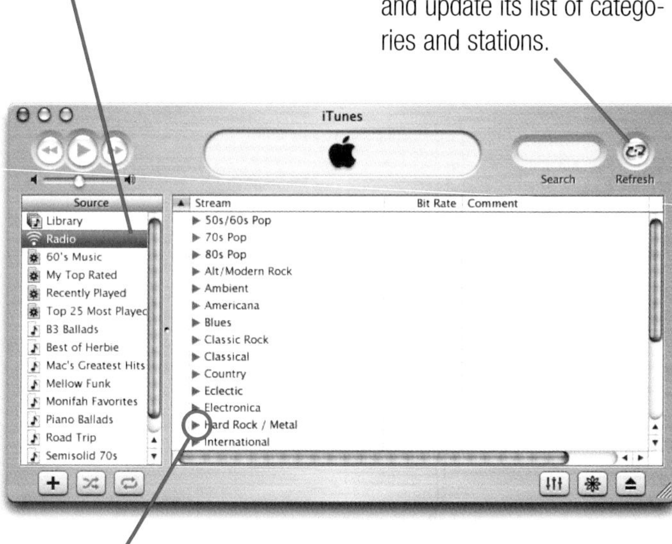

iTunes groups Internet radio stations by genre; to display the stations in a genre, double-click the genre name or click on the triangle to its left.

Bandwidth: Internet Radio's Antenna

The quality of your Internet radio "reception" depends in part on the speed of your Internet connection.

With Internet radio, information listed in the Bit Rate column is particularly important. It reflects not only how much the audio has been compressed, but also how fast a connection you'll need in order to listen without interruption. For example, if you have a 56 kbps modem connection, you won't be able to listen to a stream whose bit rate is higher than 56 kbps. (Indeed, even a 56 kbps stream may hiccup occasionally.)

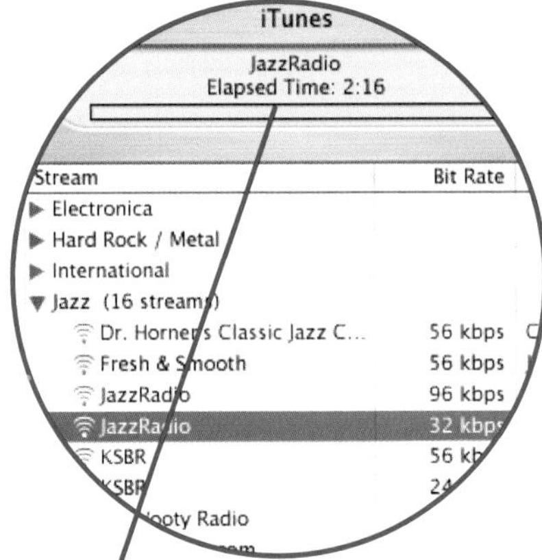

iTunes shows how long you've been listening to a stream. Notice that when you're listening to a live stream, there is no control for skipping forward and backward within a song.

To listen to a station, double-click the station's name.

How Streaming Works

When you begin playing back an Internet radio stream, iTunes connects to a streaming server, which downloads several seconds' worth of audio into an area of memory called a *buffer*. When the buffer is full, playback begins. The player then continues downloading audio into the buffer while simultaneously playing back the audio that it has already buffered. It's this just-in-time downloading that gives streaming its near-immediate gratification—most of the time, anyway.

If Internet congestion or connection problems interrupt the incoming stream, the buffer may empty completely, stalling playback while the buffer refills.

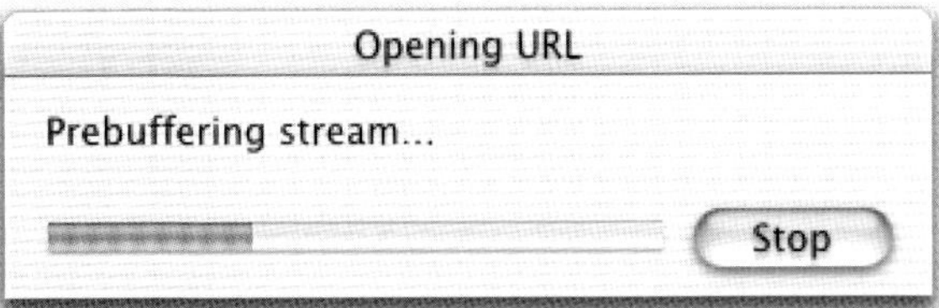

Internet Radio: The Rest of the Story

Do you want to go from being a listener to being a broadcaster? The easiest way to set up your own Internet radio station is to use the Live365 broadcasting service (www.live365.com).

For a monthly fee of under $10, Live365 will dish out up to 100MB worth of MP3 tracks. You upload your tracks to Live365's servers, create playlists, and just like that, you're a broadcaster. Your station might even end up in the iTunes Radio Tuner listing.

If you have a fast, continuous Internet connection, you can also run your own streaming server and dish out MP3s directly from your iTunes music library. Apple's free QuickTime Streaming Server can serve up MP3 files, and any Internet user with an MP3 program—iTunes, RealOne, WinAmp, and so on—will be able to tune in.

You can download the QuickTime Streaming Server at www.apple.com/quicktime/products/qtss/. But take note: while the server is well designed, setting it up isn't as straightforward as using iTunes or the other iLife programs.

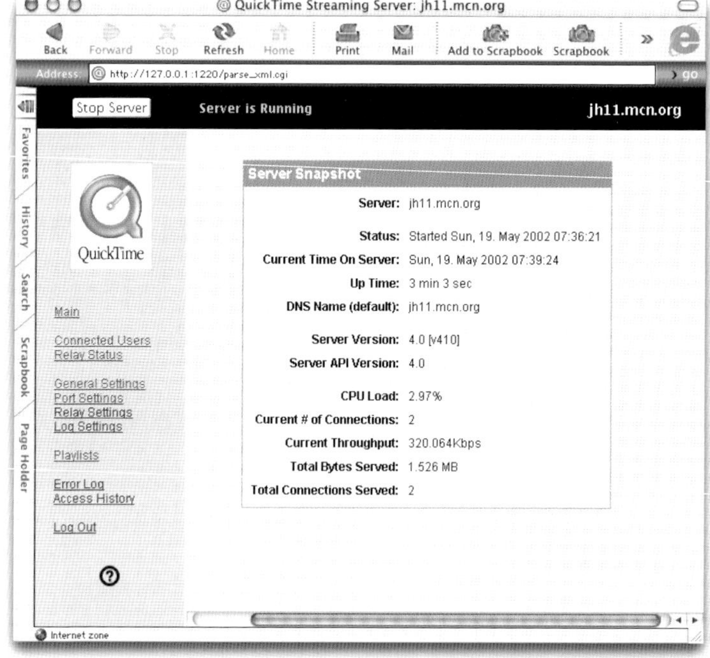

You configure and monitor the free QuickTime Streaming Server using your Web browser. Note that operating your own streaming server may require you to pay licensing fees to the copyright holders of the music you broadcast. For details on the licensing controversies swirling around Internet radio, see www.saveinternetradio.org.

You can also use QuickTime Streaming Server to set up a "local" radio station that broadcasts on your home or office network. Using the QuickTime Streaming Server administrator screens, configure your media directory to be your iTunes Music folder. Then you can create QuickTime Streaming Server playlists and tune in your music from any computer on your network.

Get links to Internet radio tools.
www.macilife.com/itunes

Internet Radio and Playlists

You can drag Internet radio station listings into playlists as though they were standalone MP3 tracks. Because Internet radio stations broadcast continuously, iTunes won't switch from one station to the next when it plays back the playlist.

Still, an Internet radio playlist can be a handy way to create a list of favorite Internet radio stations. Drag your favorite stations into a playlist, and you can access them with one mouse click—no need to activate the Radio Tuner and then open various genres to find the station you want.

Recording Internet Radio Streams

Internet radio streams aren't saved on your hard drive—like conventional radio, Internet radio is a fleeting phenomenon.

Or is it? The truth is, there are a couple of ways you can record Internet radio streams. The easiest way is to use Johann Huguenin's iNet Stream Archiver. With this $15 shareware program, you can create bookmarks of your favorite Internet radio stations by dragging the stations' listings from the iTunes window. You can then record their streams on your hard drive, optionally using a timer function to start and stop recording.

iNet Stream Archiver is limited to recording MP3 streams. To record streams in other formats—for example, Windows Media or QuickTime—use Rogue Amoeba Software's Audio Hijack. This program can record audio from nearly any program that makes noise. An "audio VCR" feature lets you set up timers that automatically start and stop recording at specific times.

Audio Hijack also includes numerous audio-enhancing features that can add reverberation and other effects. The slightly costlier Audio Hijack Pro adds additional goodies, including the ability to pause recording.

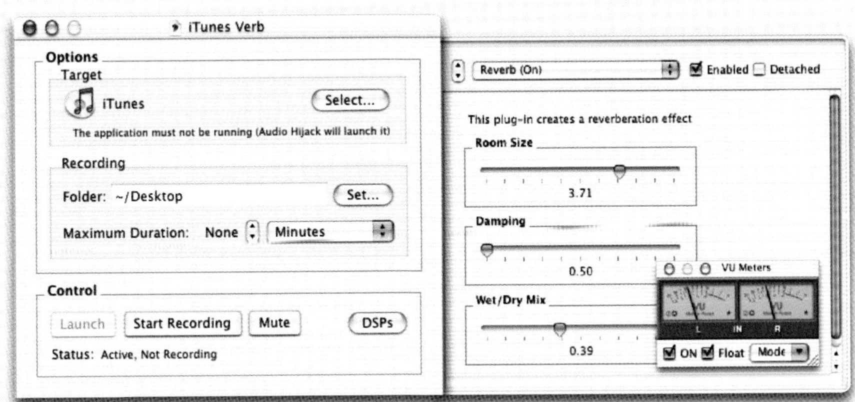

Analog to Digital: Converting Tapes and Albums

If you're like me, you're desperate to recapture the past: you want to create MP3 files from audio cassettes and vinyl albums.

Bridging the gap between the analog and digital worlds requires some software and hardware. The process involves connecting your Mac to an audio source, such as a cassette deck or stereo system, and then using recording software to save the audio on your hard drive as it plays back. You can encode the resulting files into MP3 format and add them to your iTunes music library.

Depending on your Mac, you may need an audio-input adapter in order to connect an audio source to the computer. If your Mac doesn't have an audio-input jack, you'll need an adapter such as Griffin Technology's iMic (below), which is inexpensive and does a fine job. Griffin and many other companies also sell high-end audio hardware that you might prefer if you're an audiophile.

Step 1. Make the Connections

Recording analog sources is easiest when you connect the Mac to the audio output of a stereo system. This will enable you to record anything your stereo can play, from vinyl albums to cassettes to FM radio.

Most stereo receivers have auxiliary output jacks on their back panels. To make the connection, use a cable with two RCA phono plugs on one end and a ⅛-inch stereo miniplug on the other. Connect the phono plugs to the receiver's output jacks, and the miniplug to the input jack on your Mac or audio adapter.

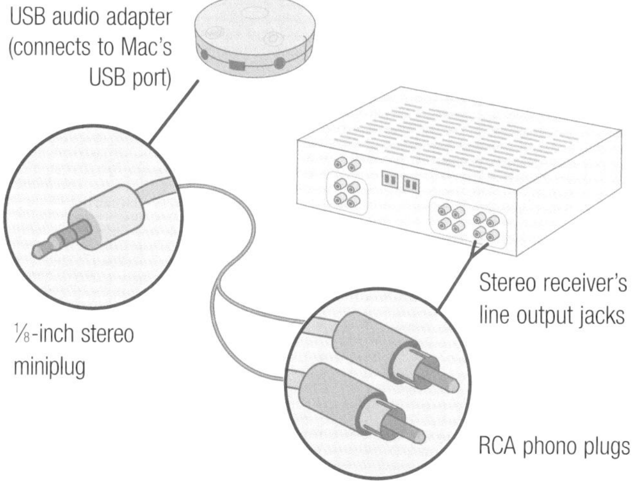

Step 2. Prepare to Record

Before you record, set your audio levels properly: you want the audio signal to be as loud as possible without distorting the sound.

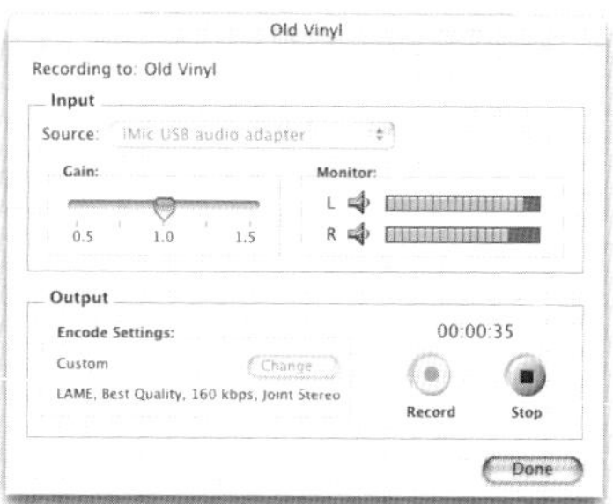

Fire up your audio recording software (N2MP3 Professional is shown here), and adjust its recording levels so that the loudest passages of music fully illuminate the volume meters.

See the process of digitizing a record and converting it to MP3.
Converting Records into MP3s

GO TO DVD

Step 3. Record

First, do a test recording. Activate your software's Record mode and begin playing back the original audio, preferably a loud passage. After a minute or two, stop and play back the recorded audio to verify that the recording levels you set are correct. Listen for distortion in loud passages; if you hear any, decrease the levels slightly.

Once you've arrived at the correct setting for recording levels, record the original audio in its entirety.

Step 4. Encode as MP3

If you aren't recording directly to MP3 format, you'll need to convert the recording (which is likely in AIFF format) into MP3 format. You can use iTunes to do this: press the Option key and choose Convert to MP3 from the Advanced menu, and then locate and double-click on the recording you just made. iTunes will convert the track and store the resulting MP3 file in your iTunes library.

iTunes can also convert multiple tracks in one operation. After choosing Convert to MP3, simply ⌘-click on each file you want to import.

Before converting, you might want to adjust iTunes' encoding settings by using the Preferences command as described on page 22. Some MP3 buffs lower the bit rate for music that originated on analog media, on the theory that a higher bit rate would be wasted on it. You might try a bit rate of 96 kbps, with VBR turned on. Consider doing some tests and letting your ears be the judge.

Choosing an Audio Recording Program

Plenty of audio-recording programs are available, ranging from free programs such as TC Works' SparkME to commercial programs such as Bias' Peak.

A fine utility for recording analog audio is Proteron Software's N2MP3 Professional. This powerhouse program can record directly into MP3 format, thus saving you an additional step. It also includes several MP3 encoders, including one called LAME, whose sound quality many MP3 gurus prefer to the encoder built into iTunes.

One of my favorite programs for recording analog audio is CD Spin Doctor, included with Roxio's Toast Titanium CD burning software. CD Spin Doctor creates AIFF files, which you can encode into MP3 format using iTunes.

A few features make CD Spin Doctor particularly ideal for converting analog recordings into digital form. One is the Auto-Define Tracks command: choose it, and CD Spin Doctor scans a recording, detects the silence between each song, and then divides the recording into multiple tracks. This makes it easy to record one side of an album and then divvy it up into separate tracks.

CD Spin Doctor has noise and pop filters that can clean up abused records, as well as an "exciter" filter that enhances old recordings by beefing up bass and improving the sense of stereo separation.

There's also Griffin Technology's Final Vinyl, which I use on the DVD. You'll find links to these and other audio programs on this book's companion Web site.

iTunes Tips

Crossfading Between Songs

You hear it on the radio all the time: as one song nears its end, it begins to fade as the next song starts to play. You can recreate this effect in iTunes. First, choose Preferences from the iTunes menu, click the Effects button, and then check the Crossfade Playback box.

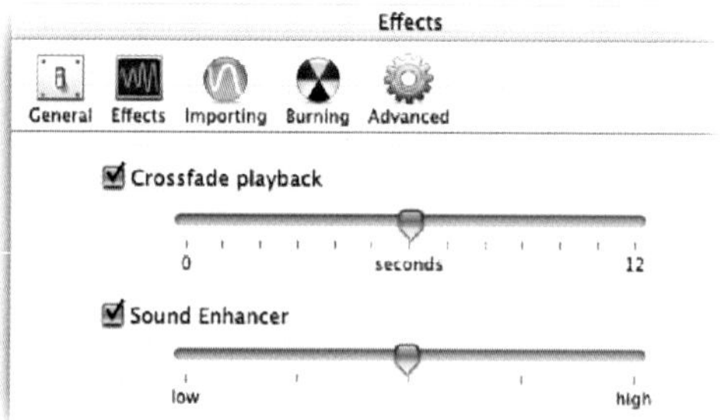

Use the slider to adjust the length of the crossfade effect.

With crossfading, one song fades out...

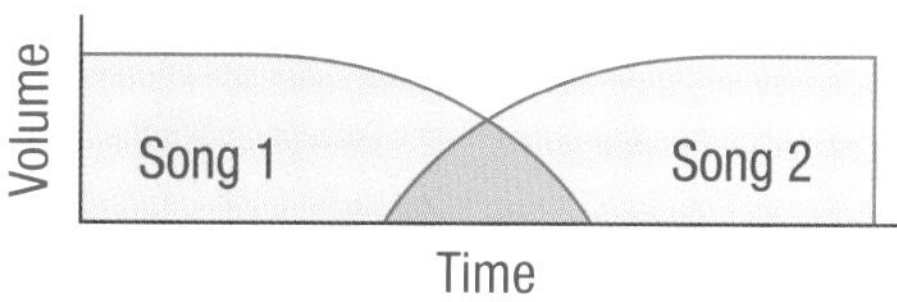

...as the next song fades in.

Using the Sound Enhancer

You can add aural punch by improving what audio gurus call *presence*, the perception that the instruments are right in the room with you. To do this, use the Sound Enhancer option in the Effects tab of the Preferences dialog box. Drag the slider toward the High setting, and you may notice brighter-sounding high frequencies and an enhanced sense of stereo separation. Experiment with the setting that sounds best for your ears—and your audio equipment.

Adjusting a Song's Volume Level

When you create a playlist containing songs from numerous albums, you may notice some songs are louder than others. One way to compensate for this is by adjusting the playback volume for specific songs. First, Control-click on a song and then choose Get Info from the contextual pop-up menu.

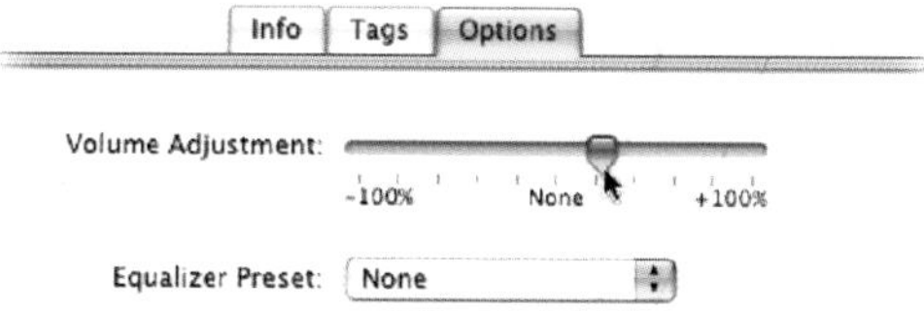

In the Options tab of the Song Information dialog box, drag the Volume Adjustment slider to decrease or increase the song's playback volume.

Tips for the iTunes Library

Adding MP3s from Other Sources

Chances are most of the MP3s you work with will be ones you've created from your own audio CDs. But you can also buy downloadable MP3 tracks from music sites such as MP3.com; many music sites also offer free MP3s.

And, although record industry executives wouldn't want me to say so, you can also download MP3s using utilities such as LimeWire (www.limewire.com) to access file-sharing networks such as Gnutella. Note that downloading via Gnutella may make you a thief—most of the tracks available through file-swapping networks have been shared without the permission of their copyright holders.

Regardless of where your other MP3s come from, you can add them to your iTunes music library by simply dragging them into the iTunes window or by using the File menu's Add to Library command.

Optimizing Levels with Sound Check

A faster alternative to adjusting playback levels for individual songs is to use the Sound Check option, which optimizes playback volumes so that all songs play back with similar volume levels. To turn Sound Check on, choose Preferences from the iTunes menu, click the Effects button, then check the Sound Check box.

Customizing Your Columns

You can specify which columns of information iTunes displays in its windows—to remove columns you never use or to add ones that iTunes normally doesn't display. One way is by using the Edit menu's View Options command. Here's an easier way: Control-click on any column heading, and uncheck or check columns in the shortcut menu. You can also use the shortcut menu to automatically resize columns to fit the longest item in each one.

You can also change the order of the columns themselves, moving them left and right to suit your tastes. To move a column, click on its heading and then drag left or right.

Keeping Your Library Organized

iTunes normally stores your music in the Music folder, as described on page 25. If you download an MP3 file from the Internet and drag it into the iTunes window, you'll actually have two copies of the MP3 file on your hard drive.

If you don't want this—if you'd prefer to have your music files scattered throughout your hard drive—choose Preferences from the iTunes menu, click the Advanced button, and then uncheck the box labeled Copy Files to iTunes Music Folder When Adding to Library. You can also temporarily override the copying feature: press Option while dragging a file into the iTunes window. Note, though, that having music scattered across your hard drive makes backing up your music library much more cumbersome.

If you already have files scattered across your hard drive and you want to move them all to the Music folder, choose Consolidate Library from the Advanced menu.

More iTunes Tips

Adding One Playlist to Another

You can add the entire contents of one playlist to other playlists. In the Source area of the iTunes window, simply drag one playlist to another.

If you've opened multiple windows as described on page 30, you can also drag a playlist's name to an open playlist window. In the example shown here, I'm adding the contents of the Blue Six playlist to the Mellow Funk playlist.

Two Ways to Shuffle

Normally, the iTunes shuffle feature plays back songs in random order. You can, however, also choose to shuffle by *album*. In its album-shuffle mode, iTunes plays back an entire album in its original song order and then randomly chooses another album and plays all of it. It's an interesting variation on the random-playback theme that you might want to try.

To use album shuffle, choose Preferences from the iTunes menu, click the Advanced button, and in the Shuffle By area, click the Album button.

Everyone's a Critic: Rating Your Songs

iTunes lets you express your inner music critic by assigning a rating of between one and five stars to songs. You don't have to assign ratings, but if you do, you can use ratings as a criterion when creating smart playlists.

You can also sort your music library or playlists in order of your favorites: simply click on the My Rating column heading.

The fastest way to rate a song is to Control-click on it and then choose the desired rating from the My Rating pop-up menu.

You can also rate songs by clicking within the My Ratings column in the iTunes window or by opening the Options tab of the Song Info dialog box. In both cases, simply click the tiny dots

that represent placeholders for each star. Drag to the right to add stars, or to the left to remove them.

And finally, you can rate the song that is currently playing by using the iTunes icon in your dock. Click on the iTunes icon and hold down the mouse button for a moment—a pop-up menu appears. Use the My Ratings submenu to assign a rating.

The How and Why Behind Specifying Compilations

Chances are you have some compilation CDs in your music collection: *Solid Gold 70s, The Best of Bartok, Tuvanese Throat Singing Mania*, and so on. You can have iTunes store the MP3 files for compilations in a separate folder within your iTunes Music folder. This helps reduce folder clutter and makes it easier to locate and manage your MP3 files.

For example, say you have a compilation CD that contains tracks from a dozen different artists. Normally, iTunes creates a separate folder for each artist—even though that folder might contain just one MP3 file. But if you designate those songs as being part of a compilation, iTunes will store all of those tracks together in their own folder.

To tell iTunes that a song is part of a compilation, select the song and choose Get Info from the File menu or press ⌘-I. In the Tags area of the Song Information window, check the Part of a Compilation box. As with other tag-editing tasks, you can do this for multiple songs at once by selecting them all before choosing Get Info.

iTunes stores compilations within a folder whose name is, you guessed it, Compilations. Within this folder, iTunes creates a separate folder for each compilation you've specified.

Some Program to Watch Over Me

While you're listening, iTunes is watching: the program keeps track of how many times you listen to a song and when you last listened to it.

iTunes displays this audio odometer in its Play Count and Last Played columns. This means you can sort your music library or a playlist according to how many times you listened to a song (click the Play Count column heading) or when you last listened to it (click the Last Played column heading). Note that you'll probably have to scroll the iTunes window to the right to see these columns.

You can also use these data as criteria when creating a smart playlist (see page 32)—have iTunes create a playlist of your favorite songs or of those you haven't listened to lately.

Adding On: Scripts and Beyond

I've already mentioned that you can enhance the capabilities of iTunes through AppleScripts that automate iTunes in various ways.

You can also enhance the iTunes visualizer—the feature that displays those psychedelic patterns as your music plays back—by adding plug-ins. Visualizer plug-ins may not be as practical as AppleScripts, but on-screen psychedelics can often be more fun than practicalities.

Here's how to download and install iTunes AppleScripts and visualizer plug-ins, as well as information on some other programs that can round out the audio spoke of your digital hub.

Visualize Cool Graphics

If you're a fan of the iTunes visualizer, try out some of the free visualizer plug-ins available on the Web. My favorite is Andy O'Meara's free G-Force, which goes well beyond the built-in iTunes visualizer. For example, you can "play" G-Force—controlling its patterns and colors—by pressing keys on your keyboard as a song plays back.

You can find G-Force and other visualizer plug-ins by going to download Web sites.

Most visualizers include installation programs that tuck the plug-ins into the appropriate spot. But, just for the record, iTunes visualizer plug-ins generally live within the iTunes folder of your Library folder.

Automating with AppleScript

AppleScript is a powerful automation technology that is part of the Mac OS and many Mac programs, including iTunes. AppleScript puts your Mac on autopilot: when you run a script, its commands can control one or more programs and make them perform a series of steps.

Dozens of useful scripts are available for iTunes. You might start by downloading the set of scripts created by Apple (www.apple.com/applescript/itunes). After you've experimented with them, sprint to Doug's AppleScripts for iTunes (www.malcolmadams.com/itunes), where you'll find the best collection of iTunes AppleScripts.

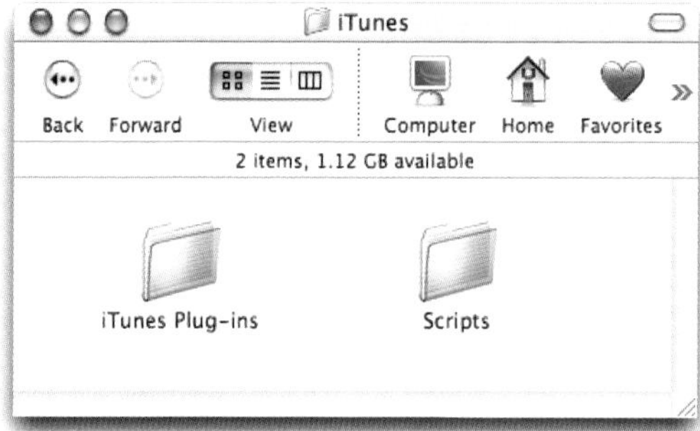

After you've downloaded an iTunes AppleScript, you need to move it to a specific place in order for iTunes to recognize it. First, quit iTunes. Then, click the Home button or choose Home from the Finder's Go menu. Next, locate and open the Library folder, and then locate and open the iTunes folder. Create a folder named Scripts inside this folder and stash your scripts here.

Beyond iTunes: Completing Your Audio Arsenal

Several programs can work with iTunes to expand its capabilities. I've mentioned some in previous sections—N2MP3 Professional, iNet Stream Archiver, and LimeWire, for example. A few more favorites are described here; for links to even more audio add-ons, visit *The Macintosh iLife* Web site.

iHam on iRye

Obviously named by over-caffeinated programmers, iHam on iRye is an interesting program that lets you control iTunes from a different Mac—think of it as a remote control for iTunes. First, set up the iHam on iRye server on the Mac containing iTunes and your music library. You can then use the iHam on iRye client program to connect to the server and play back songs and playlists. iPickles sold separately.

Toast Titanium

Roxio's Toast Titanium is a burning program for serious CD arsonists. This application can burn DVDs as well as audio and data CDs, and provides more control over the burning process. Just one example: while iTunes puts the same amount of time between each song on a CD, Toast Titanium lets you specify a different interval for each song. Toast Titanium also includes the CD Spin Doctor audio-recording program discussed on page 45.

Toast also works together with iTunes. As shown above, you can drag and drop songs from iTunes directly into Toast.

Panic's Audion

Audion combines ripping, playback, Internet radio, powerful playlist features, visualizers, and CD burning into one program. Sound like iTunes? Audion goes well beyond. For example, Audion supports a variety of MP3 encoders, rather than just one. It also lets you slow down the playback of a song—handy for musicians trying to figure out a complicated riff. Audion lets you play back two MP3s simultaneously and mix between them. With Audion's Alarm Clock command, you can have a song or playlist wake you up.

There's much more to Audion than I've described here. Suffice it to say that if you're into MP3, you should download the free trial version and audition Audion.

Books on Bytes: Listening to Audiobooks

iTunes isn't just about tunes. You can also use it to listen to recorded *audiobooks* that you can buy and download from Audible.com (www.audible.com). Listen to a novel on your next flight, burn it to a CD so you can listen to it in the car, or transfer it to your iPod and listen while you jog. Audible.com offers audio versions of novels, magazines, newspapers, comedy shows, and much more.

Working with audiobooks is easy, but it's a bit trickier than working with ordinary MP3 files. You must first set up an account with Audible.com to obtain a user name and a password. The first time you add an audiobook to your iTunes library, you will be asked to specify this information.

And to ensure that your Mac handles audiobooks correctly, be sure iTunes is set up to handle Internet playback. Quit your Web browser and email program, then choose Preferences from the iTunes menu. Click the General button at the top of the Preferences window, and click the Set button that appears next to the label Use iTunes for Internet Music Playback.

Now your Mac is ready to read aloud.

Working with Audiobooks

After you've visited www.audible.com and created an account, you're ready to buy and listen to audiobooks.

Step 1. Purchase and Download the Audiobook

When choosing an audiobook, you typically have a choice of formats, which are numbered 1 through 4. The iPod supports formats 2, 3, and 4. Which should you use? If you're using a modem connection, you might choose format 2—its files are smaller and thus download faster. If you have a fast connection, you might lean toward formats 3 or 4. They sound better, but they'll take longer to download and use more disk space on your Mac and iPod.

Step 2. Add the Audiobook to Your iTunes Library

When you download an audiobook, its icon appears on your Mac's desktop. Audiobooks end with the file extension .aa. Drag this icon into the iTunes window.

Step 3. Specify Account Information

The first time you add an audiobook to iTunes, you must specify the user name and password you created when signing up at Audible.com. iTunes contacts Audible.com to verify your account information.

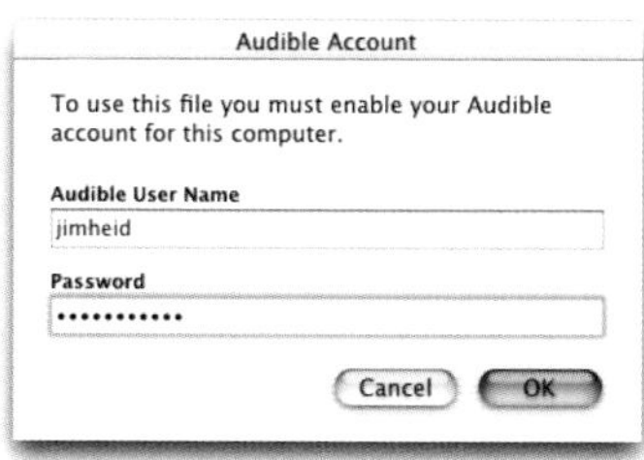

Contacting Audible
Verifying Audible account information...
Stop

Step 4. Listen

An audiobook appears in your iTunes library, just like any other song. You can listen to it, apply equalization to it, and burn it to a CD.

Audiobooks Tips

One Account on Up to Three Computers

You can use one Audible.com account with up to three computers. This enables you to move audiobooks between, say, your Mac at home, your PowerBook, and your Mac at work. If you try to add an account to a fourth computer, an error message appears. If you want to add the account to that computer, you must remove the account from one of the other three.

To remove an account, choose Remove Audible Account from the Advanced menu.

The Equalizer and Audiobooks

To improve the sound quality of audiobooks, try applying the Spoken Word equalizer setting.

Audiobookmarks

The audiobook format provides bookmarks: when you pause or stop an audiobook, iTunes creates a bookmark at the point where you stopped. When you resume playing the audiobook, playback resumes at the bookmark's position.

It gets better. The iPod also supports audiobookmarks, and it synchronizes them with iTunes when you synchronize your music library. This synchronization process works in both directions: if you pause an audiobook on your iPod, the bookmark is transferred to your Mac when you sync. Thus, you can use your iPod to start listening to an audiobook on your evening commute, then use your iMac to pick up where you left off when you get home.

Burning a Book

To burn an audiobook to a CD, create a playlist and drag the audiobook to the playlist. Next, select the playlist and click the Burn CD button.

If your audiobook is longer than roughly one hour, it won't fit on a standard audio CD. For lengthy audiobooks, you'll have to tell iTunes what portion you want to burn. Select the audiobook, then choose Get Info from the File menu. Next, click the Options tab and set up the Start Time and Stop Time boxes as shown here.

Start Time: 0:00
Stop Time: 1:00:00

Enter these values to burn the first hour.

Start Time: 1:00:00
Stop Time: 2:00:00

Enter these values to burn the second hour.

iPod: Music to Go

It's hard to appreciate the significance of the iPod until you load it up with hundreds of songs and begin carrying it around with you.

Then it hits you: all of your favorite songs are right there with you, ready to play—in the car, on a walk, in the living room, on a plane. There's no finding and fumbling with CDs, and every song is only a couple of button presses away.

Several factors work together to make the iPod the best portable music player, starting with its capacity: no other portable player of its size can store as many tunes.

Another factor is the iPod's integration with iTunes: connect the iPod to your Mac, and iTunes automatically synchronizes your music library and playlists. And, the synchronization occurs over FireWire, which is many times faster than the USB connections used by other portable players.

And finally, there's the iPod's versatility. Its ability to store contact information, your calendar, appointment schedule, and other files make the iPod more than a portable music player.

Life with an iPod

Step 1. Build a Music Library

Use the techniques described earlier in this section to import songs from audio CDs, assign equalization settings (optional), edit song information (if necessary), and create playlists.

Step 2. Transfer to the iPod

Connect the iPod to your Mac using the included FireWire cable. iTunes copies your music library and playlists to the iPod.

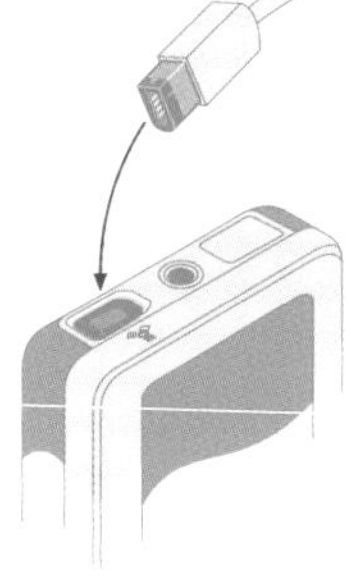

While the iPod is connected, its battery charges. The battery charges to 80 percent of its capacity in an hour, and charges fully in about three hours.

You can adjust settings for updating the music on your iPod by using the iPod Preferences dialog box, described on the following pages.

Watch an iPod synchronization session.
Synchronizing with an iPod

Step 3. Listen and Repeat

Disconnect the iPod and start listening. When you modify your iTunes music library or playlists, you can update the iPod's contents to match by simply connecting the iPod again.

You can use the headphones jack to connect the iPod to a stereo system or other audio hardware, such as an FM transmitter. To connect to a stereo system, use a cable with a ⅛-inch miniplug on one end and two RCA phono plugs on the other. Connect the phono plugs to an available input on the back of your system.

To the right of the iPod's audio-output jack is the Hold button. Slide it to the left to disable the iPod's buttons. This is useful when you're transporting the iPod in a briefcase or purse, where its buttons could get pressed, causing the battery to drain.

To back up to the previous list of choices, press the Menu button.

The battery gauge shows how much power remains.

Use the scroll wheel to move the menu highlight up and down, and to adjust the playback volume.

The iPod's menu system uses a "drill-down" scheme: select an option and press the Select button, and you drill down one level to another menu or list of choices.

To skip to the previous or next song, press the Previous or Next button.

To choose an item in a menu, press the Select button.

To pause and resume playback, press the Play/Pause button. To turn off the iPod, press and hold this button for a few seconds.

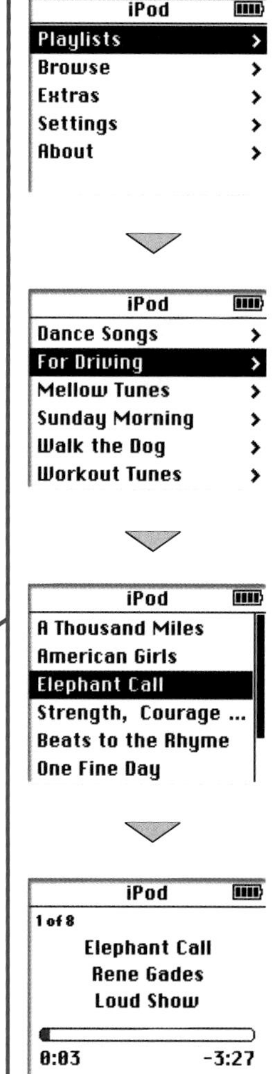

Setting iPod Preferences

Normally, iTunes will synchronize all your playlists and your entire music library, or at least as much of it as will fit on the iPod.

But there may be times when you want to manually control which playlists and songs iTunes copies to the iPod. Maybe your iTunes music library is larger than will fit on the iPod, requiring you to specify what you want to copy. Or maybe you listen to some songs on your Mac but not on your iPod, and you don't want to waste iPod disk space by copying those songs.

Whatever the reason, you can use the iPod Preferences dialog box to specify updating preferences.

You can also use this dialog box to activate *FireWire disk mode*, in which the iPod appears on your desktop just like a hard drive (which, of course, it is). In FireWire disk mode, you can use the Mac's Finder to copy files to and from the iPod's hard drive. This is a handy way to shuttle documents to and from work, or to carry backups of important programs or files with you on the road.

Opening iPod Preferences

When you connect the iPod to the Mac and start iTunes, the iPod appears in the Source pane of the iTunes window, and an iPod preferences icon appears next to the Equalizer button.

The graph shows how much iPod disk space you've used and how much remains.

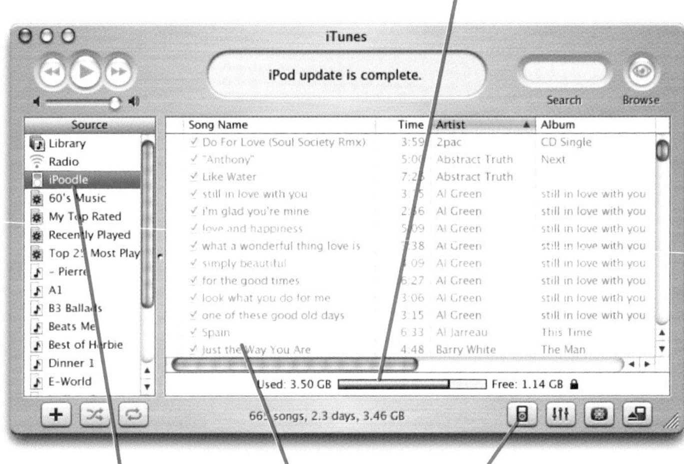

To rename the iPod, click its name and then type a new name. The name appears in iTunes, as shown above, and in the Finder (left) when the iPod is in FireWire disk mode. It also appears in the iPod's Info screen.

To display the iPod Preferences dialog box, click the Options button (🅾).

If iTunes is configured to update automatically (below), the iPod's contents appear dimmed (above) and you can't manually change them.

iPod Preferences

- (●) Automatically update all songs and playlists
- ( ) Automatically update selected playlists only:

iPod Preferences Settings

To control which playlists are copied, click this option and check the box next to each playlist you want to copy.

Normally, iTunes copies everything when you connect the iPod.

iPod Preferences

Automatically update all songs and playlists
Automatically update selected playlists only:
- Pierre
60's Music
A1
B3 Ballads
Beats Me
Manually manage songs and playlists
Open iTunes when attached
Enable FireWire disk use
Only update checked songs
Cancel OK

To update songs and playlists by hand, click this option. After you click OK, the iPod's contents in the iTunes window are no longer dimmed, and you can drag songs and playlists from iTunes to the iPod. See "Manual Management" on page 58.

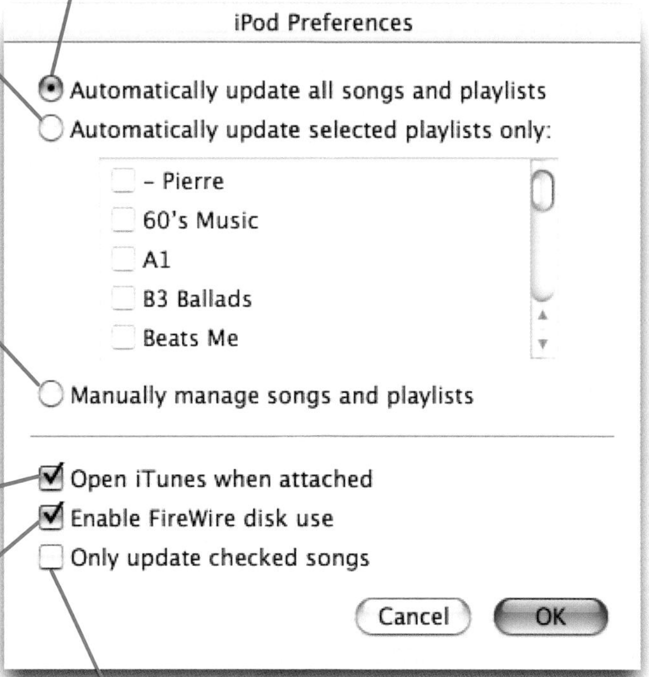

To have your Mac automatically start iTunes when you connect the iPod, choose this option.

To use the iPod as a FireWire hard drive, choose this option. (You must do so to add contacts and notes to the iPod; see page 60.)

If you've chosen automatic updating but don't want to copy all new songs to the iPod, check this box and then, in the Library, uncheck any new songs that you do not want copied. When you next update the iPod, only the new songs that are checked will be copied to it.

iPod Tips

Here are some tips for getting more out of your iPod and appreciating its finer points.

Browsing by Album

Looking for a way to access songs by album? It isn't obvious, but it's there: go to Browse, then choose Artists, then choose All.

Scrubbing within a Song

You can quickly move around, or scrub, within a song while it plays. Press the Select button, and the elapsed-time gauge on the iPod's screen is replaced with a little diamond—just like the one iTunes displays during playback. Using the scroll wheel, move the diamond left and right to scrub within the song.

Extending Battery Life

To get the longest playing times, turn off the screen's backlighting, avoid jumping between songs frequently (the hard drive is one of the iPod's biggest power consumers), and use the Settings menu to turn off the iPod's equalizer. And remember, you can play songs when the iPod is plugged in to its power adapter. If you put the iPod in manual-updating mode or use one of the iPod utilities discussed here, you can even play songs while the iPod is connected to (and charging from) the Mac.

iPod Utilities

Apple built a simple anti-piracy system into the iPod: its music files are stored in an invisible folder on the iPod's hard drive. Thus, you can't use the Finder to copy music files from the iPod to your hard drive. Music transfer is a one-way street: from the Mac to the iPod.

However, several free or inexpensive utilities let you directly access the MP3 files on an iPod. I'm fond of Flying Mouse Software's PodMaster 1000 ($8). It lets you access the MP3s on an iPod's hard drive, play them back, and view their ID3 tags.

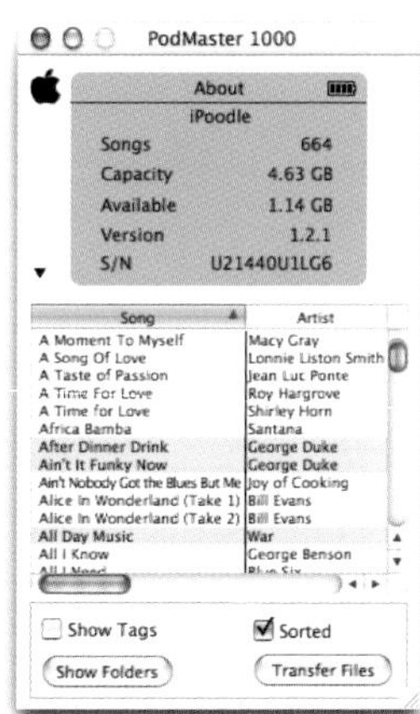

Other direct-access utilities for Mac OS X include Podestal, PodUtil, and iPod2iTunes, all of which are available on software-download sites.

Manual Management

When you have the iPod set up for manual updating, you can use iTunes to create playlists that exist only on the iPod. In the Source area of the iTunes window, select the iPod and then create the new playlist.

When manual updating is active, you must manually unmount the iPod when you're done with it. You can do this in iTunes (select the iPod in the Source list and then click the Eject button) or by using the Finder (drag the iPod's icon to the Trash or select it and press ⌘-E).

If you ever decide to switch back to iTunes' automatic updating mode, iTunes will replace the iPod's contents with the current music library and playlists.

Playing While Charging

When the iPod is connected to the Mac, its menus aren't available, preventing you from playing music located on the iPod. One way to work around this is to put the iPod in manual-updating mode, as described previously. You can then play tunes on the iPod by using the iTunes window. The other technique is to use a direct-access utility such as PodMaster 1000, which can play songs directly from the iPod regardless of the current iTunes updating mode.

The Stereo Connection

Don't just listen to your iPod through headphones—connect it to your home or car stereo system, too. To connect the iPod to a stereo system, use a cable with a ⅛-inch stereo miniplug on one end and two RCA phono plugs on the other. Plug the miniplug into the iPod, and connect the phono plugs into a spare set of inputs on the back of your stereo—they're usually labeled AUX or something similar.

One way to listen to an iPod in the car is by using a cassette adapter, available at Radio Shack and other electronics stores. Plug the adapter's cable into the iPod, and insert the adapter into your car's cassette deck.

You can also use an FM transmitter, which plugs into the iPod and then transmits its signal so that you can tune it in on your radio. Most FM transmitters don't work all that well, though I've found one that does. It's available from C. Crane Company (www.ccradio.com).

Incidentally, an FM transmitter is also a great way to beam your Mac's audio signal throughout the house—tune in streaming Internet radio on your kitchen-table radio.

FireWire Disk Mode

FireWire disk mode is not only convenient for shuttling documents between two locations, it's also handy for storing often-used programs. For example, you might stash a direct-access utility such as Podestal on your iPod so you can conveniently copy songs to your Mac at home and at the office.

iPod Key Sequences

To Do This	Do This
Turn off the iPod	Hold down Play/Pause for two seconds.
Restart the iPod	Hold down Menu and Play/Pause until the Apple logo appears on the screen (five to 10 seconds).
Force the iPod into FireWire disk mode (useful if you're using an old Mac or Windows PC containing a non-powered FireWire add-on card)	Restart (see above), then immediately hold down Previous and Next.
Have the iPod scan its hard drive for problems	Restart, then immediately hold down Previous, Next, Menu, and Select. Note: Don't jostle the iPod during disk scanning.
Have the iPod perform self-diagnostic tests	Restart, then immediately hold down Previous, Next, and Select.
Play the built-in Breakout game	Go to Extras > Game.

iPod as Address Book and More

You can store more than just music on your iPod. You can also store names and addresses and short text notes.

The iPod's address book feature is made possible by an Internet standard called vCard. All current email programs support vCard, as does the Mac OS X Address Book program. You'll also find support for vCard in Palm- and PocketPC-based hand-held computers and even some cell phones.

Mac programmers, intrepid folks that they are, have taken the vCard ball and run with it. Numerous utilities are available that let you peck out notes and store them in vCard format, or that let you convert notes and calendar entries from Microsoft Entourage into vCard format. So your iPod's Contacts menu isn't just an address book—it can store any text tidbits you want.

Before you can add vCards to your iPod, you must activate the iPod's FireWire disk mode. With the iPod connected, open iTunes and click the iPod Preferences button. In the iPod Preferences dialog box, check the Enable FireWire Disk Use box. Remember to remove the iPod's icon from your desktop before disconnecting the iPod from your Mac.

Adding Contacts from Microsoft Entourage X

In order for the iPod to recognize vCards, you must store them in the iPod's Contacts folder. To copy contacts from Microsoft Entourage to the iPod, open Entourage X's address book and select the contacts you want to copy to the iPod. Next, drag those contacts to the iPod's Contacts folder.

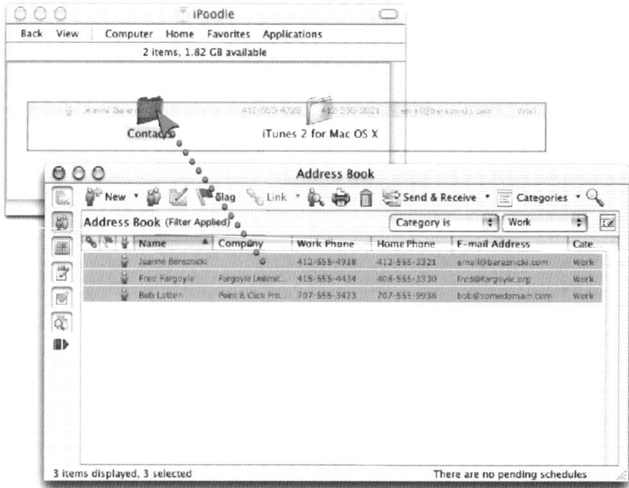

Deleting Contacts

To remove contacts from the iPod, open the Contacts folder, select the contacts you don't want, and drag them to the Trash.

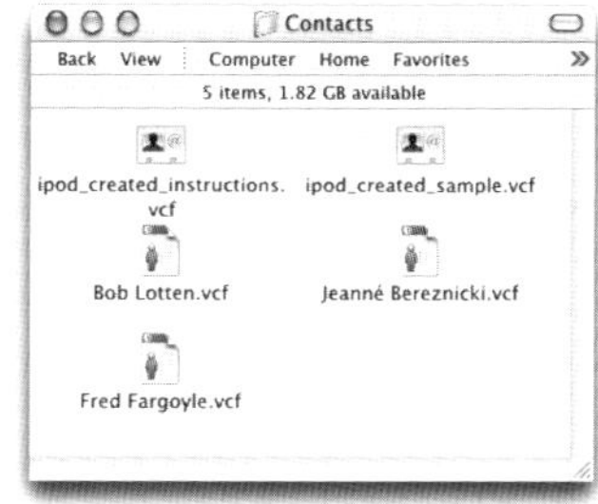

Find these and other iPod utilities.
www.macilife.com/itunes

Just the Text

Jonathan Chaffer's iPod Text Editor is simplicity itself: type a note title and text, then save the note as a contact.

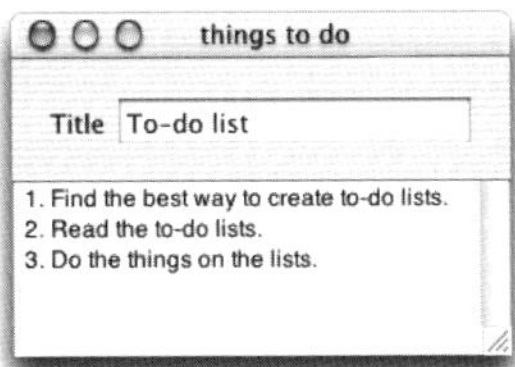

iPod Scripts

Numerous programmers have created useful AppleScripts for the iPod that enable you to manage playlists, copy songs, and more. The best source for these scripts is Doug Adams' excellent Doug's AppleScripts for iTunes site, mentioned earlier.

All the News That's Fit to Pod

PodNews is an ambitious (and free) utility that downloads news, sports scores, horoscopes, and other information from the Internet, converts it into vCards, and then transfers it to your iPod.

The iPod's Entourage

Email and more—to go. Michael Zapp's iPod-It can export calendar events, email, notes, and contacts from Microsoft Entourage X. iPod-It can also download news headlines and iCal calendars.

Miniature Marvel: Inside the iPod

No other portable music player combines high capacity, small size, and ease of use as effectively as Apple's iPod.

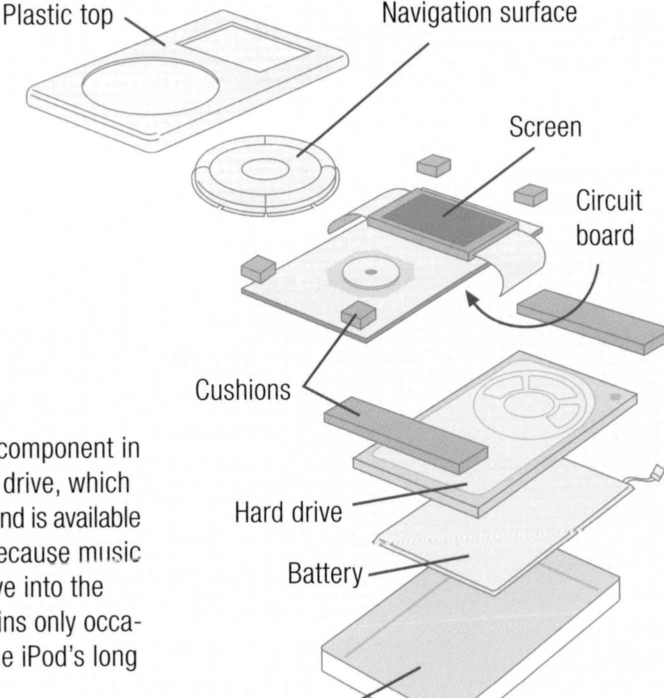

The single most expensive component in the iPod is its Toshiba hard drive, which uses a 1.8-inch disk platter and is available in a variety of capacities. Because music is loaded from the hard drive into the iPod's memory, the drive spins only occasionally, making possible the iPod's long battery life.

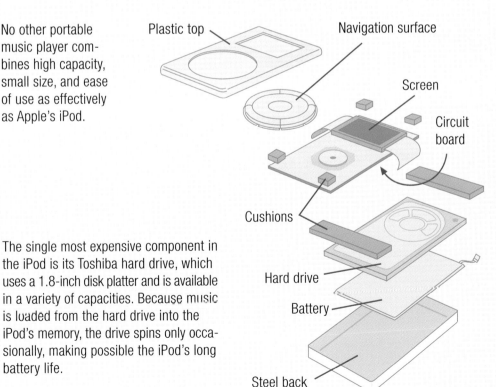

The iPod's LCD screen sits atop a main circuit board that contains 32MB of memory, as well as circuitry that handles playback, FireWire communications, and more.

The iPod's lithium-ion battery is three millimeters thick and manufactured by Sony Corp.

The 5GB iPod model uses a mechanical scroll wheel; its higher-capacity siblings use a touchpad-like surface that has no moving parts.

iPod as Calendar: Using iCal

With Apple's iCal software, you can keep track of appointments, schedules, and events of all kinds. You can create multiple calendars—for example, one for personal events such as birthdays and another for work appointments.

Use iCal to display multiple calendars at once to quickly identify schedule conflicts. You can also share calendars—with friends, coworkers, or complete strangers—by *publishing* them through your .Mac account.

You can even download and use calendars that other people have created. Hundreds of free calendars are available in categories ranging from TV schedules to holidays to the phases of the moon. To learn more about iCal and get your own copy, visit www.apple.com/ical.

What does all this have to do with the iPod? Simply this: You can copy your calendars to the iPod and view them on the road. You can also set up alarms in iCal and have your iPod beep to notify you of important appointments. Or TV shows.

So your iPod isn't just a pocket-sized jukebox and address book—it's a calendar, too.

Copying Calendars to the iPod

To copy a calendar to the iPod, export it, saving the exported calendar in the iPod's Calendars folder.

Step 1. Get Connected

Connect the iPod to your Mac and activate the iPod's FireWire disk mode (described on page 57).

Step 2. Export or Copy the Calendar

In iCal's Calendars list, select the calendar you want to export and then choose Export from the File menu. In the Export dialog box, navigate to your iPod's Calendars folder. Type a name and click the Export button. Unmount your iPod by dragging its icon to the Trash. You can now access the calendar using the iPod's menus, as described to the right.

You may also have calendar files that originated somewhere other than in your copy of iCal—perhaps you downloaded a calendar from a Web site, or someone emailed it to you as an attachment, or you simply copied it from a different Mac. To add a calendar file to the iPod, drag its icon into the Calendars folder.

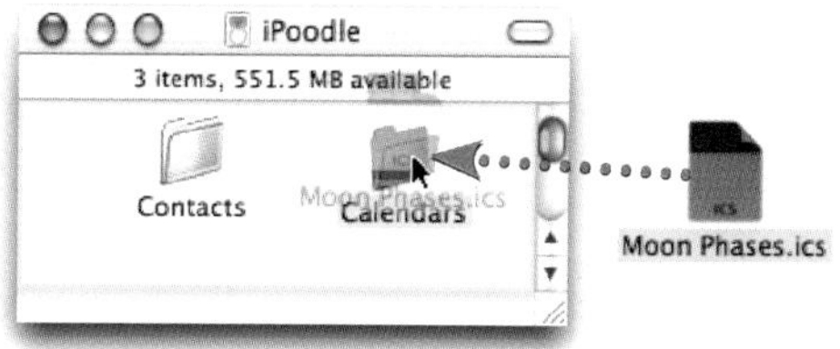

You can also use Apple's iSync program to automatically synchronize calendars between your Mac and your iPod. To learn more about iSync, visit www.apple.com/isync.

Find iCal utilities, sites, and AppleScripts.
www.macilife.com/ical

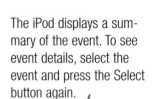

Navigating Calendars and Events

As with music and addresses, the iPod uses a drill-down menu scheme for calendars and events: the deeper you go, the more detail you get.

To display calendars, go to Extras > Calendars.

Each calendar appears as a separate menu item. To display a specific calendar, use the scroll wheel to highlight it, then press the iPod's Select button.

Days that have events associated with them are indicated with a small dot. To see a day's events, highlight the day, then press the iPod's Select button.

The iPod displays a summary of the event. To see event details, select the event and press the Select button again.

Calendar Tips

Silencing Alarms

If you've used iCal to specify that some events have alarms, your iPod will beep at the specified times. But there may be times when you don't want the iPod to beep.

To silence the iPod's alarms, go to Settings > Alarms where you'll find three options: On (the iPod beeps and the alarm text appears on the iPod's screen); Silent (no beep but the alarm text still appears); and Off (no beep or alarm text).

Dates of All Kinds

You don't use iCal to manage your schedule? Don't let that stop you from sampling the world of calendars that other people have published on the Web. You can download hundreds of calendars in dozens of categories: sports schedules, TV schedules, lunar phases, celebrity personal appearances, holidays of all kinds, and more.

One place to find calendars is Apple's iCal Web site, but the ultimate collection of calendars lives at an independent site called iCalShare (www.icalshare.com). I downloaded the Moon Phases calendar, and now my iPod knows the phases of the moon through the year 2015.

So even if you don't use iCal to manage your appointments, you might find it a useful tool for keeping track of events that take place elsewhere in the solar system.

iCal Calling iTunes

Doug Adams' iCal Calling iTunes is a slick AppleScript that turns iCal and iTunes into a musical alarm clock: it enables iTunes to play a specific playlist at a time you specify.

iCal Calling iTunes is a cinch to use. Simply create an iCal event whose name is the same as one of your iTunes playlists. When the event time arrives, iTunes begins playing the playlist.

iPhoto: Organizing and Sharing Images

The Macintosh **iLife**

iPhoto at a Glance

Millions of photographs lead lives of loneliness, trapped in unorganized boxes where they're never seen. Their digital brethren often share the same fate, exiled to cluttered folders on a hard drive and rarely opened.

With iPhoto, you can free your photos—and organize, print, and share them, too. iPhoto simplifies the entire process. You begin by *importing* images from a digital camera, your hard drive, a CD from a photofinisher, or other source. Then you can create *albums,* organizing the images in whatever order you want.

Along the way, you might also use iPhoto's editing features to retouch flaws, improve brightness and contrast, remove red-eye, and crop out unwanted portions of images. And you might use iPhoto's keyword features to help you file and locate images.

When you've finished organizing and editing images, you can share them in several ways, from printing them to publishing them to creating on-screen slide shows, complete with music from your iTunes library.

Welcome to the Photo Liberation Society.

Add an album. Play a slide show. View information. Rotate images.

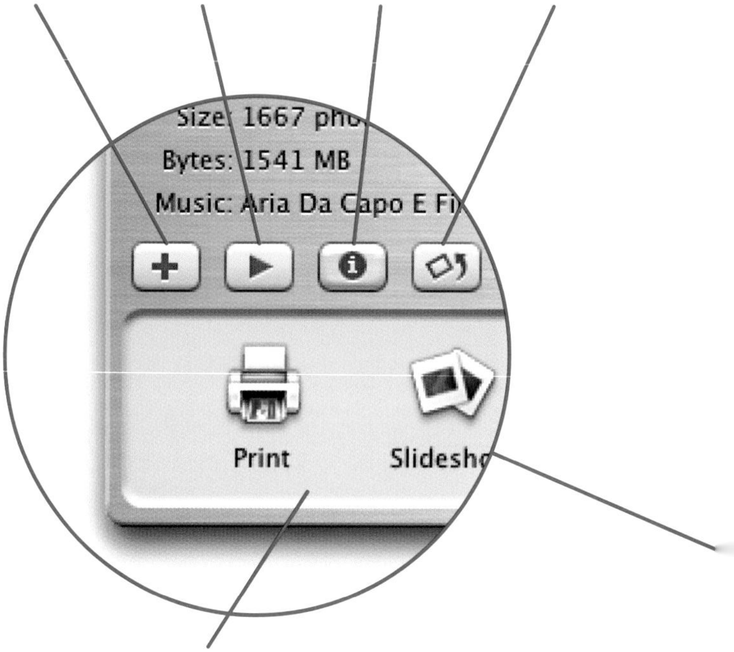

This window pane changes depending on which mode button you've selected. The Organize pane, shown here, contains the iPhoto functions you're likely to use often.

See iPhoto in action.
iPhoto: Organizing and Sharing Images

To quickly see the last set of images you imported, click Last Import.

The Photo Library contains all the images you import into iPhoto, whether from a digital camera or a disk file (page 70). Each set of images you import is called a *roll*.

To resize the album area, drag this vertical bar left or right.

You can name each roll of images. To show a roll's images, click on the triangle next to the roll's name. Click the triangle again to hide the images.

If your photos aren't being displayed by roll, choose Film Rolls from the View menu.

You can assemble photos into albums, and then share the albums (page 76).

The Trash holds photos you delete; photos aren't removed from your hard drive until you empty the Trash by choosing Empty Trash from the File menu.

You can view and edit information and comments for images or entire rolls (page 72).

These four buttons switch between each of iPhoto's primary modes.

To change the size of the photos displayed in iPhoto's window, drag the size slider.

Use the Burn button to archive photos on CDs or DVDs (page 100).

The Essentials of Digital Imaging

Like the digital audio world and other specialized fields, digital imaging has its own jargon and technical concepts to understand. You can accomplish a lot in iPhoto without having to know these things, but a solid foundation in imaging essentials will help you get more out of iPhoto, your digital camera, and other imaging hardware.

There are a few key points to take away from this little lesson. First, although iPhoto works beautifully with digital cameras, it can also accept images that you've scanned or received from a photofinisher.

Second, those images must be in JPEG format. iPhoto will often accept images in other formats, but the program is designed to work with JPEG images.

And finally, the concept of resolution will arise again and again in your digital imaging endeavors. You'll want big, high-resolution images for good-quality prints, and small, low-resolution images for convenient emailing to friends and family. As described on pages 88 and 89, you can use iPhoto to create low-resolution versions of your images.

Where Digital Images Come From

iPhoto can work with digital images from a variety of sources.

Digital camera

Digital cameras are more plentiful and capable than ever. The key factor that differentiates cameras is *resolution*: how many *pixels* of information they store in each image. Entry-level cameras typically provide two-megapixel resolution; you can get a good-quality 8- by 10-inch print from an uncropped two-megapixel image.

Most digital cameras connect to the Mac's USB port. Images are usually stored on removable-media cards; you can also transfer images into iPhoto by connecting a *media reader* to the Mac and inserting the memory card into the reader.

Scanner

With a scanner, you can create digital images from photographs and other hard-copy originals.

Scanners also connect via USB, although some high-end models connect via FireWire. Save your scanned images in JPEG format, and then add them to iPhoto by dragging their icons into the iPhoto window.

For tips on getting high-quality scans, visit www.scantips.com.

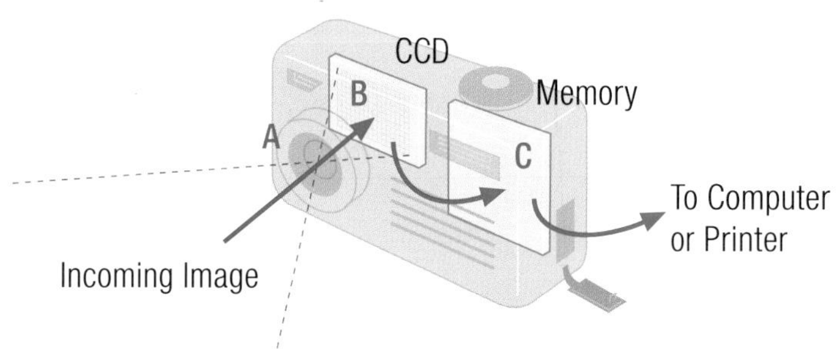

In a digital camera, the image is focused by the lens (A) onto the CCD (B), where tiny, light-sensitive diodes called photosites convert photons into electrons. Those electrical values are converted into digital data and stored by a memory card or other medium (C), from which they can be transferred to a computer or printer.

Compact disc

For an extra charge, most photofinishers will burn your images on a compact disc in Kodak Picture CD format. You get not only prints and negatives, but also a CD that you use with the Mac.

To learn more about Picture CD, go to www.kodak.com and search for *picture cd.*

Internet

Many photofinishers also provide extra-cost Internet delivery options. After processing and scanning your film, they send you an email containing a Web address where you can view and download images. After downloading images, you can drag their icons into iPhoto's window.

A Short Glossary of Imaging Terms

artifacts Visible flaws in an image, often as a result of excessive *compression* or when you try to create a large print from a low-resolution image.

CompactFlash A removable-memory storage medium commonly used by digital cameras. A CompactFlash card measures 43 by 36 by 3.3 mm. The thicker *Type 2* cards are 5.5 mm wide.

compression The process of making image files use less storage space, usually by removing information that our eyes don't detect anyway. The most common form of image compression is *JPEG.*

EXIF Pronounced *ex-if*, a standard file format used by virtually all of today's digital cameras. EXIF files use JPEG compression but also contain

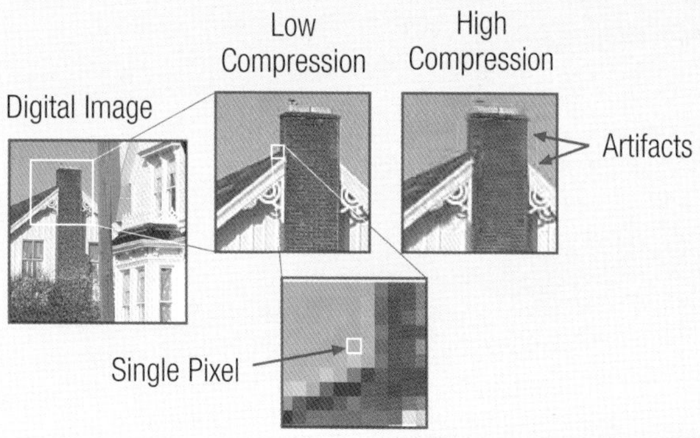

details about each image: the date and time it was taken, its resolution, the type of camera used, the exposure settings, and more. iPhoto retrieves and stores EXIF information when you import images. EXIF stands for *Exchangeable Image File.*

JPEG Pronounced *jay-peg*, the most common format for storing digital camera images, and the format that iPhoto is designed to use. Like MP3, JPEG is a *lossy* compression format: it shrinks files by discarding information that we can't perceive anyway. And as with MP3, there are varying degrees of JPEG compression; many imaging programs enable you to specify how heavily JPEG images are compressed. Note that a heavily compressed JPEG image can contain *artifacts.* JPEG stands for *Joint Photographic Experts Group.*

megapixel One million pixels.

pixel Short for *picture element*, the smallest building block of an image. The number of pixels that a camera or scanner captures determines the *resolution* of the image.

resolution **1.** The size of an image, expressed in pixels. For example, an image whose resolution is 640 by 480 contains 480 vertical rows of pixels, each containing 640 pixels from left to right. Common resolutions for digital camera images are 640 by 480, 1280 by 960, 1600 by 1200, 2048 by 1536, and 2272 by 1704.
2. A measure of the capabilities of a digital camera or scanner.

SmartMedia A commonly used design for removable-memory storage cards. SmartMedia cards measure 45 by 37 by .76 mm.

Importing Photos into iPhoto

The first step in assembling a digital photo library is to import photos into iPhoto.

iPhoto can directly import photos from many digital cameras. (See a list at www.apple.com/iphoto/compatibility/.) You can specify that iPhoto delete the images from the camera after importing them.

You can also import photos by dragging them from the Finder into the iPhoto window, or by using the Import command in the File menu. You might take this approach if you have scanned JPEG images on your hard drive or if you're using a media reader.

Each time you import images, iPhoto creates a new roll (as in roll of film—get it?). Even when you import just one image, iPhoto creates a roll for it.

Importing from a Camera

First, connect your camera to one of your Mac's USB ports (the port on the keyboard is particularly convenient) and turn the camera on.

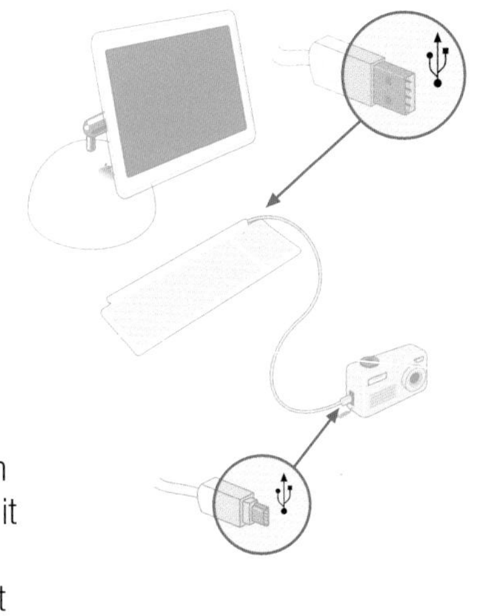

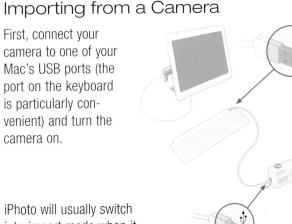

iPhoto will usually switch into import mode when it detects the camera. If it doesn't, click the Import button.

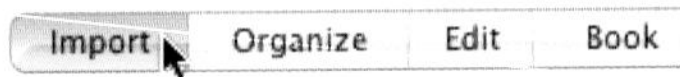

iPhoto displays information about the camera and its images here.

To begin importing the images, click Import.

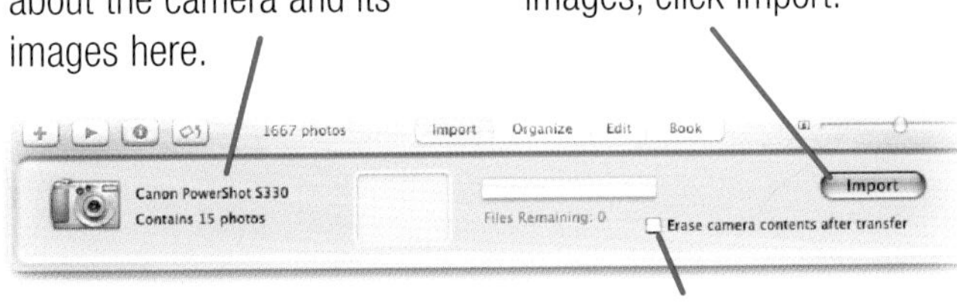

To have iPhoto delete the images in the camera after importing them, check this box.

As it imports, iPhoto displays small thumbnail versions of each image and shows how many images remain to be imported.

After you've finished importing images, you can disconnect your camera. Before you do, however, check to see if its icon appears on your Finder desktop. If its icon does appear, drag it to the Trash or select it and press ⌘-E before disconnecting the camera.

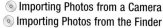

See how to import photos.
Importing Photos from a Camera
Importing Photos from the Finder

Importing from the Finder

To import an entire folder full of images, simply drag the folder into the iPhoto window.

iPhoto gives the new roll the same name as the folder that its images came from. You can rename the roll using the technique on page 73.

To import only some images, select their icons and then drag them into the iPhoto window.

Importing from Email

A friend has emailed some photos to you, and you want to add them to your iPhoto library. Here's how: First, save the photos on your Mac's desktop. Next, drag them into the iPhoto window as shown above. Finally, delete the photos from your desktop.

Note: If you use the Mac OS X Mail program, you don't even have to save the photos on your desktop first. Simply drag them from the email message into the iPhoto window.

Importing from PhotoCDs and Picture CDs

iPhoto can also import images saved on a Kodak PhotoCD or Picture CD. (PhotoCD is an older format that you aren't likely to see too often. Picture CD is a newer format that most photofinishers use.)

With a PhotoCD, you can't simply drag images from the CD into iPhoto's window. Instead, switch iPhoto into Import mode, insert the CD, and then click the Import button in the bottom-right corner of the iPhoto window.

For a Picture CD, choose Import from iPhoto's File menu, locate the Picture CD, and then locate and double-click the folder named Pictures. Finally, click the Open button. Or, use the Finder to open the Pictures folder on the CD and then drag images into iPhoto's window.

Where iPhoto Stores Your Photos

When you import photos, iPhoto stores them in a folder called iPhoto Library, located inside the Pictures folder.

Get in the habit of backing up the iPhoto Library folder frequently to avoid losing your images to a hardware or software problem. iPhoto's burning features are ideal for backing up photos (see page 100).

And whatever you do, don't futz with the files inside this folder—renaming or moving them could cause iPhoto to have problems finding your photos.

When you import images that are already stored on your hard drive, iPhoto makes duplicate copies of them in your iPhoto Library folder. To avoid wasting disk space, you might want to delete the original files after importing them into iPhoto. You can store your iPhoto Library folder elsewhere, such as on an external hard drive. For details, see page 102.

After the Import: Getting Organized

iPhoto forces some organization on you by storing each set of imported images as a separate roll. Even if you never use iPhoto's other organizational features, you're still ahead of the old shoebox photo-filing system: you will always be able to view your photos in chronological order.

But don't stop there. Take the time to use at least some of iPhoto's other organizational aids, which let you give titles to rolls and individual images, and assign comments and keywords to images to make them easier to find.

Titles are names or brief descriptions that you assign to photos and rolls: Party Photos, Mary at the Beach, and so on. iPhoto can use these titles as captions for its Web photo albums and books. You can also have iPhoto display titles below each thumbnail image.

There's one more benefit to assigning titles to photos: when you're working in iDVD, you can search for a photo by typing part of its title in the photo media browser's Search box.

Take advantage of iPhoto's filing features, and you'll be able locate images in, well, a flash.

Assigning Titles to Images

To assign a title to an image, select the image and type a name in the Title box.

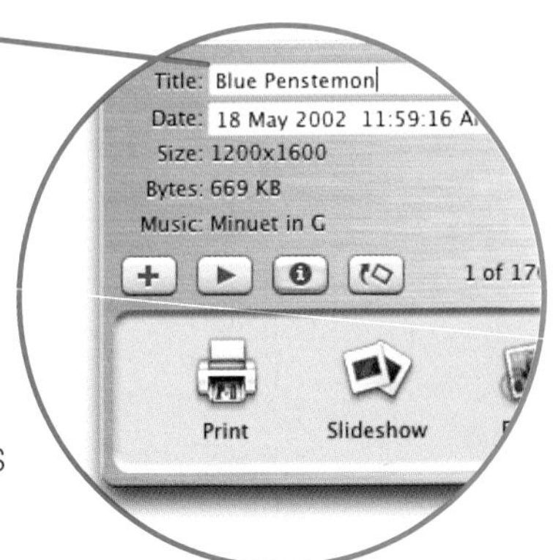

With the Set Title To command in the Edit menu, you can also have iPhoto assign titles to one or more photos for you. iPhoto can use an image's file name, timestamp, or roll name as a title.

Assigning Comments

You can also assign a comment to a photo; think of a comment as the text you'd normally write on the back of a photograph. You can search for photos based on comments, and iPhoto can use comments as captions for the photos in a book.

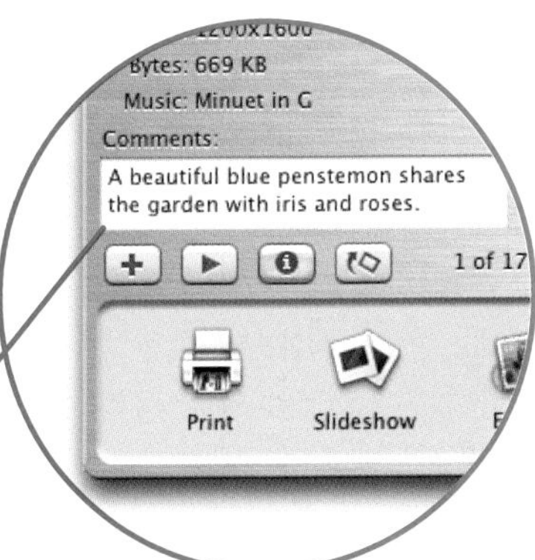

To display the Comments box, click the button.

To assign a comment, select the photo and type the comment in the Comments box.

See how to rotate and title images.
Rotating Vertical Photos
Naming a Roll
Assigning Titles to Photos
GO TO DVD

Assigning Titles to Rolls

iPhoto gives a newly imported roll a bland name consisting of a number and the date you imported its images. Use the Title box to give rolls names that are more descriptive.

To title a roll, select it by clicking on its name, then type a title in the Title box.

You can also edit the date of a roll or a single image. This is handy if your digital camera's built-in clock wasn't set correctly or if you want a roll's date to reflect the day you shot its images, not the day you imported them.

After importing images, rotate photos shot in vertical orientation. Select the photo or photos and then click the rotate button (⟲) or press ⌘-R (to rotate counterclockwise) or ⌘-Shift-R (to rotate clockwise).

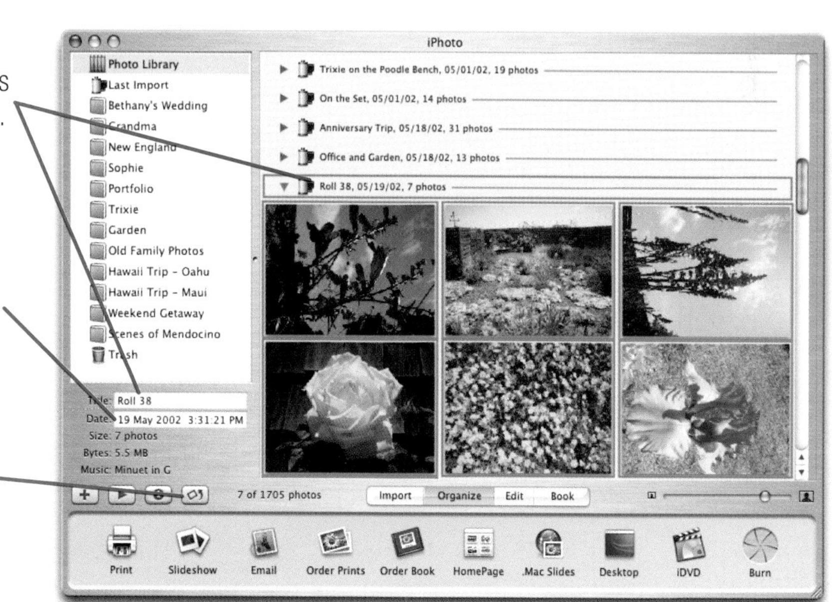

Tips for Working with Rolls

Changing the Sort Order

iPhoto displays rolls chronologically, with the oldest roll at the top of the window. To have your newest rolls appear at the top, choose Preferences from the iPhoto menu and click the Place Most Recent Photos at the Top check box.

Hide Rolls You Aren't Using

To the left of each roll's name is a tiny, down-pointing triangle: click it, and iPhoto collapses the roll, hiding its images. I like to collapse every roll whose photos I don't need to see at the moment. This clears the clutter in my iPhoto window and speeds up scrolling and changing the size of thumbnails.

A related tip: press the Option key while clicking on a collapsed roll's triangle, and iPhoto expands every roll in your library. Similarly, to collapse every roll, Option-click on the down-pointing triangle of any roll.

Viewing Rolls

If iPhoto isn't displaying individual rolls, and is instead showing all the photos in your library, choose Film Rolls from the View menu. When this command has a check mark next to it, iPhoto displays your library sorted by roll.

Assigning and Editing Keywords

Chances are that many of your photos fall into specific categories: baby photos, scenic shots, and so on. By creating and assigning *keywords*, you make related images easier to find.

Keywords are labels useful for categorizing and locating all the photos of a given kind: vacation shots, baby pictures, mug shots, you name it.

iPhoto has five predefined keywords that cover common categories. But you can replace the existing ones to cover the kinds of photos you take, and you can add as many new keywords as you like.

You can assign multiple keywords to a single image. For example, if you have a Beach keyword, a Dog keyword, and a Summer keyword, you assign all three to a photo of your dog taken at the beach in July.

To create and assign keywords, choose Keywords from the Edit menu (or press ⌘-K). This displays the Keywords/Search window.

For details on searching for keywords and comments, see "Searching for Photos" on page 84.

Assigning Keywords

To assign a keyword, display the Keywords/Search window by choosing Keywords from the Edit menu.

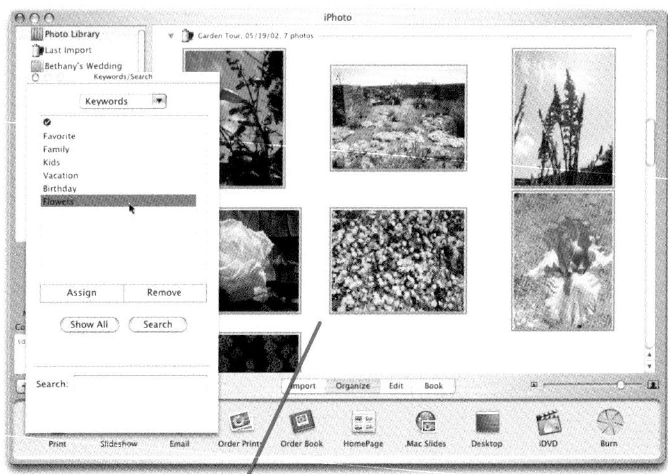

Tip: To display keywords alongside your photos, choose Keywords from the View menu (or press Shift-⌘-K).

Step 1.

Select the photo or photos to which you want to assign keywords.

Step 2.

Click one or more keywords.

Step 3.

Click Assign.

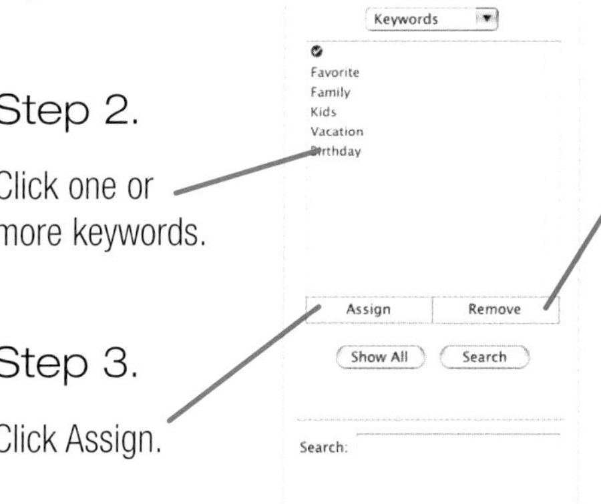

To remove a keyword from a photo, select the photo and click Remove.

Creating and Editing Keywords

You can create new keywords to describe the types of photos you take.

Step 1.

Choose New from the pop-up menu at the top of the Keywords/Search window.

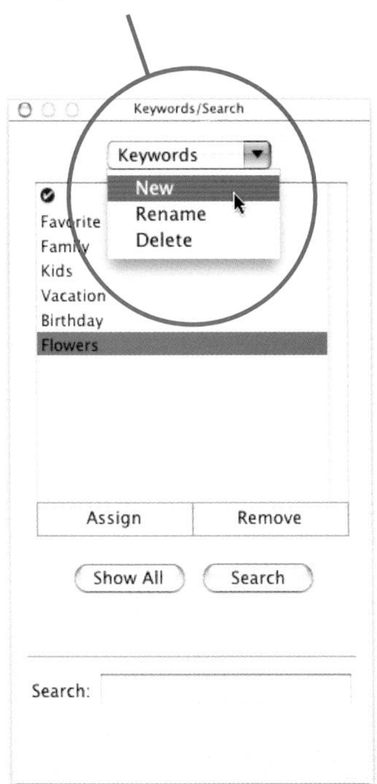

Step 2.

Type the new keyword's name.

Renaming Keywords

To rename an existing keyword, select it and choose Rename from the Keywords pop-up menu. Then, type a new name.

If you've already assigned a given keyword to some photos, think twice about renaming that keyword. If you do rename it, the photos to which you've assigned that keyword will inherit the new keyword.

For example, say you've assigned a Friends keyword to photos of all your friends. If you later rename the Friends keyword to Enemies, all the photos of your friends will take on the new keyword.

Creating Albums

Getting photos back from a lab is always exciting, but what's really fun is creating a photo album that turns a collection of photos into a story.

An iPhoto album contains a series of photographs sequenced in an order that helps tell a story or document an event.

Creating albums in iPhoto is a simple matter of dragging thumbnail images. You can add and remove photos to and from albums at any time, and you can sequence the photos in whatever order you like. You can even include the same photo in many different albums.

The photos in an album might be from one roll, or from a dozen different rolls. Just as an iTunes playlist lets you create your own music compilations, an iPhoto album lets you create your own image compilations.

And once you create albums, you can share them in a variety of ways.

Step 1: Create an Empty Album

To create a new album, choose New Album from the File menu or click the Add Album button (+).

Step 2: Name the Album

iPhoto asks you to name the new album.

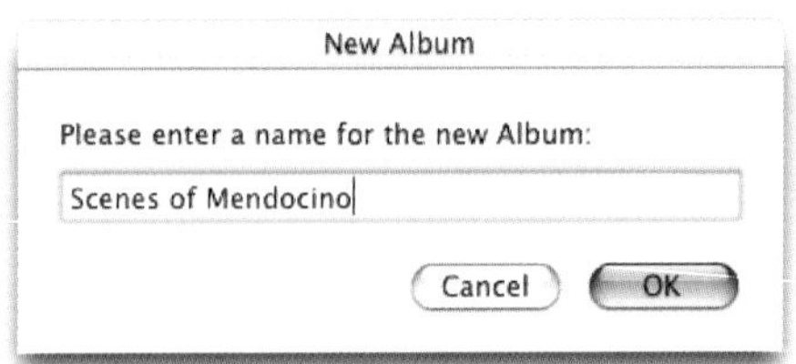

Step 3: Add Photos

After you've named the album, begin dragging photos into it. You can drag photos one at a time, or select multiple photos and drag them in all at once.

As you drag, iPhoto indicates how many photos you've selected.

See techniques for working with albums and selecting photos.
Creating an Album
Shortcuts for Selecting Photos
Fine-Tuning an Album

A Shortcut for Creating Albums

You can create an album and add images to it in one step. Select one or more images and drag them to a blank spot of the Photo Library list area. iPhoto creates a new album and adds the photos to it.

When you use this technique, iPhoto gives the new album a generic name, such as *Album-1*. To rename the album, double-click its name and type a new name.

Tips for Selecting Photos

Selecting photos is a common activity in iPhoto: you select photos in order to delete them, add them to an album, move them around within an album, and more.

When working with multiple photos, remember the standard Mac OS selection shortcuts: To select a range of photos, click on the first one and Shift-click on the last one. To select multiple photos that aren't adjacent to each other, press ⌘ while clicking on each photo.

Organizing an Album

The order of the photos in an album is important: when you create slide shows, books, or Web photo galleries, iPhoto presents the photos in the order in which they appear in the album.

Once you've created an album, you may want to fine-tune the order of its photos.

To edit an album, click on its name.

To change the order of the photos, drag them. Here, the flower close-up is being moved so it will appear after the other two garden shots.

Don't want a photo in an album after all? Select it and press the Delete key. This removes the photo from the album, but not from your hard drive or Photo Library.

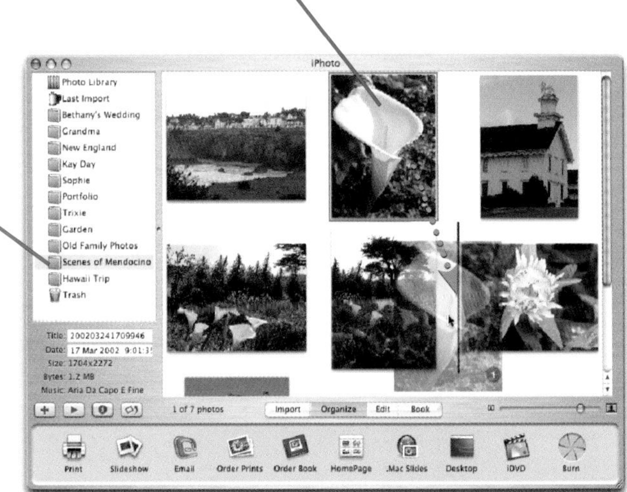

Basic Photo Editing

Many photos can benefit from some tweaking. Maybe you'd like to crop out that huge telephone pole that distracts from your subject. Maybe the exposure is too light, too dark, or lacks contrast. Or maybe the camera's flash gave your subject's eyes the dreaded red-eye flaw.

iPhoto's edit mode can fix these problems and others. And it does so in a clever way that doesn't replace your original image: if you don't like your edits, choose Revert to Original from the File menu.

iPhoto's editing features address many common image problems, but iPhoto isn't a full-fledged digital darkroom—you can't, for example, darken only a portion of an image. For advanced image editing, you'll want a program such as Adobe Photoshop or its less-expensive but still powerful sibling, Photoshop Elements.

If you have a separate image-editing program, you can set up iPhoto to work along with it. For details, see the section "Using iPhoto with Other Imaging Programs," on page 83.

Editing Essentials

To switch to iPhoto's edit mode, select a photo—either in the iPhoto Library or in an album—and click the Edit button. Or, simply double-click the photo.

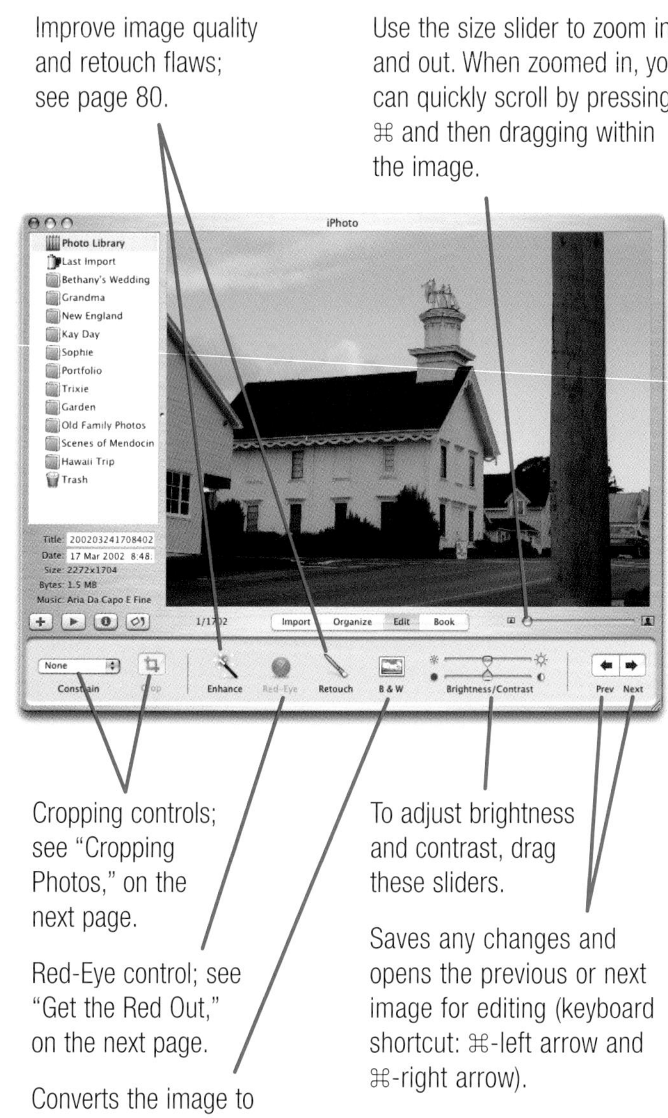

Improve image quality and retouch flaws; see page 80.
Use the size slider to zoom in and out. When zoomed in, you can quickly scroll by pressing ⌘ and then dragging within the image.
Cropping controls; see "Cropping Photos," on the next page.
Red-Eye control; see "Get the Red Out," on the next page.
Converts the image to black and white.
To adjust brightness and contrast, drag these sliders.
Saves any changes and opens the previous or next image for editing (keyboard shortcut: ⌘-left arrow and ⌘-right arrow).

See techniques for cropping photos.
Cropping Photos

Cropping Photos

To crop out unwanted portions of a photo, first click and drag within the image to indicate which portion you want to retain.

Drag to create a selection. To move the selection, drag within it. To resize it, drag any corner. To start over, click on the image anywhere outside the selection.

If you have a specific output destination in mind for the photo, choose the most appropriate option from the Constrain pop-up menu. For example, if you plan to print a vertically oriented 5 by 7 photo, choose 5 x 7 Portrait. iPhoto restricts the proportions of the cropping area to match the option you choose. To create a cropping selection of any size, choose None.

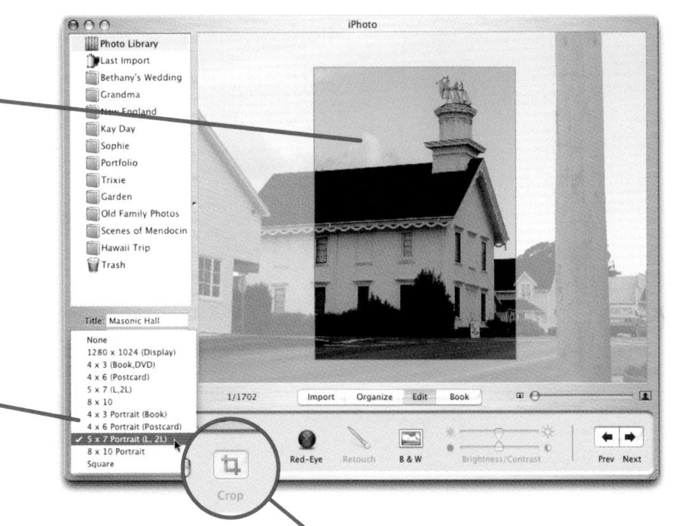

To apply the crop area to the image, click Crop.

Get the Red Out

Red-eye is a common problem caused by the bright light of an electronic flash reflecting off a subject's retinas and the blood vessels around them.

Be sure the Constrain pop-up menu is set to None, then drag to select the subject's eyes.

To apply the fix, click the Red-Eye button.

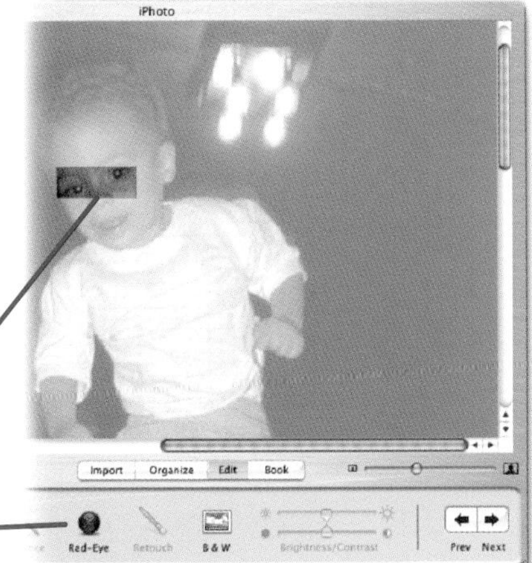

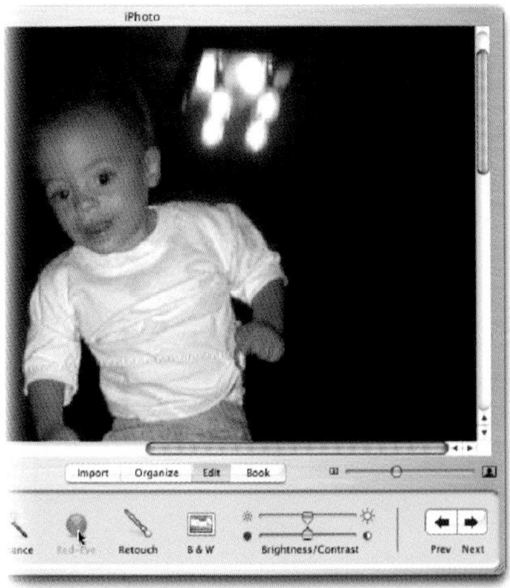

Enhancing and Retouching Photos

Some photos need work. Old photos can appear faded, their color washed out by Father Time. They might also have scratches and creases brought on by decades of shoebox imprisonment.

New photos can often benefit from some enhancement, too. That shot you took in a dark room with the flash turned off—its color could use some punching up. That family photo you want to use as a holiday card—the clan might look better with fewer wrinkles and blemishes.

iPhoto's Enhance and Retouch tools are ideal for tasks like these. With the Enhance tool, you can improve a photo's colors and exposure, and rescue a photo you might otherwise delete. With the Retouch tool, you can remove minor scratches and blemishes, not to mention that chocolate smudge on your kid's face.

Both tools enable you to view before-and-after versions of your work: press the Control key, and iPhoto shows you what the image looked like before you began retouching and enhancing. And you can always backtrack one step by using the Undo command, or return to Square One by choosing Revert to Original from the File menu.

As with iPhoto's other editing features, the Enhance and Retouch tools appear in iPhoto's edit mode. If you aren't familiar with how to switch to edit mode, see "Basic Photo Editing" on page 78.

Using One-Click Enhance

To apply one-click enhance, click the Enhance icon in the Edit pane at the bottom of the iPhoto window.

Before: This dimly lit shot is barely visible.

After: iPhoto has let the dogs out.

Tips

As you may have noticed, the Enhance tool improves image quality by adjusting brightness, contrast, and color balance all at the same time. To see what your image looked like before you clicked Enhance, press and hold down the Control key (that's Control, not ⌘).

If at first you don't succeed, click, click again. Each time you click Enhance, iPhoto processes the image again. But too much enhancement can make an image appear grainy and artificial. If that happens, choose Undo Enhance Photo from the Edit menu as many times as needed to backtrack.

See how to enhance and retouch photos.
Enhancing a Photo
Retouching a Photo

Using the Retouch Tool

To use the Retouch tool, click the Retouch icon in the Edit pane.

To remove a flaw, position the crosshair pointer over the flaw and then drag away from the flaw in short strokes.

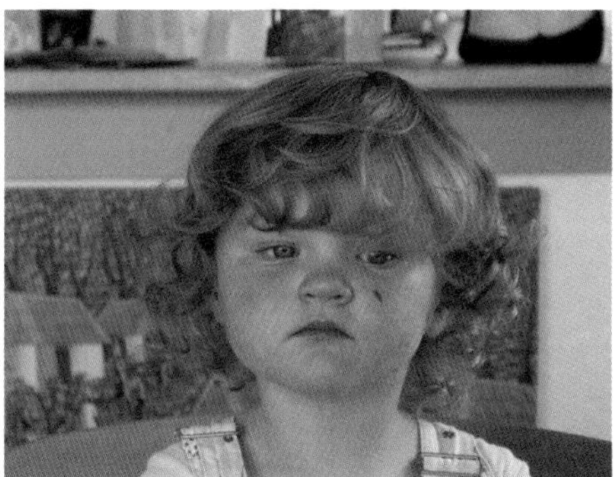

Before: Cute kid, but a little dirty.

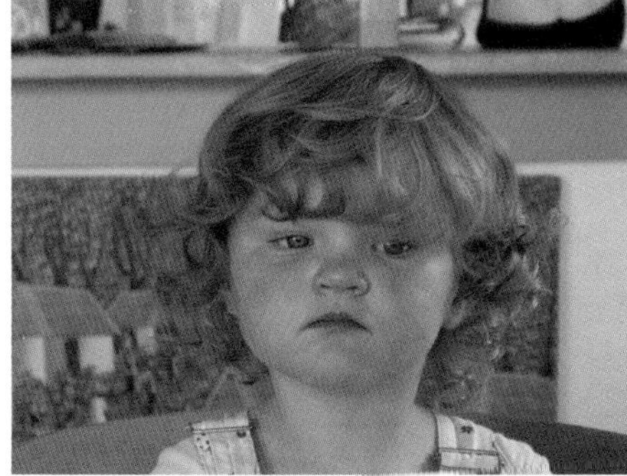

After: We lost the dirt, but kept the freckles.

Tips

As with the Enhance tool, you can temporarily see what your image looked like before you began retouching by pressing and holding down the Control key.

To retouch with more precision, use the size slider to zoom in on the area of the image that you're working on.

When the Retouch tool is active, you can't use the ⌘-drag technique to scroll a zoomed-in photo. Use the scroll bars and scroll arrows to scroll, or deactivate the Retouch tool by clicking its icon again.

You can undo each mouse click by choosing Undo Retouch from the Edit menu. To undo all of your retouching, choose Revert to Original from the File menu. Note that you'll also lose any other edits, such as cropping.

Scratches are best removed by rubbing the mouse pointer over a scratch until it disappears. That's because iPhoto learns the pattern on either side of a scratch, and rubbing makes this pattern easier to learn. Also, some scratches disappear faster if you rub at a ninety-degree angle to the scratch. Experiment and undo as needed.

Using the Edit Window

Normally, iPhoto displays the image you're editing within the iPhoto window itself. But iPhoto also provides a separate edit window that you may prefer. One reason to use an edit window is that you can have multiple edit windows open simultaneously, enabling you to compare images. And the edit window has some features that the Edit pane lacks.

Displaying the Edit Window

To open an image in a separate window, press the Option key while double-clicking on the image. You can also use the Preferences command to have iPhoto always use the separate window when you double-click on an image.

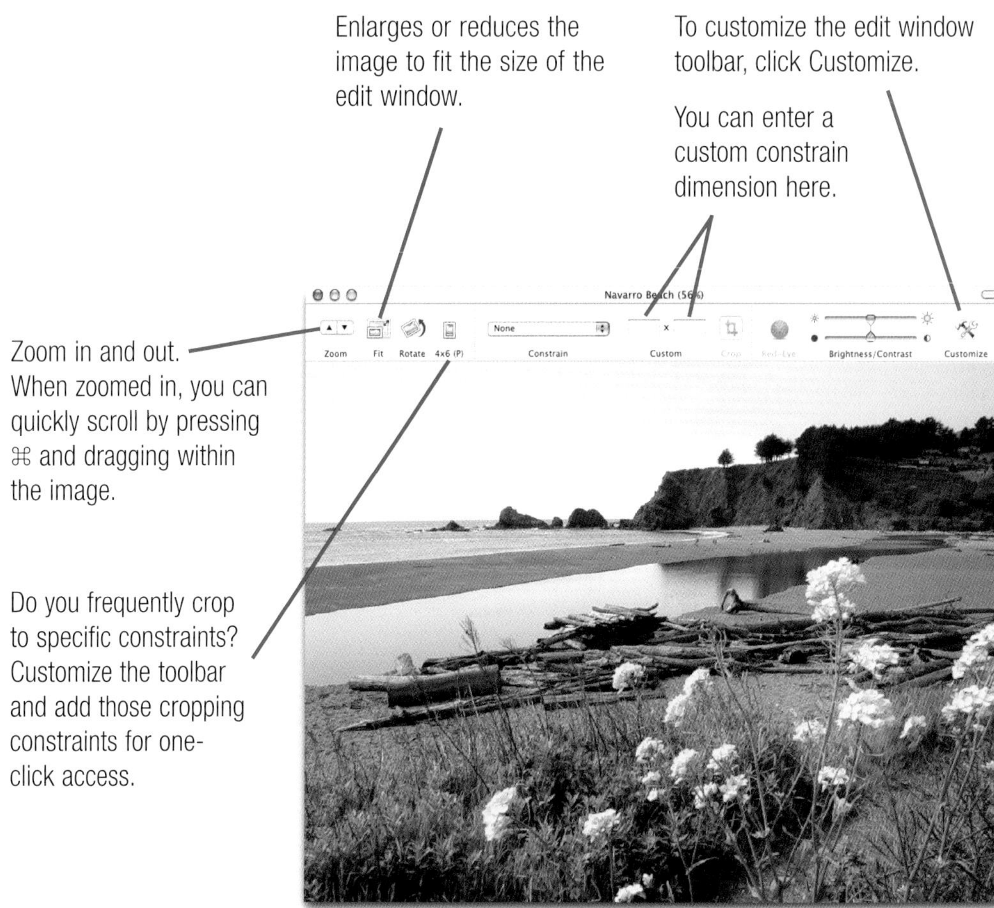

Enlarges or reduces the image to fit the size of the edit window.
To customize the edit window toolbar, click Customize.
You can enter a custom constrain dimension here.
Zoom in and out. When zoomed in, you can quickly scroll by pressing ⌘ and dragging within the image.
Do you frequently crop to specific constraints? Customize the toolbar and add those cropping constraints for one-click access.
Navarro Beach (56%)
None
Zoom
Fit
Rotate
4x6 (P)
Constrain
Custom
Brightness/Contrast
Customize

See how to display and use iPhoto's edit window.
Using the Edit Window

Using iPhoto with Other Imaging Programs

If you have Adobe Photoshop or another image editing program, you might want to set up iPhoto to work with it: when you double-click an image in iPhoto's Organize view, your Mac will switch to your image editing program, which will open the image.

Choose Preferences from the iPhoto menu, and in the area labeled Double-click, click the Opens in Other button. Next, locate and double-click your image editing program.

Don't want iPhoto to always open images in another program? Here's an easy alternative: to open a photo in a different program, simply drag the photo to the program's icon in your dock. For example, drag a photo to the Photoshop icon to open the image in Photoshop.

Restoring the Original Image

iPhoto also includes iSafetyNet. Actually, there is no feature by that name, but there might as well be: even after you've cropped and otherwise modified an image, you can always revert to the original version by selecting the image and then choosing Revert to Original from the File menu.

Customizing the Edit Window Toolbar

To customize the edit window toolbar, click its Customize button or choose Customize Toolbar from the Window menu.

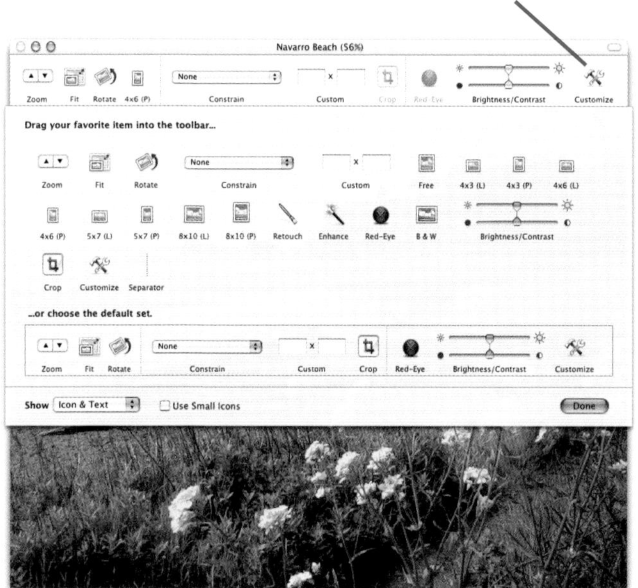

You can then add and remove tools to suit your needs.

To add a tool, drag it to the toolbar. To remove a tool you don't use, drag it off of the toolbar.

You can also rearrange tools by dragging them left and right on the toolbar. And using the Show pop-up menu, you can specify whether the toolbar appears with icons and text, with just icons, or with just text. To display small icons for each tool, check the Use Small Icons box.

Searching for Photos

If you've taken the time to assign titles, comments, and keywords to your photos, here's where your investment pays off.

Use iPhoto's search feature to quickly locate a certain photo or collection of photos. You can locate photos that match a specific keyword or combination of keywords. You can also search for text contained in a photo's comment, title, file name, or keyword. And you can search your entire photo library or just one album.

To search for photos, open the Keywords/Search window by choosing Keywords from the Edit menu or pressing ⌘-K. When you search for photos, iPhoto displays only those that meet your criteria. You can then do whatever you like with the photos you've found: edit and retouch them, add them to an album, email them, view them as a slide show, print or delete them, and so on.

Doing a lot of searching? Note that you don't have to close the Keywords/Search window. If you like, simply drag the window off to the side so you can see it and your photos at the same time.

Searching by Keywords

Step 1.

To search your entire library, make sure the Photo Library item is selected. To search within a specific album, select it.

Step 2.

Click the keyword you want to search for. You can further narrow your search by selecting additional keywords—for example, ⌘-clicking Vacation to find all photos of flowers taken on a vacation. To widen the search, ⌘-click on a highlighted keyword again to deselect it.

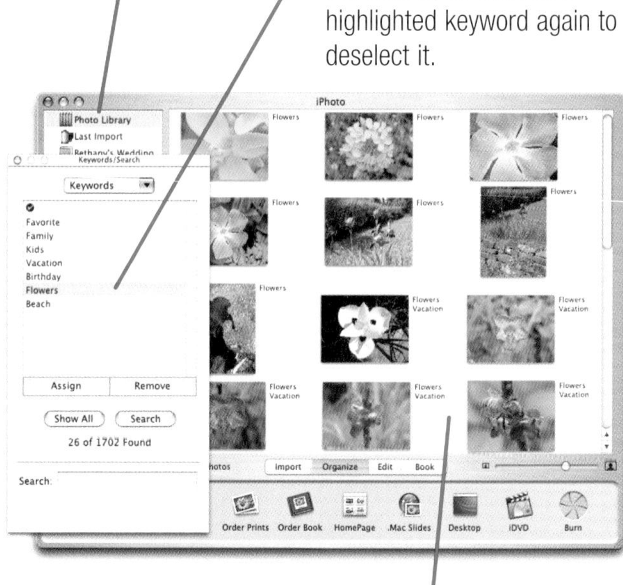

Step 3.

Click the Search button.

iPhoto displays the number of photos it found.

iPhoto displays only those photos that have the search keyword or keywords assigned to them. (To view keywords alongside each photo as shown here, choose Keywords from the View menu or press Shift-⌘-K.) To display all photos again, click the Show All button in the Keywords/Search box.

Searching for Text

The Keyword/Search window's Search box is particularly powerful. It lets you search for photos based on text in titles, comments, file names, and keywords. Building on the previous example, if I typed *flowers* in the Search box, iPhoto would find all photos with Flowers as their keyword.

Step 1.

To search your entire library, make sure the Photo Library item is selected. To search within a specific album, select it.

Step 2.

Type the text you're looking for. As you type, iPhoto narrows down the list of photos displayed to those that meet your criterion—just as iTunes narrows down the list of songs displayed as you type into its Search box. Here, iPhoto has located a photo based on text present in its title and comment.

EXIF Exposed: Getting Information About Photos

I mentioned earlier that digital cameras store information along with each photo—the date and time when the photo was taken, its exposure, the kind of camera used, and more. This is called the *EXIF* data.

iPhoto saves this EXIF data when you import photos. To view it, select a photo and choose Show Photo Info from the File menu (⌘-I).

Much of this information may not be useful to you, but some of it might. If you have more than one digital camera, for example, you can use the window's Photo tab to see which camera you used for a given shot.

If you're interested in learning more about the nuts and bolts of photography, explore the Exposure tab to see what kinds of exposure settings your camera used.

At the very least, you might just want to explore the Photo Info window to see the kind of information iPhoto is keeping track of for you.

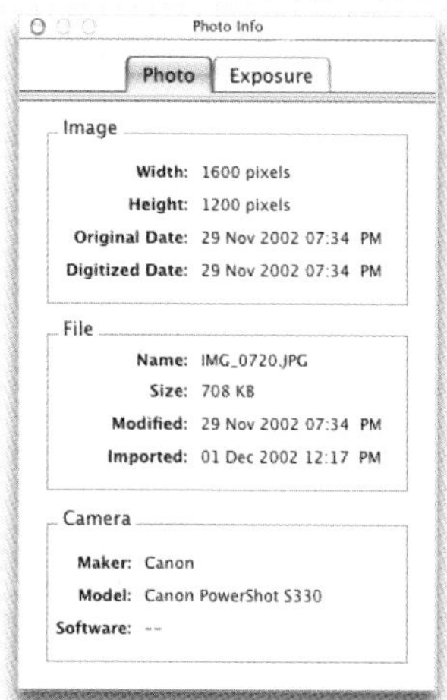

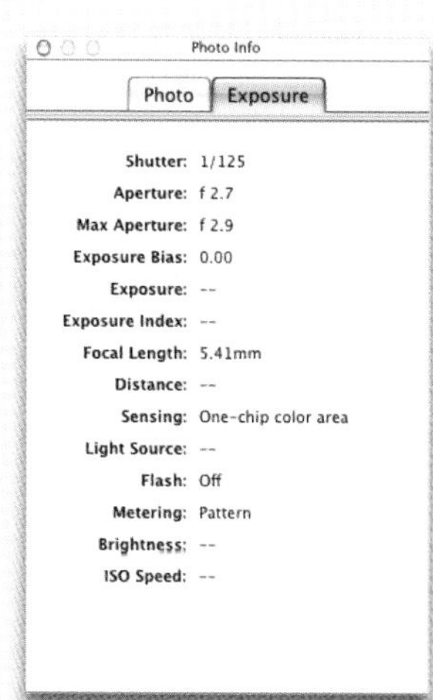

Sharing Photos on a HomePage

Everyone likes to get photos in the mail. Email, however, is another story. Too many people make the mistake of emailing massive image files that take forever to transfer, and end up bogging down their recipients' email sessions.

And because dealing with email attachments is frequently a hassle—particularly when you're emailing from a Mac to a Windows computer, or vice versa—there's a good chance the recipients will never see the images anyway.

A better way to share photos is to publish them on a Web site, specifically on an Apple HomePage. iPhoto works together with Apple's .Mac service to make Web photo albums easy to create—it takes only a couple of mouse clicks to make your images available to a global audience. You can also password-protect albums so only certain people can see them.

Note that you must have an Apple .Mac account to create a HomePage. To register for an account, go to www.mac.com.

Creating a HomePage

You can create a HomePage containing just one photo, a selection of photos, or an entire album. You don't even have to create an album to create a HomePage—you can select some images in the Photo Library and proceed directly to the HomePage button. But it's smarter to create an album, so you can control the order in which the photos appear on the HomePage.

Organize the album's photos in the order you want them to appear. To publish only a few photos, select them first.

To begin the publishing process, be sure you're connected to the Internet, then click the HomePage button.

See how to create a Web photo album.
Creating a HomePage Album

iPhoto connects with Apple's .Mac service and, after a few moments, displays a preview of your HomePage.

iPhoto uses the album name for the name of the HomePage, and uses the title you assigned to each photo as its caption. You can edit any text item in the HomePage preview.

Be sure your .Mac account name appears here.

A two-column layout displays larger thumbnail images.

Choose an image frame style here.

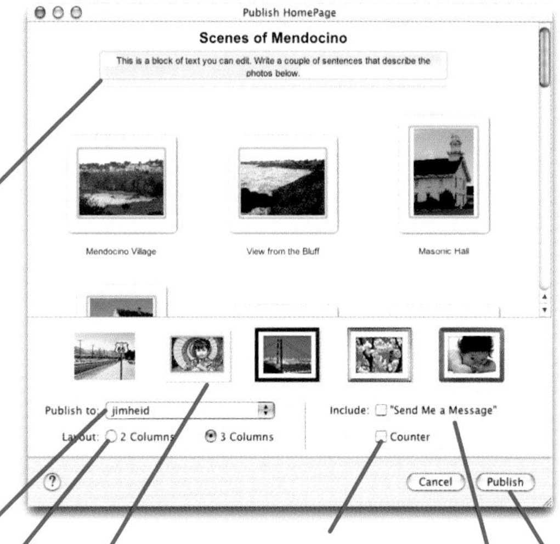

Check this box to add a counter that shows how many times your HomePage has been viewed.

Check this box to add a button that enables visitors to send you a message via Apple's iCard electronic greeting card service.

After iPhoto has transferred your photos, a dialog box displays the address of your new HomePage.

You can copy this address to the Mac's Clipboard by dragging across it, then pressing ⌘-C. Paste the address into an email message to notify people that you've published the album.

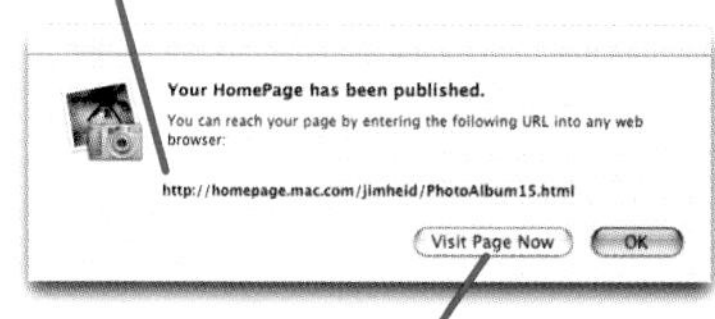

To see the new HomePage album, click Visit Page Now.

When you've finished previewing the HomePage, click Publish to transfer the images.

Editing a HomePage Album

What if you publish a HomePage album and then realize that you want to make changes? Sorry, no can do—at least not in iPhoto. But you can edit a HomePage album by going to Apple's .Mac site, logging in, and then using the .Mac editing features.

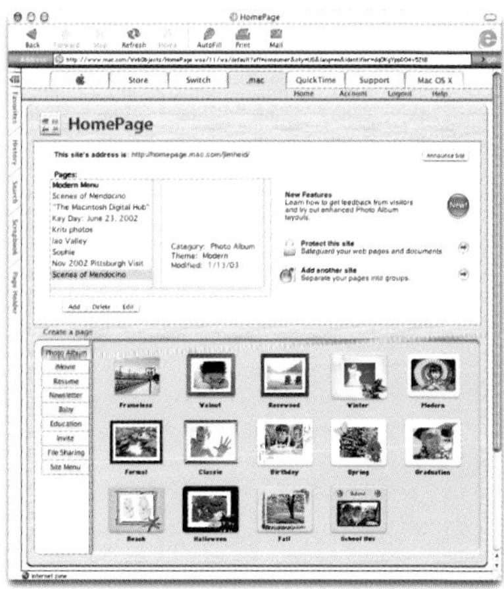

With the .Mac HomePage-editing tools, you can edit albums you've published and create several other kinds of Web pages. One of the changes you can make is to choose from a wider variety of themes (such as Birthday, Spring, and Halloween) and styles than iPhoto provides.

Sharing Photos via Email

Even after my earlier rant, I'll be the first to admit that email is the easiest way to share a few photos with someone over the Internet. It takes just a few mouse clicks—iPhoto takes care of the often tricky chores behind creating email photo attachments.

iPhoto can also make images smaller so they transfer faster. Take advantage of this feature, and you won't bog down your recipients' email sessions with huge image attachments.

Normally, iPhoto uses the Mac OS X Mail program to email photos. If you use a different email program, you can configure iPhoto to use it, as described on the next page.

Step 1: Select the Photos

Select the photos you want to email. Remember that you can select multiple photos by Shift-clicking and ⌘-clicking.

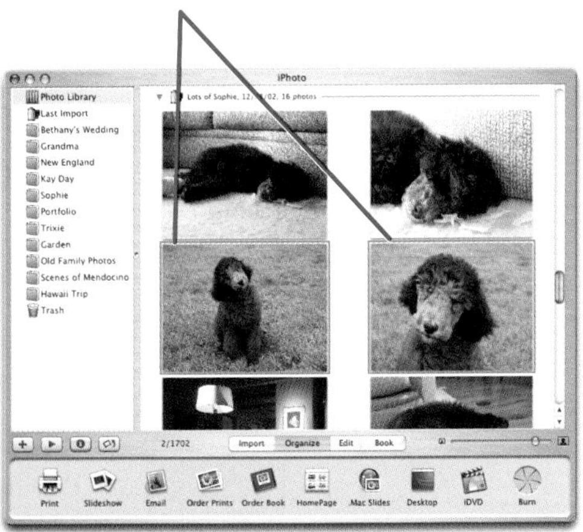

Step 2. Click the Mail Button

iPhoto displays the Mail Photo dialog box.

Step 3. Specify the Image Size

iPhoto can make the images smaller before emailing. (This doesn't change the dimensions or file sizes of your original images, which iPhoto always stores in all their high-resolution glory.)

After you've specified mail settings, click Compose.

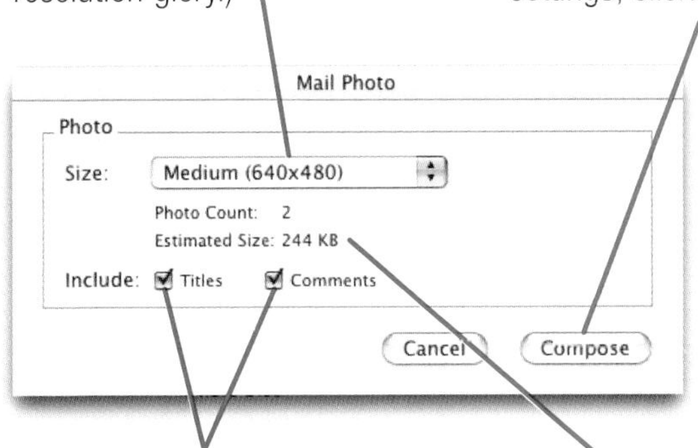

You have the option to include titles and comments along with the images—another good reason to assign this information when organizing your photos.

iPhoto estimates the size of the final attachments. If you're sending images to someone who is connecting using a modem (as opposed to a high-speed connection), try to keep the estimated size below 300KB or so. As a rule of thumb, each 100KB will take about 15 seconds to transfer over a 56kbps modem.

After iPhoto creates smaller versions, it starts Mac OS X's Mail program. Your photos are added to a new email, which you can complete and send on its way.

See how to email photos.
Emailing Photos

Tips for Emailing Photos

Setting Email Preferences

You don't use Mac OS X's email program? Me neither—I prefer Microsoft Entourage X. You can use iPhoto's Preferences command to tell iPhoto to use a program other than Mail to send your photos. Besides Mac OS X's Mail program, iPhoto can work with Microsoft Entourage, Qualcomm's Eudora, or America Online.

To change your email program preference, choose Preferences from the iPhoto menu. Then, choose your preferred email program from the pop-up menu at the bottom of the Preferences window.

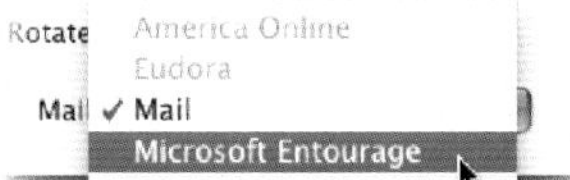

Exporting Photos By Hand

When you email a photo using iPhoto's Email button, iPhoto uses the name of the original photo's disk file as the name of the attachment. Problem is, most of your photos probably have incomprehensible filenames, such as 200203241958.jpg, that were assigned to them by your digital camera.

You might want an attachment that you send to Grandma and Grandpa to have a friendlier file name, such as holidays.jpg.

For such cases, export the photo "by hand" and then add it to an email as an attachment. Choose Export from iPhoto's File menu, and be sure the File Export tab is active.

Export the photo as described at right. Finally, switch to your email program, create a new email message, and add the photo to it as an attachment.

To make the images smaller and thus faster to transfer, type a dimension in the Width or Height box. You need type only one dimension; iPhoto will calculate the other dimension for you.

If your original image is stored in a format other than JPEG, consider choosing JPEG from this pop-up menu.

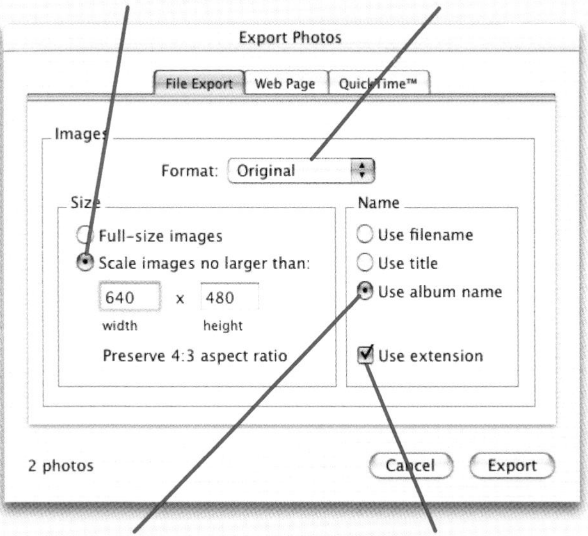

You can have iPhoto name the exported file according to its title or album name. If you're exporting just one photo, you can also type a name after clicking the Export button.

Leave this box checked to improve compatibility with Windows computers.

More Internet Sharing Options

You can also create custom Web photo albums as well as slide shows that are shared through Apple's .Mac service.

.Mac slide shows are a fun way to share photos with other Mac users. Publish some photos as .Mac slides, and other Mac OS X users can configure their Macs to use those photos as their screen savers.

You might create a custom Web album if you're a Web jockey and you already have your own Web site, perhaps one that is served by your local Internet provider rather than Apple's .Mac service. You can also burn a set of Web photo pages onto a CD and send it to anyone who has a Mac or Windows computer.

If you're a Web publisher, you can modify these pages as you see fit. You might open them in a program such as Macromedia Dreamweaver, embellish them with additional graphics or other tweaks, and then upload them to a Web site.

iPhoto's Web pages are on the bland side. You can spice up iPhoto's HTML export feature by installing Simeon Leifer's free BetterHTMLExport, available from software download sites. BetterHTMLExport provides numerous design templates for you to choose from and modify.

Chances are most of the Internet sharing you do will be through HomePage albums and email. But when you're in the mood for something completely different, iPhoto is ready.

Exporting Web Pages

You can export photos and albums as Web pages to post on sites other than an Apple HomePage. iPhoto creates small thumbnail versions of your images as well as the HTML pages that display them. (HTML stands for *HyperText Markup Language*—it's the set of codes used to design Web pages.)

To export a Web page, select some photos or an album, choose Export from the File menu, then click the Web Page tab. Specify the page appearance and dimensions of the thumbnails and the images, then click Export. In the Export dialog box, click the New Folder button to create a new folder. If you'll be publishing the pages on a Web server, I recommend naming the new folder *index*. This will cause iPhoto to create a home page named *index.html*, as required by most Web servers.

To Create a .Mac Slide Show

Step 1.

Select the photos you want to publish. To select an entire album, click its name.

Step 2.

Click the .Mac Slides button.

iPhoto connects to .Mac, then displays a message asking if you're sure you want to publish the slide show.

Step 3.

Click the Publish button.

iPhoto transfers your images to your iDisk. When the transfer is complete, a message appears enabling you to send an announcement email. The announcement contains instructions on how users can access the slide show.

To View the Slide Show

Anyone using version 10.2 or later of Mac OS X can view your slide show. You don't have to have a .Mac subscription to view .Mac slides.

Step 1.

Open Mac OS X's System Preferences, then click the Screen Effects button.

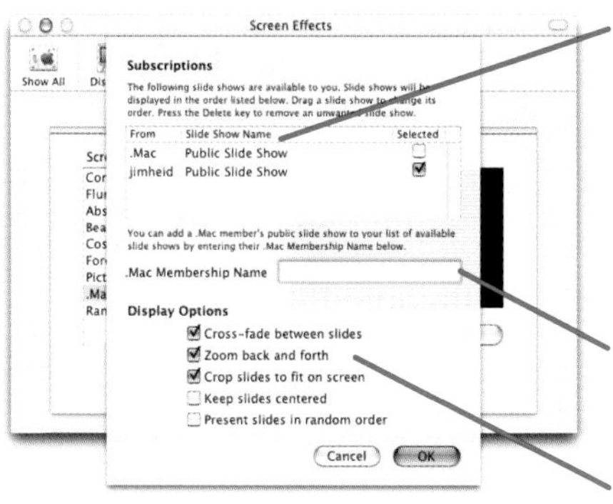

Step 2.

Click the Configure button.

Slide shows you've subscribed to appear here. Mac OS X displays each one in top-to-bottom order. To remove a slide show from the list, select it and press the Delete key. To temporarily disable one, uncheck its box. To change the order in which the slide shows display, drag them up and down in the list.

To subscribe to a user's .Mac slide show, type the user's .Mac name here—for example, *jimheid.*

Fine-tune slide show display options here.

Step 3.

Click OK.

To view the slide show, click the Test button or activate the screen effects. (Use the Activation and Hot Corners tabs to specify how and when the screen effects activate.)

Burning HTML Albums on a CD

Even if you aren't a Web jockey, there's a good reason to consider exporting an album as a set of Web pages: you can burn the exported pages onto CDs, and then mail them to others. They can view the album on their Macs or PCs using a Web browser—no attachment hassles, no long downloads.

After exporting the Web page, use the Mac OS X Finder to copy its folders and HTML pages to a blank CD-R disc. Burn the disc, eject it, and you have a photo Web site on a disc.

To view the site, simply double-click on the site's home page file. (If you followed my recommendation on the opposite page, this file is named *index.html.*)

And by the way, resist the urge to rename the site's home page file. If you change the name, the links in the Web album won't work. If you want a different name for the home page file, export the Web pages anew.

Similarly, don't rename any image files or move them from their folders.

Printing Photos and Ordering Prints

Internet photo sharing is great, but hard copy isn't dead. You might want to share photos with people who don't have computers. Or, you might want to tack a photo to a bulletin board or hang it on your wall—you'll never see "suitable for framing" stamped on an email message.

iPhoto makes hard copy easy. If you have a photo-inkjet printer, you can use iPhoto to create beautiful color prints in a variety of sizes. This assumes, of course, that your photos are both beautiful and in color.

When printing your photos, you can choose from several formatting options by using the Style pop-up menu in the Print dialog box. For example, if you choose the Sampler style, you can print pages that contain the same photo in several different sizes. With the style named N-Up, you can print up to 16 photos per page.

Another option is iPhoto's print-ordering features, which let you order photographic prints in sizes ranging from 4 by 6 inches to 20 by 30 inches.

Printing with iPhoto is straightforward, but to get the best results, you'll want to use images with a resolution high enough to yield sharp results at your chosen print size.

Printing Your Photos

iPhoto works well with today's photo-inkjet printers and lets you create prints in several sizes and formats.

To print just one photo, select it and then choose Print from the File menu (⌘-P). To print multiple photos, select them before choosing Print.

Be sure your printer is selected here.

iPhoto includes preset printing options for many popular inkjet printers. Choose the preset that best matches the type of paper you're using.

Use the Standard Prints style to create prints in common sizes. Other style options are Contact Sheet, Full Page, N-Up, Sampler, and Greeting Card (see page 107).

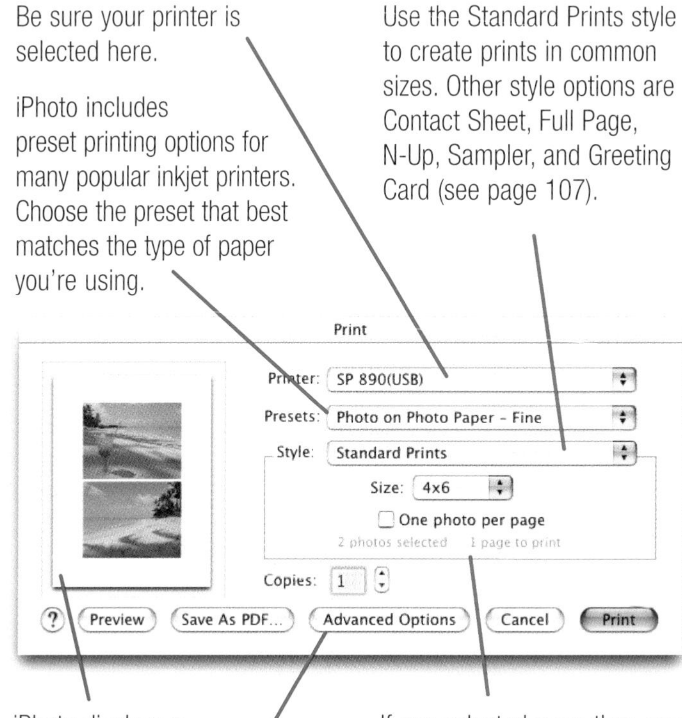

iPhoto displays a preview of your first page here.

Access additional printing options specific to your printer.

If you selected more than one photo and you're creating prints smaller than 8 by 10 inches, iPhoto lets you take better advantage of expensive photo paper by printing multiple images on each sheet. To have iPhoto center smaller prints on a full sheet of paper, click the One Photo Per Page check box.

See the print-ordering process and some fun output options.
Ordering Prints
Thinking Beyond Paper

Ordering Prints

To order prints, first select the photos you want prints of, then click the Order Prints button in iPhoto's Organize pane.

To order prints, you must first set up an Apple ID account and enable 1-Click ordering. For instructions, click the help icon in the bottom-left corner of the dialog box.

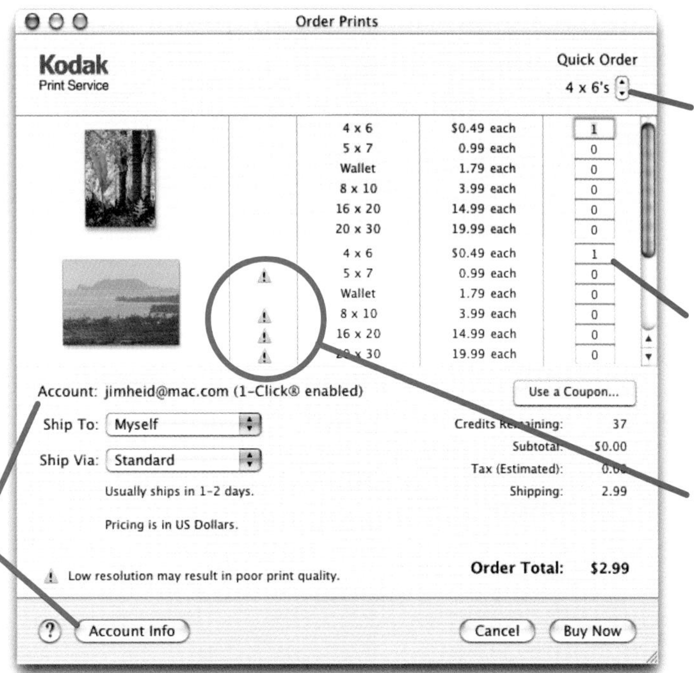

Want a 4 by 6 of every photo you selected? Specify the quantity here.

Specify how many prints you want for each size.

Low-resolution images may yield poor prints at larger sizes; see the sidebar below for details.

Resolution's Relationship to Print Quality

If you're working with low-resolution images—ones taken with a digital camera at its low-resolution setting, for example—you may see iPhoto's dreaded low-resolution warning icon when printing, ordering prints, or creating a book.

This is iPhoto's way ⚠ of telling you that an image doesn't have enough pixels—enough digital information—to yield a good-quality print at the size that you've chosen.

Don't feel obligated to cancel a print job or an order if you see this warning. I've ordered books containing low-resolution images and they still look beautiful.

Yes, some artifacts are visible at times, but I'd rather have a memorable book with some flawed photos than no book at all.

The table here lists the minimum resolution an image should have to yield a good print at various sizes.

Print Sizes and Resolution

For This Print Size (Inches)	Image Resolution Should be at Least (Pixels)
Wallet	320 by 240
4 by 6	640 by 480
5 by 7	1024 by 768
8 by 10	1536 by 1024
16 by 20 or larger	1600 by 1200

Creating Books

With iPhoto's Book button and Apple's help, you can turn an album of photos into a hard-bound, linen-covered book. iPhoto books make spectacular gifts and are ideal for promotional portfolios and other business applications, too.

To create a book, first create an album containing the photos you want to publish, in the order you want them to appear. Then, click iPhoto's Book button to display the Book pane.

Next, choose a theme design from the Theme pop-up menu. Finally, arrange the photos and text captions on each page as described here.

To order your finished book, click the Order Book button in the Book pane or in iPhoto's Organize pane. At this phase, you can choose a color for the book's linen cover. Color options include black, burgundy, light gray, or navy.

One last note: Because of the printing method used to create iPhoto books, Apple recommends against including black-and-white photos in a book.

Browsing Books

iPhoto provides a variety of book designs, called *themes*.

Catalog

Places up to eight photos on a page, with room for captions and descriptions.

Classic

Symmetrical page designs with up to four photos per page, with captions in the elegant Baskerville typeface.

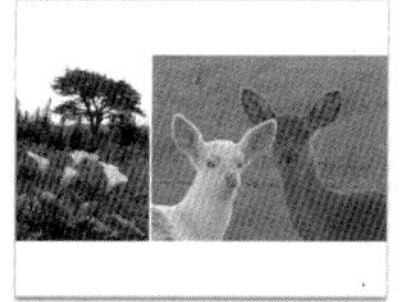

Picture Book

Positions photos as bleeds—the photos extend to the edges of the page. This theme provides no captions or titles.

Portfolio

Allows up to four photos per page and provides for captions and titles.

Story Book

Positions photos askew on the page and leaves room for storytelling.

Year Book

Allows for up to 32 photos per page—ideal for a class yearbook or a collection of police mug shots.

See an iPhoto book come together.
Creating a Book

Designing a Book

You design a book one page at a time. iPhoto displays a thumbnail version of the current page; to zoom in on the thumbnail, use the size slider. You can edit the text on each page and choose a different design from the Page Design pop-up menu.

Each theme has a variety of page designs; choose a design here. Some designs place more photos on each page than others.

Tips: To apply a page design to all subsequent pages in the book, press the Option key while choosing the design. And if you're working with low-resolution images, use a design that puts several images on a page. Each image will be smaller, and thus more likely to print with acceptable quality.

To work on a different page, select it. To move a page within the book, drag it left or right.

Note: Moving a page also changes the order of the photos in your album.

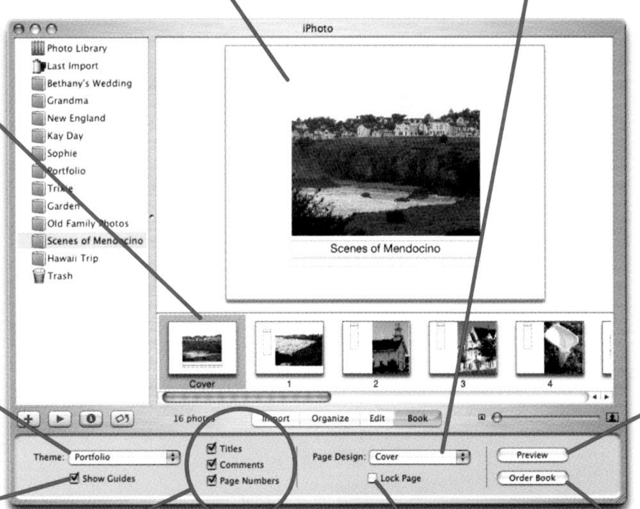

The Portfolio theme is my favorite; I like its contemporary, elegant look.

To preview the book, click Preview. You can also use the book preview window to edit captions.

To hide the faint lines that iPhoto draws on-screen around title and comment boxes, uncheck this box. Either way, these lines will not print.

You can include titles, comments, and page numbers in your book.

Tip: You can change the formatting of these items by selecting the text you want to change, and then using the Font command in the Edit menu.

When you change the number of photos on a page, iPhoto changes the placement of all photos on subsequent pages. To ensure that the photos on the page you're working on will remain on that page, click Lock Page.

When you're ready to order your book, click Order Book.

Creating Slide Shows

With iPhoto's slide show feature, you can display on-screen slide shows, complete with background music from your iTunes music library. iPhoto even gives you a lovely cross-dissolve effect—one photo fades out as the next one fades in.

Most of the time, you'll want to add photos to an album before viewing them as a slide show. That way, you can arrange the photos in a sequence that best tells your story.

But, when you're after immediate gratification—if you want to screen a roll of images immediately after importing them, for example—you can view a slide show from a series of images you've selected in the Photo Library.

You can view your slide shows on the Mac's screen or, if you're using a PowerBook with an S-video jack, you can connect the computer to a TV set to view the slide show on a television. You can also connect your Mac to a video projector and show your slide show on a big screen.

Somebody get the lights.

Creating a Slide Show

Step 1.

Select the photos you want to show.
To show an entire album, select the album.

Step 2.

Click the Slideshow button in iPhoto's Organize pane.
The Slideshow Settings dialog box appears.

Displays the photos in random order instead of in the order they appear in the iPhoto window.

When this box is checked, iPhoto repeats the slide show until time itself comes to an end or until you press the Esc key or the mouse button, whichever comes first.

To have a silent slide show, uncheck this box.

To sort the song list, click on a column heading. You can move the columns by dragging them, and you can resize them by dragging their boundaries.

You can audition a song by double-clicking it or by selecting it and pressing the ▶ button.

To narrow down the list of songs displayed, type part or all of a song or artist name here.

You can choose any iTunes playlist from this pop-up menu.

Type a duration for each image or click the up and down arrows to set a duration.

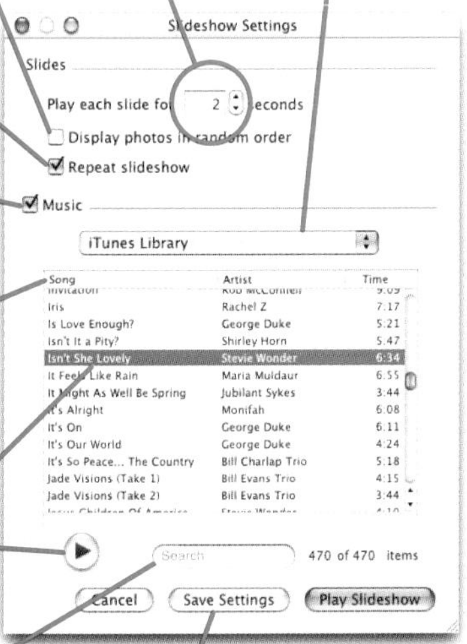

To save your song selection without actually viewing the slide show, click Save Settings.

Step 3.

Click the Play Slideshow button.

GO TO DVD

Watch an iPhoto slide show come together.
Creating a Slide Show

Assigning Songs to Albums

You can assign a different song to each of your albums. When you view a particular album as a slide show, iPhoto plays the song you've assigned to it.

To assign a song to a specific album, start iTunes and position its window so you can see it and your iPhoto albums. Then, simply drag a song to an album.

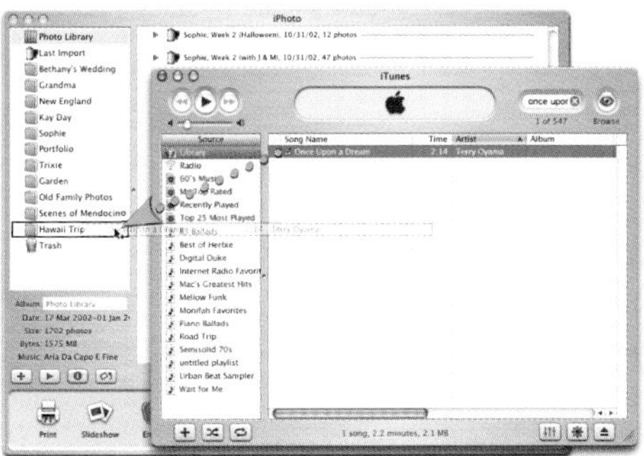

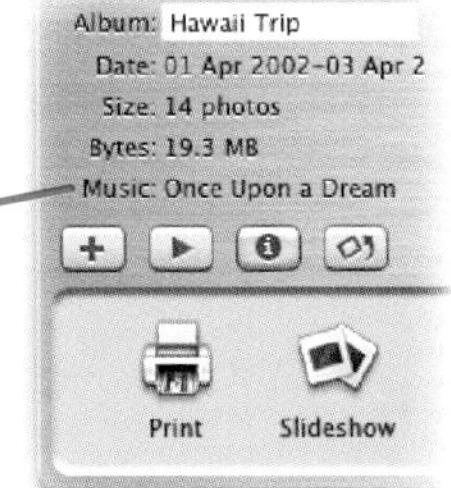

The song you've assigned to the album appears in iPhoto's information area.

Tip: You can also drag a song to the Photo Library and the Last Import items. When you drag a song to the Photo Library item, iPhoto asks if you want to make that song the default slide show music. If you click OK, iPhoto will assign that song to all future albums you create. (You can always change this song assignment manually.)

Slide Show Keyboard Controls

To pause a slide show, press the spacebar. If the slide show has music, the music will continue to play but the images won't change. To resume the slide show, press the spacebar again.

To adjust the speed of the slide show, use the up arrow and down arrow keys. To manually move through the slide show, use the left and right arrow keys.

Videotaping a Slide Show

Many PowerBooks have S-video jacks that enable you to display their screen images on a TV set or record them using a camcorder or videocassette recorder. You can take advantage of these TV-savvy Macs to record a slide show on tape.

First, connect the PowerBook's S-video connector to a camcorder or VCR, open System Preferences, and use Displays to turn on video mirroring.

Next, press your video deck's Record button, and begin playing back the slide show.

To record the background music, too, connect the Mac's speaker jack to your video deck's audio-input jacks.

More Ways to Share Photos

You can export a series of images in QuickTime movie format, again adding a music soundtrack if you like. You can publish the resulting movie on a Web site, burn it to a CD, or bring it into iDVD and burn it to a DVD.

Looking for still more ways to share? Redecorate your Macintosh desktop with your favorite photo. Or, use a set of photos as a screen saver. iPhoto makes it easy to do both.

It's obvious: If your digital photos aren't getting seen, it isn't iPhoto's fault.

Exporting Photos as Movies

Why export still images in a movie format? Because iPhoto will add a music soundtrack and cross-dissolves between images. Think of an iPhoto QuickTime movie as a portable slide show. Email it, post it on a Web site, or burn it to a CD or DVD—it will play back on any Mac or Windows computer that has QuickTime installed.

Portable slide show: An iPhoto-created QuickTime movie playing back in the QuickTime Player program.

You can import an iPhoto-created QuickTime movie into iDVD and burn it to a DVD disc. In fact, given that iDVD's slide show feature lacks a cross-dissolve effect, you might prefer to use iPhoto QuickTime movies to present photos on DVDs. However, further proving that life is a game of trade-offs, iPhoto lacks iDVD's ability to time a slide show to a piece of music. In an iPhoto QuickTime movie, the music stops abruptly after the last image displays.

To export images as a QuickTime movie, select a set of images or switch to an album. Next, choose Export from the File menu.

Specify the duration for each image to display.

You can specify that iPhoto add a background color or background image to the movie. The color or image appears whenever the dimensions of the currently displayed photo don't match that of the movie itself. (For example, in a 640 by 480 movie, the background will be visible in photos shot in vertical orientation.) The background will also be visible at the beginning and end of the movie—before the first image fades in and after the last image fades out.

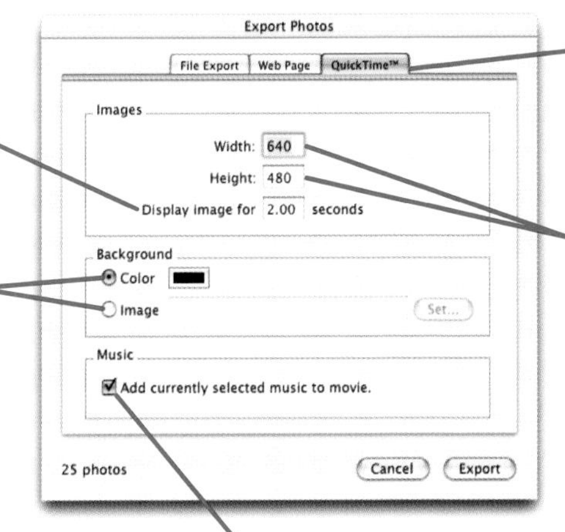

Click the QuickTime tab to access movie-export options.

Specify the desired dimensions for the movie, in pixels. The preset values shown here work well, but if you specify smaller dimensions, such as 320 by 240, you'll get a smaller movie file—useful if you plan to distribute the movie over the Internet.

When this box is checked, iPhoto uses the last song you selected as the soundtrack for the movie. To create a silent movie, uncheck this box.

Using Photos as Desktop Images and Screen Savers

The Organize pane's Desktop button lets you share photos with yourself. Select a photo and click Desktop, and iPhoto replaces the Mac's desktop with the photo you selected.

If you select multiple photos or an album, your desktop image will change as you work, complete with a cross-dissolve effect between images. It's an iPhoto slide show applied to your desktop.

Warning: Using vacation photos as desktop images has been proven to cause wanderlust.

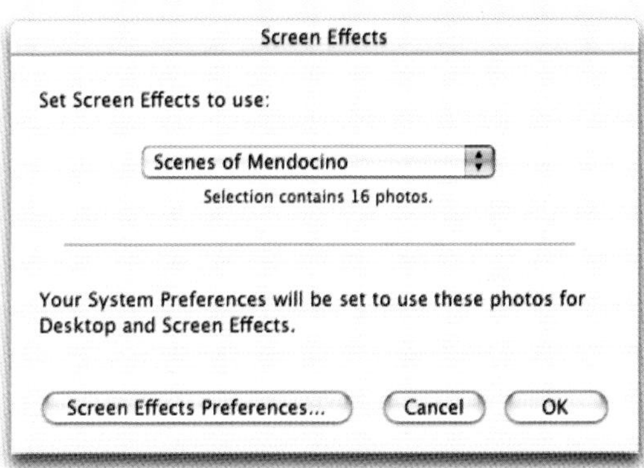

Burning Photos to CDs and DVDs

The phrase "burning photos" can strike terror into any photographer's heart, but fear not: I'm not talking about open flames here. If your Mac has a CD or DVD burner, you can save, or burn, photos onto CDs or DVDs. You can burn your entire photo library, an album or two, just a few photos, or even just one.

iPhoto's burning features make possible all manner of photo-transportation tasks. Back up your photo library: burn the entire library and then stash the disc in a safe place. Move photos and albums from one Mac to another: burn a selection, then insert the disc in another Mac to work with them there. Or send a few high-resolution photos to a friend who has a slow modem connection: burn the photos and pop the disc into the mail.

iPhoto doesn't just copy photos to a disc. It creates a full-fledged iPhoto library on the disc. That library contains the images' titles and keywords, any albums that you burned, and even original versions of images you've retouched or cropped. Think of an iPhoto-burned disc as a portable iPhoto library.

iPhoto's burning features are compatible with any CD or DVD burner supported by Mac OS X. If you can burn with iTunes, you can burn with iPhoto, too. To burn to DVD discs in iPhoto, however, you must use Mac OS X version 10.2 (Jaguar) or a later version.

Now back away from that fire extinguisher—we've got some burning to do.

Burning Basics

Burning photos involves selecting what you want to burn, then clicking the Burn button a couple of times.

Step 1.

Select photos.

Use the selection techniques discussed on page 77 to specify which photos to burn. Remember that you can also select multiple albums by Shift-clicking or ⌘-clicking on each one.

Step 2.

Click the Burn button.

iPhoto asks you to insert a blank disc.

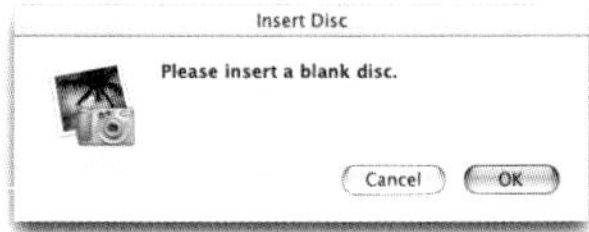

Step 3.

Insert a blank disc and click OK.

iPhoto displays information about the pending burn in its information area. You can add or remove photos to or from the selection, and iPhoto will update its information area accordingly.

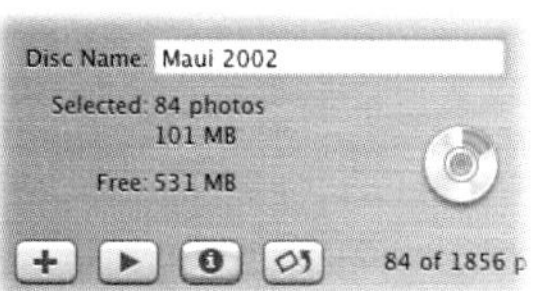

Tip: Give your disc a descriptive name by typing in the Disc Name box.

Step 4:

Click the Burn button again.

iPhoto displays another dialog box. To cancel the burn, click Cancel. To proceed, click Burn.

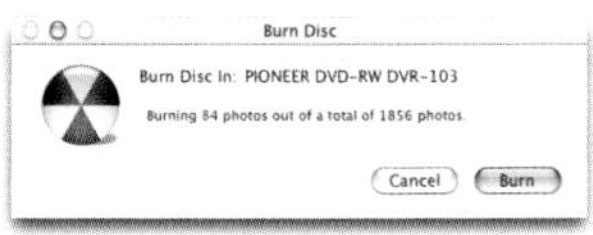

iPhoto prepares the images, then burns and verifies the contents of the disc.

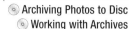

See how to archive photos and work with archives.
Archiving Photos to Disc
Working with Archives

Copying an Album from a Burned Disc

You've burned an album to disc, and now you want to copy the entire album to your hard drive (or someone else's) in order to work on the photos. Here's how.

First, select the album in the photo library list.

Next, select all the photos in the album. (A quick way to do this: select one photo then press ⌘-A.)

Finally, drag the selected photos into a blank area of the photo album list. iPhoto creates a new album, which you'll probably want to rename, and adds the photos to it.

Working with Burned Discs

When you insert a disc burned in iPhoto, the disc appears in iPhoto's photo library list. To see its photos, select the disc's name. Note that the disc's photos aren't in the iPhoto library on your hard drive—they're in the iPhoto library on the disc.

If the disc contains multiple albums, a small triangle appears next to the disc's name. To view the disc's albums, click the triangle.

You can display photos on a disc using the same techniques that you use to display photos stored in your iPhoto library. You can also order prints, display slide shows, create desktop images, and export images and QuickTime movies.

However, you can't crop, retouch, or otherwise edit photos stored on a CD or DVD. To edit a photo, add it to your library by dragging it to the Photo Library item or to an album.

How iPhoto Burns (And How to Take Advantage of It)

Prior to the actual burn, iPhoto creates a *disk image* on your Mac desktop. This is a faux disk that serves as a temporary holding area for the photos: iPhoto creates the disk image, copies the photos there, burns the disk image to your blank medium, and then deletes the disk image.

With this tip, you can save this disk image on your hard drive. Why bother? One reason might be to burn additional discs using Roxio's Toast Titanium software. Burning multiple discs with Toast is faster than with iPhoto, which performs the time-consuming process of creating a disk image and copying photos every time you burn.

One more bonus to burning with Toast: you can rename the disc before you burn. iPhoto normally uses the bland name *iPhoto Disc* for every disc it burns. With Toast, you can give the disc a descriptive name, such as *Maui 2002 Photos*.

But timing is everything. Copy the disk image after iPhoto has finished adding photos to it, but before iPhoto deletes the disk image from your hard drive. The best time to copy the disk image is when iPhoto is actually burning. During the burn, hide iPhoto and return to the Finder. Next, press the Option key and then drag the disk image to your hard drive icon or into a specific folder, if you like. (Pressing Option tells the Finder to copy the disk image instead of creating an alias to it.)

Finally, drag the saved disk image into Toast's window, rename the disc if desired (don't rename any of the files within the disc), and burn.

Creating and Managing Photo Libraries

As your photo library grows to encompass thousands of photos, locating specific images can be cumbersome. A huge photo library is also more difficult to back up, since it may not fit on a CD or even a DVD. And iPhoto itself can start to slow down when it has thousands of photos to manage.

The answer: more photo libraries. iPhoto lets you have multiple photo libraries and switch between them. If your photo library has reached gargantuan proportions, back it up and create a new, empty one.

How often should you create a new library? That depends. You might base your decision on disk space: if you back up your library by burning it to a CD-R, create a new library each time the size of your current library reaches about 650MB. That way, you can always be sure your library will fit on a CD. (To see how much space your library uses, select the Photo Library item, then look in the information area below the albums list.)

Or, you might prefer a chronological approach. If you take hundreds of photos every month (or more), consider creating a new library each month. Then again, maybe a subject-oriented approach is best for you. Use one iPhoto library to hold your family shots, and another to hold work-related shots.

You get the idea: by taking advantage of iPhoto's ability to work with multiple photo libraries, you make it easier to organize your photos—and to back them up.

Creating a New Library

Before creating a new library, you may want to back up your existing library by dragging your iPhoto Library folder to another hard drive or to a blank CD or DVD. You can also use iPhoto's Burn button to archive your library on a CD or DVD, as described on page 100.

Step 1.

Quit iPhoto.

Step 2.

Locate your iPhoto Library folder and rename it.

To quickly locate the folder, choose Home from the Finder's Go menu, then double-click the Pictures folder, where you'll find the iPhoto Library folder.

Step 3.

Start iPhoto.

iPhoto asks if you want to locate an existing library or create a new one.

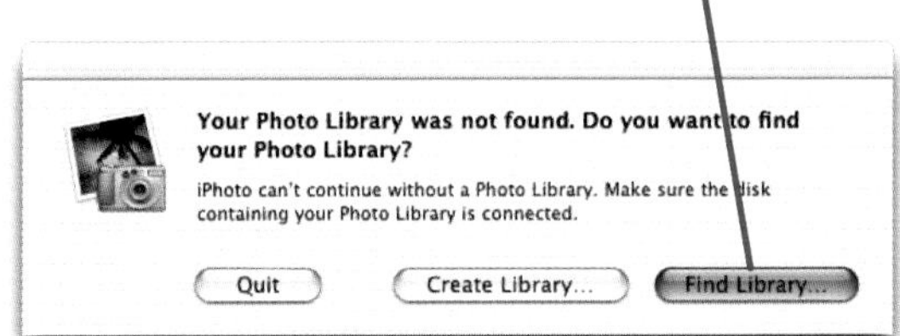

Step 4.

Click Create Library.

iPhoto proposes the name iPhoto Library, but you can type a different name if you like.

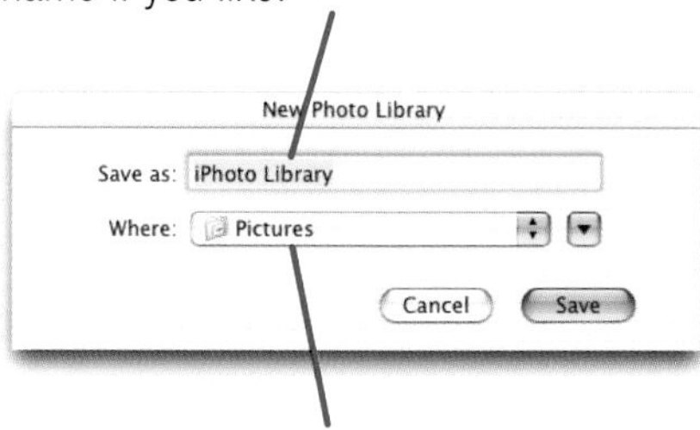

You don't need to store your library in the Pictures folder; see the sidebar below.

iPhoto creates the new, empty library.

Switching Between Libraries

There may be times when you want to switch to a different iPhoto library—for example, to access the photos in an older library. Here's how.

Step 1.

Quit iPhoto.

Step 2.

Locate your current iPhoto library folder and change its name.

Step 3.

Start iPhoto.

iPhoto asks if you want to find an existing library or create a new one.

Step 4.

Click Find Library. The Open Photo Library dialog box appears.

Step 5.

Select the library you want to use and click the Open button.

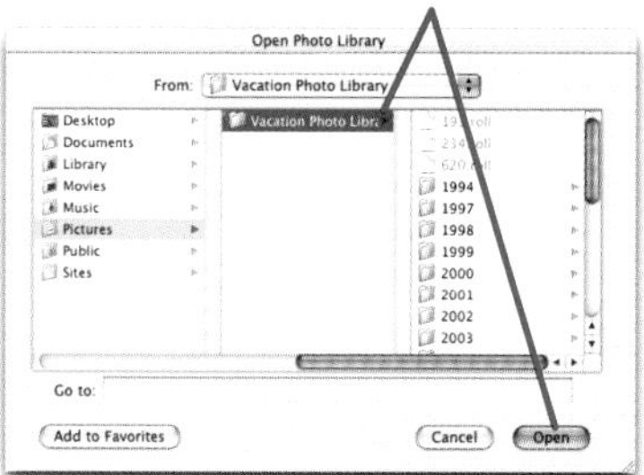

Tips for Managing Libraries and Photos

Storing Photos Elsewhere

Normally, iPhoto stores your photo library in the Pictures folder. But why be normal? You might prefer to store your library elsewhere, such as on an external FireWire hard drive.

To store your photo library elsewhere, quit iPhoto, then simply copy the iPhoto Library folder wherever you like. Restart iPhoto, click the Find Library button, and use the Open Photo Library dialog box to aim iPhoto in the right direction.

Dragging Images from iPhoto

You may want to include photos in documents that you're creating in Microsoft Word or other programs. It's easy: just drag the image from iPhoto into your document.

Dragging Photos to the Finder

If you drag an image to the Finder desktop or to a folder window, iPhoto makes a duplicate copy of the image file. Use this technique when you want to copy a photo out of your library.

You can use this technique to remove photos from a roll without deleting them from your hard drive. First, drag the photos to the Finder to make copies of them. (You might want to create a temporary folder on your desktop to hold the photos.) Next, delete the photos from the roll where they appear. Finally, re-import the photos by dragging them back into iPhoto's window, where they'll appear in their own new roll.

iPhoto Tips

AppleScripts for iPhoto

Like iTunes and iDVD, iPhoto supports the AppleScript automation technology that is part of Mac OS X. A large collection of iPhoto scripts is available, and some of the best come from Apple. You can download scripts that simplify the process of assigning keywords to photos, scripts that automate iPhoto and Photoshop, and much more. For links to my favorite iPhoto scripts, visit this book's companion Web site.

Controlling the Camera Connection

You can use the Image Capture program, included with Mac OS X, to control what happens when you connect a digital camera to your Mac. By choosing the Preferences command from the Image Capture menu, you can have the Mac start up iPhoto, start up Image Capture or a different program, or do nothing at all.

Importing Only Some Images

Speaking of Image Capture, it's the program to use when you want to import only some photos from a camera. Say you've shot twenty photos but you know only five of them are going to be keepers. Rather than import all twenty into iPhoto and then delete fifteen of them, use Image Capture.

After connecting your camera and turning it on, start up Image Capture and click its Download Some button. A window appears containing thumbnail versions of each photo.

Next, you need to tell Image Capture where to store the downloaded photos. I like to store them in a temporary folder that I create on my desktop.

From the Download Folder pop-up menu in Image Capture's toolbar, choose Other. Press ⌘-D to jump to your desktop and then click the New Folder button. Name the folder anything you like—I use the name *Import Me*. Then click the Open button.

Finally, click the Download button to download the photos you selected. Quit Image Capture, drag those photos into your iPhoto window, and delete the temporary folder.

Yes, it's a bit of work, but it's the best technique to use if your camera contains dozens of images and you know you'll only be keeping a small selection of them.

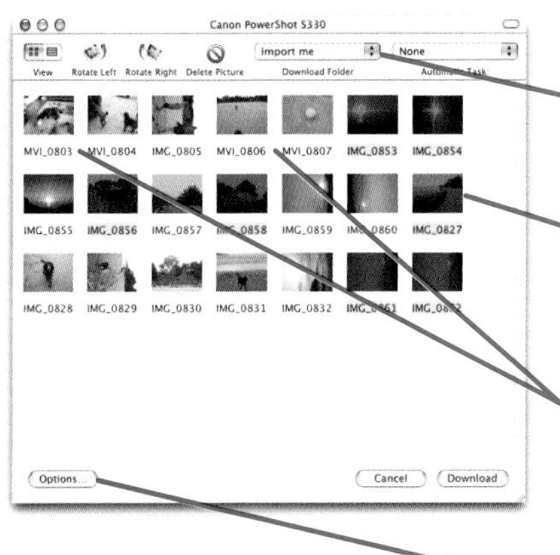

Use the Download Folder pop-up menu to specify where you want downloaded items to be stored.

Select the photos you want to download, remembering to Shift-click and ⌘-click to select multiple photos.

Many digital cameras can also take short movies; you can use Image Capture to download them.

The Options dialog box contains some useful features, including the ability to set your camera's built-in clock to match your Mac's.

Get links to iPhoto add-ons and additional online photo services.
www.macilife.com/iphoto

GO TO WEB

Portraits & Prints

This inexpensive utility from Econ Technologies goes beyond iPhoto's printing features to let you mix and match photos of various sizes on a single sheet of paper, print holiday greeting cards, and much more. Add the companion Template Maker utility, and you can create your own printing templates.

Beyond Prints

Several online photofinishers will put your photos on more than just paper. As you can see when you view the DVD, I've had photos printed onto mugs, mouse pads, T-shirts, and even cookies. (And the cookies are actually pretty good, despite all the artificial coloring.)

I ordered my photo doodads from ClubPhoto (www.clubphoto.com), but you can also get offbeat output options from Image Edit (www.image-edit.com), Mystic Color Lab (www.mysticcolorlab.com), and Kodak's Picture Center (www.kodak.com).

Dealing with Duplicates

Here's a common scenario: you use iPhoto to import some photos from your camera, and you don't delete the photos from the camera after importing. Then, you shoot another dozen or so photos and prepare to import them. iPhoto is smart enough to know that you've already imported some of the photos, and it will ask you if you want to skip those duplicates.

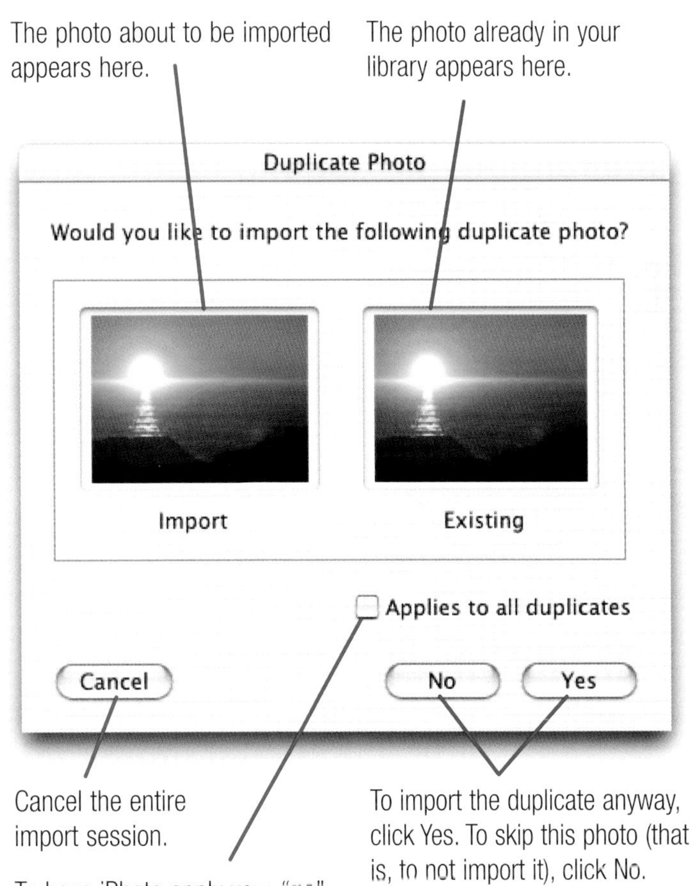
The photo about to be imported appears here.
The photo already in your library appears here.
Duplicate Photo
Would you like to import the following duplicate photo?
Import
Existing
Applies to all duplicates
Cancel
No
Yes
Cancel the entire import session.
To import the duplicate anyway, click Yes. To skip this photo (that is, to not import it), click No.
To have iPhoto apply your "no" or "yes" choice to all duplicates it finds, check this box. Your choice here applies to the current importing session only.

More iPhoto Tips

Duplicating an Album

There may be times when you'll want several versions of an album. For example, you might have one version with photos sequenced for a slide show and another version with photos organized for a book. Or you might simply want to experiment with several different photo arrangements until you find the one you like best.

iPhoto makes this kind of experimentation easy. Simply duplicate an album by selecting its name and choosing Duplicate from the File menu (⌘-D). iPhoto makes a duplicate of the album, which you can rename and experiment with.

You can make as many duplicates of an album as you like.

Printing a Contact Sheet

Photographers often create contact sheets—quick-reference prints containing small versions of multiple photos, usually an entire roll's worth on each contact sheet. (The term derives from the traditional technique: a contact sheet is created by sandwiching negatives between a piece of glass and photographic paper, and then exposing the sandwich to light.)

Specify how many images you want to appear on each row of the contact sheet.

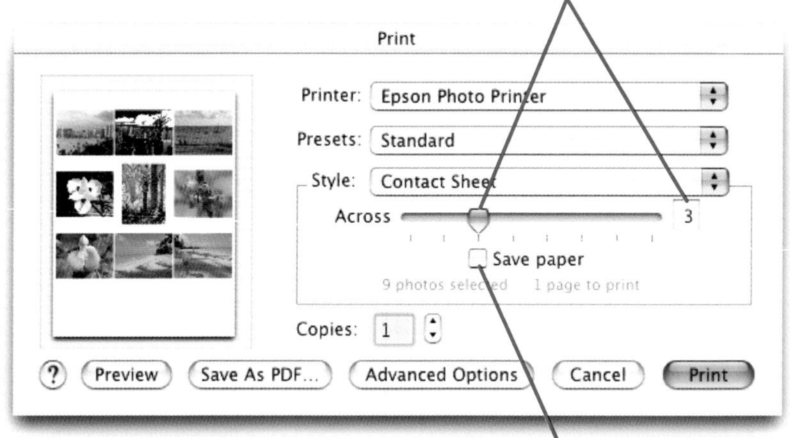

Check the Save paper box to have iPhoto print vertical images in horizontal orientation, even if you rotated them. You'll have to turn the sheet sideways to view some images, but you'll get more images on each sheet of paper.

To include only certain photos on a contact sheet, select them before choosing the Print command. You can use contact sheets to provide an at-a-glance reference for a series of photos.

But you can also use a contact sheet to squeeze several images onto a single sheet of paper.

Tip: You can use contact sheets to print multiple copies of one photo. Simply select only one photo before choosing Print.

Other Print Styles

iPhoto provides several additional print styles: Greeting Card, Full Page, N-Up, and Sampler.

The Greeting Card style formats the page so you can fold it into a card.

The Full Page style lets you create a print with one photo per page and any size margin you like, up to one inch. You might use this option when you don't care if the final print is a standard print size, such as 5 by 7 or 8 by 10.

The N-Up style prints multiple copies of a single photo on each page. You can choose to print as few as two copies per page, or as many as 16.

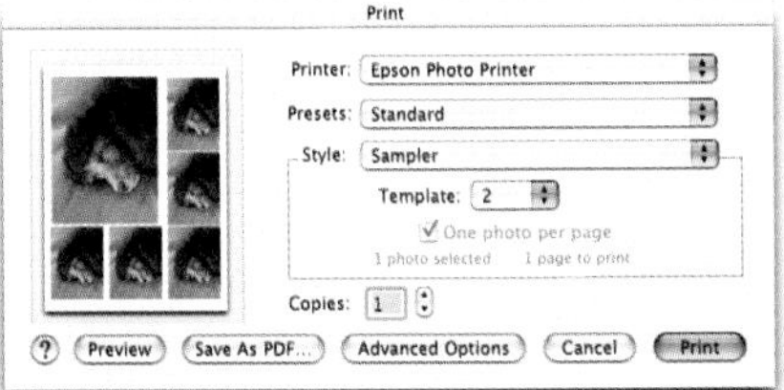

The Sampler style mixes and matches sizes on a single sheet—much like the combination of print sizes you might get from a portrait studio. This style provides two templates, which you can choose using the Template pop-up menu.

The Why and How of Duplicating Photos

You have a photo that appears in multiple albums, but you want to edit its appearance in just one album, leaving the original version unchanged in other albums.

Time for the Duplicate command: select the photo and choose Duplicate from the File menu (⌘-D). Now edit the duplicate.

You can also use the Duplicate command to create special effects for iPhoto's slide show and QuickTime movie features. Make a few duplicates of an image, and modify each duplicate in some way. Sequence each image in an album, and when you play the slide show or QuickTime movie, each version will fade into the next.

From Import to Album

If you have photos on your Finder desktop—whether on your hard drive, a Picture CD, or a digital camera's memory card—you can import them and create an album in one fell swoop. Simply drag the photos from the Finder into a blank area of the Photo Library list. iPhoto will import the photos, storing them in their own roll. iPhoto will also create an album and add the photos to it.

Stay Out of the Library

I've mentioned it before, but it bears repeating: *never* add files to or remove them from the folders inside the iPhoto Library folder. Indeed, I recommend that you don't even venture inside this folder. Renaming, moving, or otherwise modifying files inside your iPhoto Library folder is a great way to lose photos. Let iPhoto manage the library for you—add and remove photos only by dragging them into and out of the iPhoto window.

Tips for Better Digital Photography

Get Up Close

Too many photographers shy away from their subjects. Get close to show detail. If you can't get physically closer, use your camera's zoom feature, if it has one. If your camera has a macro feature, use it to take extreme close-ups of flowers, rocks, seashells, tattoos—you name it. Don't limit yourself to wide shots.

Avoid Digital Zooming

Many digital cameras supplement their optical zoom lenses with digital zoom functions that bring your subject even closer. Think twice about using digital zoom—it usually adds undesirable artifacts to an image.

Position the Horizon

In landscape shots, the position of the horizon influences the mood of the photo. To imply a vast, wide open space, put the horizon along the lower third of the frame and show lots of sky. (This obviously works best when the sky is cooperating.) To imply a sense of closeness—or if the sky is a bland shade of gray—put the horizon along the upper third, showing little sky.

This rule, like others, is meant to be broken. For example, if you're shooting a forlorn-looking desert landscape, you might want to have the horizon bisect the image to imply a sense of bleak monotony.

Kill Your Flash

I turn off my camera's built-in flash and rarely turn it on. Existing light provides a much more flattering, natural-looking image, with none of the harshness of electronic flash. Dimly lit indoor shots may have a slight blur to them, but I'll take blur over the radioactive look of flash any day.

Master Your Camera

Many digital cameras have manual-exposure modes that enable you to specify shutter speed and aperture settings. Manually adjusting these settings gives you more control over tricky shots. For example, say a subject is in front of a busy background and you just can't get the shot from another angle. You can increase the shutter speed and open up the aperture to decrease the camera's *depth of field*. This will throw the background out of focus.

Beware of the Background

More accurately, *be aware* of the background. Is a tree growing out of Mary's head? If so, move yourself or Mary. Are there distracting details in the background? Find a simpler setting or get up close. Is your shadow visible in the shot? Change your position. When looking at a scene, our brains tend to ignore irrelevant things. But the camera sees all. As you compose, look at the entire frame, not just your subject.

Crop Carefully

You can often use iPhoto's cropping tool to fix composition problems. But note that cropping results in lost pixels, and that may affect your ability to produce high-quality prints. Try to do your cropping in the camera's viewfinder, not iPhoto.

Embrace Blur

A blurred photo is a ruined photo, right? Not necessarily. Blur conveys motion, something still images don't usually do. A photo with a sharp background but a car that is blurred tells you the car was in motion. To take this kind of shot, keep the camera steady and snap the shutter at the moment the car crosses the frame.

You can also convey motion by turning this formula around: If you pan along with the moving car as you snap, the car will be sharp but the background will be blurred.

Indoor shots taken without a flash will often have some motion blur to them, too, since the camera will have to take a longer exposure. I'd rather see a somewhat blurry shot of dancing partygoers than a tack-sharp, harshly lit one.

Compose Carefully

Following a couple of rules of thumb can help you compose photos that are more visually pleasing.

First, there's the age-old *rule of thirds*, in which you divide the image rectangle into thirds and place your photo's subject at or near one of the intersections of the resulting grid.

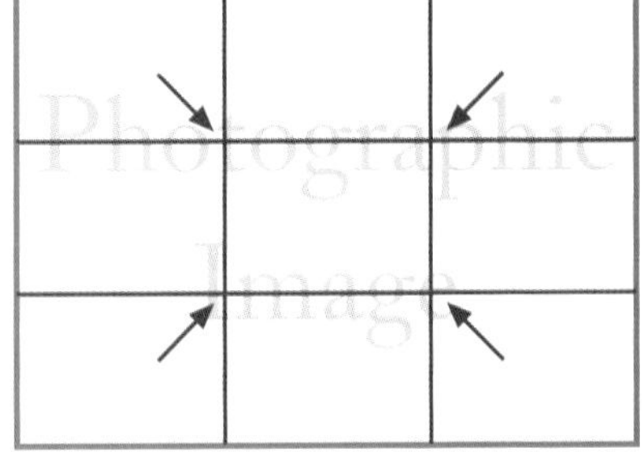

Place your photo's subject at or near these intersections.

This composition technique yields images that are more visually dynamic.

A second technique is to draw the viewer's eyes to your subject and add a sense of dynamism by using diagonal lines, such as a receding fence.

No Tripod?

If you want to take sharp photos in low light, mount your camera on a tripod. If you don't have a tripod handy, here's a workaround: turn on your camera's self-timer mode—the mode you'd usually use when you want to get yourself in the picture—then set the camera on a rigid surface and press the shutter button. Because you won't be holding the camera when the shutter goes off, you won't risk getting a blurred shot.

iMovie: Making Movies

The Macintosh **iLife**

iMovie at a Glance

Video can be a powerful vehicle for communicating an idea, setting a mood, selling a product, or bringing back a memory. It can also be great way to put people to sleep.

Video editing is the process of assembling video clips, still images, and audio into a finished package that gets your message across and keeps your audience's eyes open. Video editing is what iMovie is all about.

With iMovie, you can import video from a miniDV camcorder connected via FireWire. iMovie controls your camcorder during the importing process, stashing incoming clips on its Clips pane.

Then, you edit clips and sequence them by dragging them to the timeline, optionally adding music from your CD collection or iTunes music library and creating titles, effects, and scene transitions. When you're finished, a few mouse clicks send your efforts back out to tape or to iDVD.

You can use iMovie to edit interminable home movies, but you can also use it to assemble montages of photos from iPhoto, promotional videos, and anything else that belongs on the small screen.

Quiet on the set.

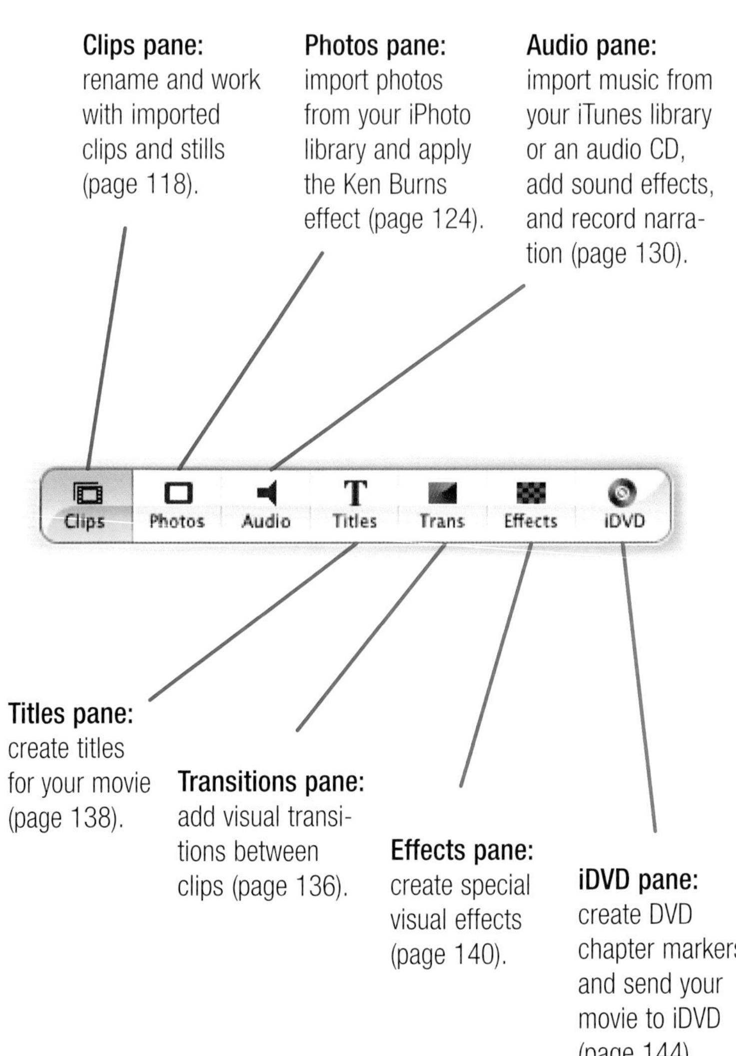
Clips pane: rename and work with imported clips and stills (page 118).
Photos pane: import photos from your iPhoto library and apply the Ken Burns effect (page 124).
Audio pane: import music from your iTunes library or an audio CD, add sound effects, and record narration (page 130).
Clips
Photos
Audio
Titles
Trans
Effects
iDVD
Titles pane: create titles for your movie (page 138).
Transitions pane: add visual transitions between clips (page 136).
Effects pane: create special visual effects (page 140).
iDVD pane: create DVD chapter markers and send your movie to iDVD (page 144).

See the movie-making process from start to finish.
iMovie: Making Movies

The monitor displays video as you import it or play it back.

Switch between the clip viewer and the timeline viewer (page 121).

The scrubber bar lets you move through and crop a clip (page 118).

Rewind, start and stop playback, and play back in full-screen mode.

Adjust the speaker's volume as you work in iMovie.

Video clips and still images that you import are stored in the Clips pane until you add them to the timeline.

The playhead indicates the current playback location. Drag it left and right to quickly move backward and forward within your movie or within a single clip.

These buttons switch between iMovie's panes, each of which lets you work with a different kind of element.

You can sequence clips by dragging them from the Clips pane to the timeline (page 120).

Drag the zoom slider to zoom in and out on the timeline.

Switch between camera mode (to import video) and edit mode (page 116).

Create slow- and fast-motion effects (page 141).

Adjust the audio levels of individual clips (page 132).

Reclaim space by emptying the iMovie trash now and then (page 119).

iMovie displays remaining free disk space here.

The Essentials of Movie Making

Editing video is the most complex task you will perform in iLife. Not that it's technically difficult—iMovie, FireWire, and the miniDV video format have made it easier than ever.

But editing video can be time consuming and labor intensive, as you can see in the iMovie segment of the DVD. Bringing media into iMovie, fine-tuning the length of clips, timing shots to match a music track, adding transitions and effects—it all takes time. But as a creative exercise, it's hard to beat.

If you're new to video editing, start small. Create a short movie—between 30 and 90 seconds. Your first effort shouldn't be an epic; it should be a short story, or even a single well-wrought paragraph. That's the best way to learn the art and science of editing—and to appreciate its magic.

Video Editing: The Big Picture

Import Assets

Bring in video from a camcorder and, optionally, add photos, MP3 music tracks, or music from a compact disc.

Trim the Fat

Use iMovie's crop markers and Crop command to discard unwanted portions of clips.

Sequence Clips

Drag clips to the timeline viewer and clip viewer to add them to your final movie.

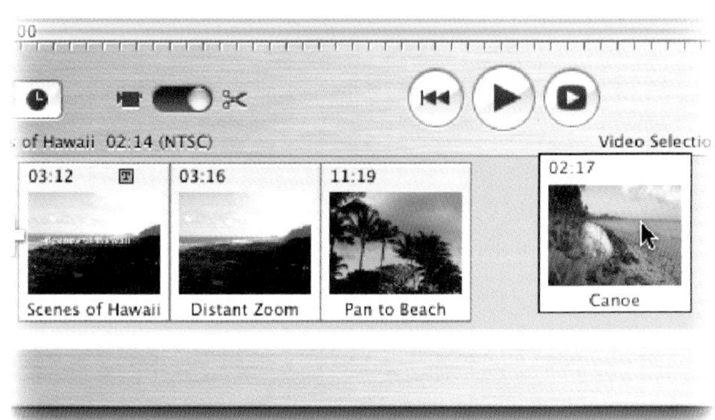

Add Eye Candy

Create transitions between clips and add titles and any special effects.

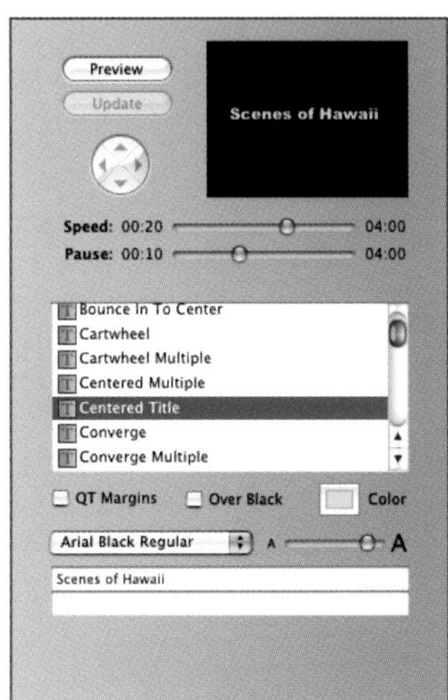

Polish

If you've added music or other audio tracks, you'll want to fine-tune audio levels for each track.

Export

Record your movie back to tape, send it to iDVD, or export it as a QuickTime movie to publish on a Web site.

A Short Glossary of Video Terms

aspect ratio The relationship of height to width in an image. A TV image has an aspect ratio of 4:3—four units of width for each three units of height.

clip A piece of video footage or a still image. A finished movie generally contains multiple clips, sequenced on the timeline.

FireWire The high-speed interface used to connect video gear, such as a miniDV camcorder, to the Mac. Also used for other devices, including hard drives and, of course, the iPod.

frame A single still image in a movie clip, and the smallest unit of a movie clip you can work with. One second of video contains 30 frames.

miniDV Often abbreviated DV, a video format that stores high-quality video and stereo audio on a tiny cassette. The miniDV format has been a major factor in the digital video revolution. In a DV camcorder, circuitry converts video and audio into digital data, which is recorded on the tape. When you import or export DV video, you're simply transferring bits across a FireWire cable. By contrast, older video formats, such as VHS and Hi-8, store audio and video in analog form.

playhead iMovie's equivalent to the blinking cursor in a word processor. As a clip plays back, the playhead moves to show where you are in relation to the entire movie or video clip.

rendering The process of creating frames for a transition, title, or effect.

transition A special effect that acts as a segue between two clips.

track An independent stream of audio or video. iMovie lets you have one video track and two separate audio tracks.

Importing Video

In video production, assets—the video clips, still images, and audio files—are the building blocks that you assemble into a finished product.

The asset you'll be working with most often is, of course, video—clips from a DV camcorder. But you may also work with still images, MP3 music tracks, narration that you record, and audio files extracted from compact discs.

Because a finished movie can comprise a large number of assets, it's a good idea to store them all in one folder. This makes it easier to back up your project and copy it to other drives.

iMovie helps you in this regard: When you create a new movie project, iMovie creates a folder and gives it the name of your movie.

Inside your project's folder is another folder called Media; this is where iMovie stores imported video clips, as well as other files it creates as you work. Don't move or rename any files within the Media folder; if you do, iMovie may not be able to open your project correctly. As a general rule, you shouldn't put any files in the Media folder yourself—let iMovie manage this folder.

Importing Video

Connect your DV camcorder to your Mac's FireWire jack.

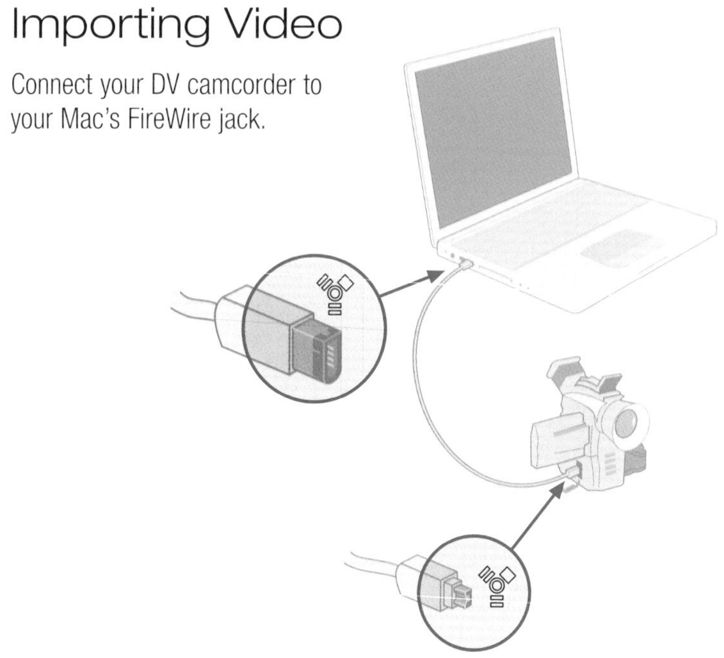

Be sure the camcorder is turned on and in its VCR mode (called VTR on some camcorders).

See the process of importing assets.
Importing Video from a Camera
Importing Photos
Importing a Music Track

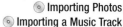

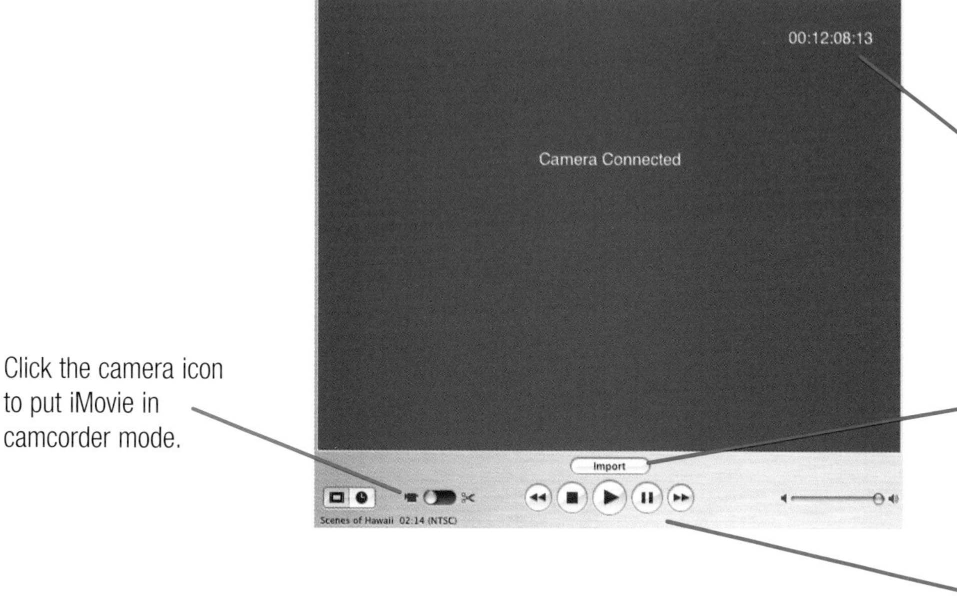

iMovie displays the time code that your camera recorded on the tape. This can help you keep track of where you are on a tape as you fast-forward or rewind.

Click the camera icon to put iMovie in camcorder mode.

To start and stop importing, click Import or press the spacebar while the tape is playing back.

When iMovie is in camcorder mode, the playback buttons control your camcorder.

iMovie displays each clip you import on the Clips pane.

Using iMovie's Scene-Detection Feature

If you had enough disk space, you could capture an entire DV cassette as a single clip—but locating individual scenes would be tedious. A better technique is to use iMovie's scene-detection feature, which causes iMovie to begin a new clip each time it detects a scene break. (Your camcorder generates a scene break automatically each time you press its record button.)

To turn on scene detection, choose Preferences from the iMovie menu, and click the check box labeled Automatically Start New Clip at Scene Break.

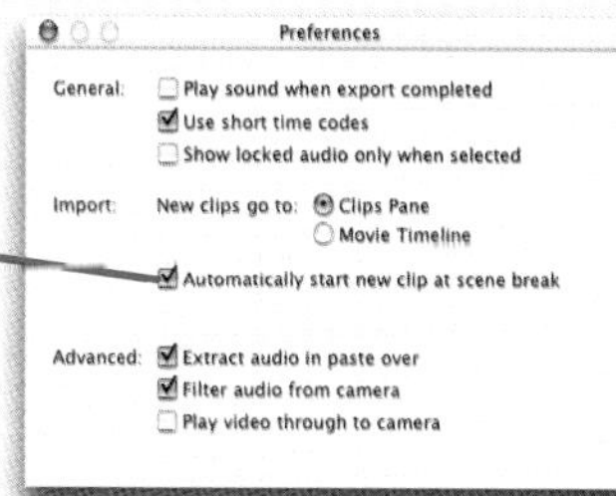

Working with Clips

After you import video and other assets, the real work (and fun) of building your movie begins.

All building projects require advance preparation, and video editing is no exception. You might begin by renaming your clips to give them descriptive names. You don't have to rename clips, but doing so can make them easier to sort out and manage.

Next, you might crop a clip to remove footage you don't want. iMovie defines cropping differently than imaging programs, such as iPhoto. When you crop a clip in iMovie, you change its length, not its dimensions—you remove seconds or minutes, not pixels. After cropping a clip, you might add it to the movie by dragging it to the timeline at the bottom of the screen.

As you perform these tasks, you'll often work with iMovie's playhead, moving it to the start of a clip, or dragging it back and forth—a process called *scrubbing*—to find the portion you want to retain.

Naming and cropping—these are the chores that prepare assets for their screen debut. And that debut occurs when you drag assets to the timeline.

Rename Your Clips

iMovie automatically names imported clips, giving them names, such as Clip 01 and Clip 02, that aren't exactly descriptive. Give your clips descriptive titles, such as Bird Close-up or Beach Long Shot, to help you identify them. To rename a clip in the Clips pane, simply click its name and type a new name. Or, double-click on a clip and type a new name in the Clip Info dialog box. You can also rename clips in the clip viewer.

Cropping Clips

Any clip you import may have extraneous junk at its beginning and end. By cropping the clip to remove this excess, you'll make a better movie and reclaim disk space as a bonus.

If you're planning to add a transition before or after a clip, make the clip a bit longer than you otherwise would.

Step 1. First, select the clip you want to crop. You can also crop a clip that you've already added to the timeline.

Step 2. Click in the dashed ruler area beneath the monitor, then drag the triangular crop markers left and right to mark the footage you want to keep. To review your selection, drag the playhead left and right.

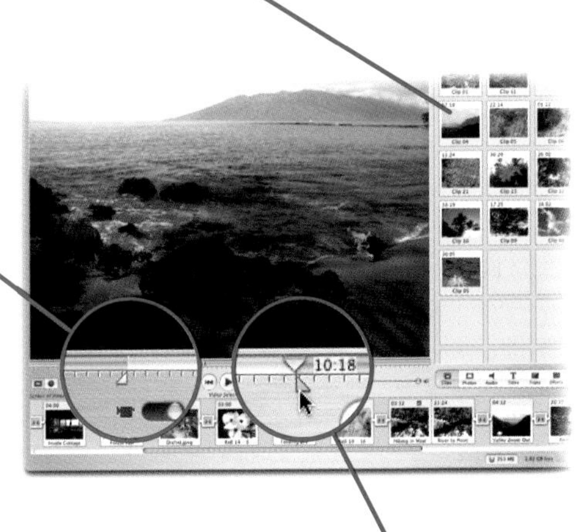

Step 3. To perform the crop, choose Crop from the Edit menu (or press ⌘-K).

As you adjust the crop markers, iMovie tells you how long the cropped clip will be.

See techniques for working with clips.
Naming Clips
Cropping a Clip
Working with the Timeline

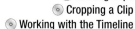

Controlling What Plays Back

You already know that clicking the play button or pressing the spacebar begins playback. You may have noticed that *what* iMovie plays back depends on what is selected.

You can choose to play just one item—a clip, a title, a transition, and so on—by selecting that item, then clicking on the play button or hitting the spacebar. This can be a handy way to check out a title or transition you've just added. Along the same lines, to play back a portion of your project, select those items by Shift-clicking, then start playback.

To play an entire project, deselect everything (press ⌘-D or click in a blank area of the timeline). Next, press your keyboard's Home key to move the playhead to the beginning of the movie, and then begin playback.

Emptying the Trash

When you crop a clip, iMovie puts its discarded portion in the Trash—not the same Trash the Finder provides for discarding unwanted files, but a separate, iMovie-specific Trash. Reclaim disk space by emptying iMovie's Trash as you work (choose Empty Trash from the File menu). But if you've done a lot of cropping, emptying the Trash can take a few minutes, so wait until you're ready to take a break. And note that once you empty iMovie's Trash, you can't reclaim footage that you've cropped out.

Reclaiming the Past

You're working on your movie and realize that a shot you cropped really needs to be longer after all. If you haven't emptied the Trash, you can restore the cropped footage. Select the clip, then choose Restore Clip Media from the Advanced menu.

The Keys to Precision

To fine-tune a crop marker's position, select the crop marker and press the keyboard's left and right arrow keys to move the marker in one-frame increments. To move in 10-frame increments, press Shift along with the arrow key. These keyboard controls work throughout iMovie.

Trimming Clips (and the Pros and Cons of Jump Cuts)

The cropping technique I described on the opposite page is the most common method of removing unwanted footage from a clip. But there's another technique: trimming.

Trimming is the opposite of cropping. When you crop, you use the crop markers to indicate which portion of a clip you want to keep. When you trim, you use the crop markers to indicate what you want to delete. Drag the crop markers left and right to mark the footage that you want to toss to the cutting room floor. Then, press your keyboard's Delete key or choose Clear from the Edit menu.

It's best to use trimming to remove footage from the very beginning or very end of a clip. If you delete footage from the middle of a video clip, you'll end up with an awkward, visually jarring jump in the action. In movie-making terms, this kind of sloppy splice is called a *jump cut*, and it's usually a bad thing, a sign of shoddy movie-making.

Then again, one director's flaw might be another's effect. Jump cuts are common special effects in music videos and other "arty" productions.

To avoid a jump cut, put a cutaway or reaction shot at the point where the jump cut would be (see page 122). If you don't have a cutaway or reaction shot, put a three- to five-second cross-dissolve transition at the jump cut point. This is called a *soft cut,* and it's common in documentaries and newscasts.

Timeline Techniques: Adding Clips to a Movie

A clip in the Clips pane is like a baseball player on the bench. To put the clip on the playing field, you must add it to the timeline.

Select the clip, then drag it to the timeline.

Timeline Tips

You can add multiple clips to the timeline at once. Select each clip by Shift-clicking on it, then drag the clips to the timeline as a group. You can also select multiple clips by dragging a selection rectangle around them; click the narrow gray border between clips to begin drawing the selection.

You can also add clips to the timeline by pasting them. Select a clip in the Clips pane—or a clip that's already in the timeline—and cut or copy, then paste. If the playhead is at the end of the timeline, that's where the pasted clip appears. If you select a clip that's already in the timeline before you paste, the pasted clip appears immediately to the right of that clip.

See iMovie's timeline and clip viewer in action.
Working with the Timeline
Switching to the Clip Viewer

Timeline Versus Clip: Which Viewer to Use?

You can view your project's march of time in either of two ways: using the timeline viewer or the clip viewer. Each viewer has its strengths, and you're likely to switch between them frequently as you work on a movie. To switch between views, click the clip viewer button or the timeline viewer button.

The Clip Viewer

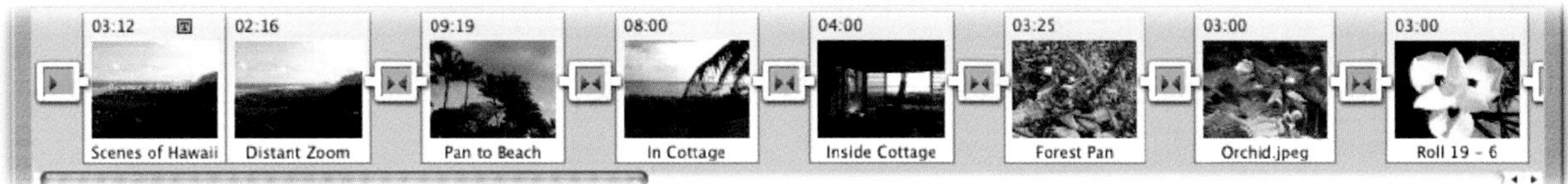

The clip viewer shows large thumbnail versions of each clip. In this viewer, you can change the order of clips by dragging them left and right. You can also rename clips here. However, this viewer does not show audio tracks or provide audio controls. The clip viewer is ideal when you're first assembling a movie or you want to experiment with different clip sequences. When it's time for audio fine-tuning and other precise work, switch to the timeline viewer.

The Timeline Viewer

The timeline viewer adds two audio tracks and controls for adjusting audio levels and creating slow- or fast-motion effects. You can't drag to change the order of clips in this view. Use the timeline viewer when you're working with audio tracks, or when you want to speed up or slow down video. When you want to swap the order of clips around, switch to the clip viewer.

Editing Techniques and Tips

Creating Cutaways

A *cutaway* is a common video-production technique. Think of Barbara Walters nodding solemnly while Fabio describes what kind of tree he'd like to be. Or maybe the video changes to show a close-up of Grandma's garden as she talks about it. To create edits like these, use the Advanced menu's Paste Over at Playhead command.

Step 1. Get Your Shots

Begin planning cutaway shots when shooting your video. After Grandma talks about her garden, shoot some close-ups of the plants she talked about. While you're shooting the school play, grab a couple of shots of the audience laughing or clapping. Or after you've shot an interview, move the camera to shoot a few seconds of the interviewer nodding. (In TV news, this kind of shot is called a *noddie.*)

Tip: Still have an old VHS or 8mm camcorder? Dust it off, pop it on a tripod, and use it to shoot short cutaway shots. Dub the footage to your miniDV camcorder, then import it into iMovie. The video quality won't match exactly, but your viewers may never notice. And your cutaways will be authentic rather than staged.

Make sure your primary and cutaway footage exist as separate clips.

Step 2. Set Up for the Edit

With your footage imported, you're ready to set up for the edit.

If your footage is one large clip, you need to split it into multiple clips. To do so, drag the clip to the timeline, position the playhead where you want to split the clip, and choose Split Video Clip at Playhead from the Edit menu (⌘-T).

With cutaway shots, you retain the audio from the primary clip and discard the audio from the cutaway shot. iMovie does this for you: choose Preferences from the iMovie menu and be sure the Extract Audio in Paste Over box is checked.

Step 3. Crop the Cutaway

The next step is to crop your cutaway shot to the appropriate length. In iMovie's Clips pane, select the cutaway shot. In the monitor, drag the crop markers left and right to mark what you want to keep. Finally, choose Crop (⌘-K) from the Edit menu.

Step 4. Insert the Cutaway

Now you're ready to insert the cutaway. Position iMovie's playhead at the desired cutaway point, then add the cutaway shot.

First, position the primary footage in the timeline.

Next, select the cropped cutaway shot in the Clips pane and choose Copy from the Edit menu.

Position the playhead at the spot where you want the cutaway to occur, and choose Paste Over at Playhead from the Advanced menu.

See how to save an image from a clip.
Creating a Freeze Frame

iMovie pastes the cutaway footage into the timeline beginning at the playhead's position.

iMovie extracts the audio from the primary clip and puts it in Audio Track 1.

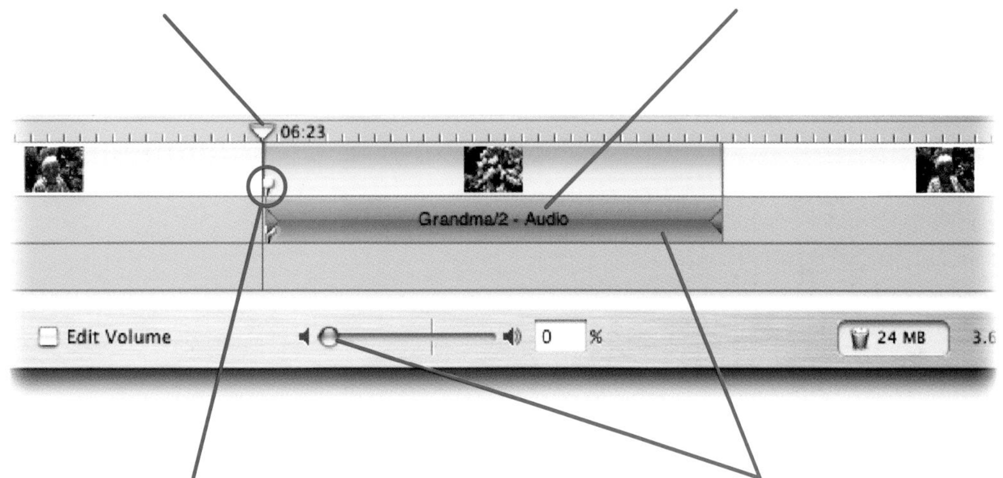

The pushpin icons indicate the audio is locked to the video above it. If you move the video, the audio will move along with it, maintaining synchronization between audio and video.

Your final step is to mute the cutaway clip's audio. To do so, select it and then drag the volume slider all the way to the left.

Creating a Freeze Frame

With the File menu's Save Frame As command, you can create a PICT or JPEG image file containing the currently displayed video frame. Here's one scenario where you might use it: you've made a movie of Junior scoring the game-winning goal, and you've got a great close-up of his smiling face as his teammates hoist him up on their shoulders. If you create a still image of that shot, you can place the still at the end of your movie and add closing credits to it. When played back, the action will freeze on Junior's happy mug as the credits roll.

To create a still, position the playhead so the frame you want is visible in iMovie's monitor. Next, choose Save Frame As from the File menu. In the Save dialog box, choose PICT from the Format pop-up menu, and then save. (For a good-housekeeping merit badge, stash the still in the folder that contains your movie.) Now, import the PICT and add it to your movie.

Adding Photos to Movies

Photographs are mainstays of many types of movies, especially montages and documentaries. With the iPhoto browser in iMovie, you can add photos from your iPhoto library to your movies. You can also add photos that aren't stored in your iPhoto library by using the File menu's Import command.

When adding photos to movies, consider taking advantage of iMovie's *Ken Burns effect* to add a sense of dynamism to your stills. Why name a feature after a filmmaker? Think about Ken Burns' documentaries and how his camera appears to move across still images. For example, a shot might begin with a close-up of a weary face and then zoom out to reveal a Civil War battlefield scene.

That's the Ken Burns effect. Now, Ken Burns himself would probably call it by its traditional filmmaking terms: *pan and scan* or *pan and zoom*. These terms reflect the fact that you can have two different kinds of motion: panning (moving across an image) and zooming (moving in or out).

Whatever the effect's name, its result is the same: it adds motion and life to otherwise static images.

Adding a Photo from Your iPhoto Library

Step 1.

Click the Photos button.

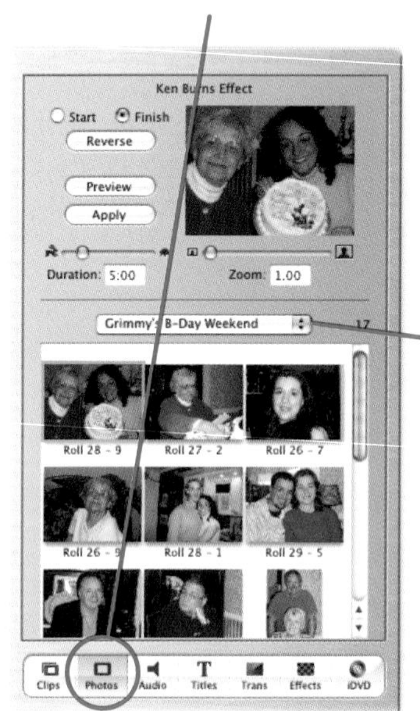

To view a specific album, choose its name from the pop-up menu.

Step 2.

Select the photo. You can select multiple photos by Shift-clicking or ⌘-clicking on them.

See how to work with photos.
Using the iPhoto Browser
Applying the Ken Burns Effect

Step 3.

Adjust the duration and zoom settings as desired.

To pan-zoom a photo, you must specify the start and finish settings for the move: that is, how you want the photo to look when it first appears, and how you want it to look at the end of its duration.

Displays the results of your settings in the preview monitor.

iMovie applies the settings and adds the photo or photos to the timeline. As an alternative to clicking Apply, you can also drag the photo or photos to the timeline.

Reverses your settings—for example, turns a zoom in into a zoom out.

When zoomed in on a photo, drag the photo using the hand pointer to specify which part of it you want to see.

Ken Burns Effect
Start
Finish
Reverse
Preview
Apply
Duration: 5:00
Zoom: 1.00

To specify the length of time you want the image to appear, drag the slider or type in the box. (Values are in seconds and frames. For example, for a 5½ second duration, type 5:15.)

Specify the desired start and finish zoom settings by dragging the slider or typing in the box. To change the starting zoom setting, click the Start button before adjusting the zoom setting. Similarly, to change the ending zoom setting, first click Finish. To not apply any zooming, specify start and finish zoom settings of 1.00.

Note: The Ken Burns effect is sticky. That is, iMovie remembers the last set of pan and zoom settings that you used and applies them to future photos.

Using Photos that Aren't in Your iPhoto Library

You can also work with images that aren't stored in your iPhoto library.

Step 1. Choose Import from the File menu (or press Shift-⌘-I).

Step 2. Select the photo, Shift-clicking or ⌘-clicking to select multiple images.

Step 3. Click Open.

iMovie adds the photo or photos to the Clips pane.

When you import a photo this way, iMovie applies the current Ken Burns effect settings to the photo. You can change those settings using the techniques described in "Changing Ken Burns Settings" on the next page.

Alternatively, if you know what Ken Burns settings you want, you can set them up first and then import the photo.

Working with the Ken Burns Effect

There's more to Ken Burns than meets the eye. Here are some tips to help you get more out of this powerful effect.

Changing Ken Burns Settings

You've applied the Ken Burns effect and now decide you want to change the clip's pan, zoom, or duration settings. To do so, select the clip in the timeline and click the Photos button. Now make the desired adjustments and click Apply.

Note that if you have transitions on either side of the clip, iMovie will need to recreate them, since they contain frames that will no longer match the new clip. iMovie displays a message warning you that the transition will have to be "re-rendered."

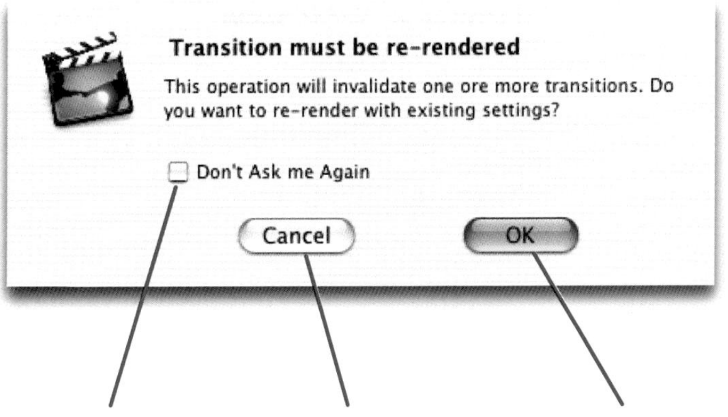
Transition must be re-rendered
This operation will invalidate one ore more transitions. Do you want to re-render with existing settings?
Don't Ask me Again
Cancel
OK

To always have iMovie re-render transitions, check this box.

To cancel the new Ken Burns settings and keep the old clips, click Cancel.

To re-render adjacent transitions, click OK.

Watch Your Proportions

If you plan to show a photo at actual size (that is, a zoom setting of 1.00), be sure the photo's proportions match the 4:3 aspect ratio of television—otherwise, the image won't completely fill the screen.

Most digital camera images have these proportions. You can use iPhoto to crop those that don't: in the Constrain pop-up menu in iPhoto's Edit pane, choose the option 4 x 3 (Book, DVD).

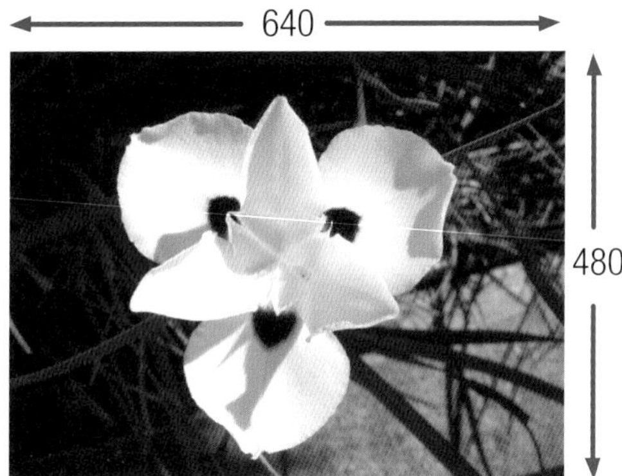
640
480

A standard TV image has an aspect ratio of 4:3—four units of width for every three units of height.

If you don't want to crop the image, here's a quick workaround: use the Zoom slider to zoom in just enough so that the image fills the preview area. That way, you won't end up with unsightly black borders around part of the photo.

Image Resolution and Zooming

iMovie imports photos at their full resolution. This enables you to zoom in on part of a photo and still retain image sharpness.

However, if you zoom in on a low-resolution image or one that you've cropped heavily in iPhoto, you will probably notice some chunky-looking pixelation. So think twice about zooming in on low-resolution images unless you want that pixelated look.

Zoom to Tell a Story

Creative use of zooming can help tell your story. When you zoom in, you gradually focus the viewer's attention on one portion of the scene. You tell the viewer, "Now that you have the big picture, this is what you should pay attention to."

When you zoom out, you reveal additional details about the scene, increasing the viewer's sense of context. You tell the viewer, "Now that you've seen that, look at these other things to learn how they relate to each other."

Go Slow

Unless you're after a special effect, avoid very fast pans and zooms. It's better to pan and zoom slowly to enable your viewers to absorb the changes in the scene.

Generally, a zoom speed of 0.05 to 0.1 per second gives a pleasing result. For example, a five-second clip should have a difference between start and finish zoom of about 0.5.

Vary Your Zoom Direction

Variety is the spice of zooming. If you're creating a photo montage and zooming each image, consider alternating between zooming in and zooming out. For example, zoom in on one image, then zoom out on the next.

A fine example of this technique lives within Mac OS X itself: Mac OS X's screen effects (in System Preferences) alternate between zooming in and zooming out.

The Need to Render

When you import a photo or apply the Ken Burns effect, iMovie must render the video frames that represent your efforts. This is called rendering, and it's described in more detail on page 137.

Older versions of iMovie didn't have to render photos. That's because they weren't able to pan-zoom the photos, nor did they import photos at full resolution.

Using Photos Without Ken Burns

You don't have to use the Ken Burns effect. To use a photo without any panning or zooming, simply drag the photo to the timeline and press ⌘-period when iMovie begins rendering. iMovie will give you a static clip whose duration matches the setting of the Duration slider.

This also works with photos that you import using the Import command: press ⌘-period after choosing a photo to import, and iMovie won't apply the Ken Burns setting to it.

Advanced Ken Burns Techniques

Ken Burns has some limitations. One is that you can't "hold" on a certain frame. You might want to have a 10-second clip in which the photo zooms for the first eight seconds and then remains static for the last two. Or maybe you want to zoom in partway, freeze for a couple of seconds, and then continue zooming.

Ken can't do that.

Another limitation is that you can't combine multiple moves in a single clip. For example, you might want to pan across a photo and then zoom in on part of it. Ken can't do that, either.

At least not without a little finessing. It's actually possible to accomplish both of these tasks in iMovie. Here's how.

Holding on a Frame

Holding on a frame involves saving a frame from a Ken Burns-generated clip and then adding it to the timeline.

Step 1.

Set up the Ken Burns effect as desired and then apply it, as described on pages 124-127.

Step 2.

Select the clip that iMovie has rendered, then move the playhead to its last frame.

Step 3.

Use the File menu's Save Frame As command to save this frame as a still image. Save the frame as a PICT file, storing it in your project folder. (See page 123 for more details on saving frames as still images.)

Step 4.

Choose Import from the File menu and import the PICT file you just created. When iMovie begins rendering the imported image, press ⌘-period. (See page 127 for more details on interrupting image rendering.)

Step 5.

Drag the still image to the timeline and crop it to the desired length.

Variations

You can also reverse this process: start by holding on a frame, and then pan and zoom. First, apply the Ken Burns effect, then save the first frame of the resulting clip as a PICT image. Import that image, cancel rendering, and position the still image before the Ken Burns clip.

Another variation involves inserting a still image in the middle of a Ken Burns move so that panning and zooming stops and then resumes. For this trick, apply the Ken Burns effect and then split the resulting clip where you want to hold on a frame. (To split a clip, position the playhead at the desired split point and choose Split Video Clip at Playhead from the Edit menu.)

Next, save the last frame of the first half of the clip (or the first frame of the second half). Import this frame, cancel rendering, and drag it between the two halves.

Get links to the pan-zoom tools discussed here.
www.macilife.com/iMovie

GO TO WEB

Combining Moves

Combining two kinds of moves involves importing the same photo twice and applying different Ken Burns settings each time.

Step 1.

Set up the first Ken Burns move as desired and then apply it.

Step 2.

In the iPhoto browser, select a different photo, and then select the same photo that you selected for Step 1.

This tricks iMovie into preparing to create a new clip instead of updating the one you just created.

Step 3.

In the Ken Burns Effect area of the Photos pane, click the Reverse button.

Reverse

This reverses the Ken Burns settings that you set up for Step 1: its end point becomes the new start point.

Step 4.

Set up the second Ken Burns move and then apply it.

Beyond Ken Burns: Other Pan-Zoom Tools

When it comes to panning and zooming, Ken Burns isn't the only game in town. Several companies offer pan-zoom tools that work with iMovie.

Photo to Movie. I highly recommend this cute little program from LQ Graphics; it works independently of iMovie and makes it very easy to create pan-zoom effects. Create your effect in Photo to Movie, export it as a QuickTime movie, and then bring it into iMovie and add it to your project.

Photo to Movie's results are superior to those created by Ken Burns effect. Photo to Movie supports what animators call *ease in* and *ease out*: rather than motion abruptly starting and ending, as it does with the Ken Burns effect, the motion starts and ends gradually. The results have a more professional appearance.

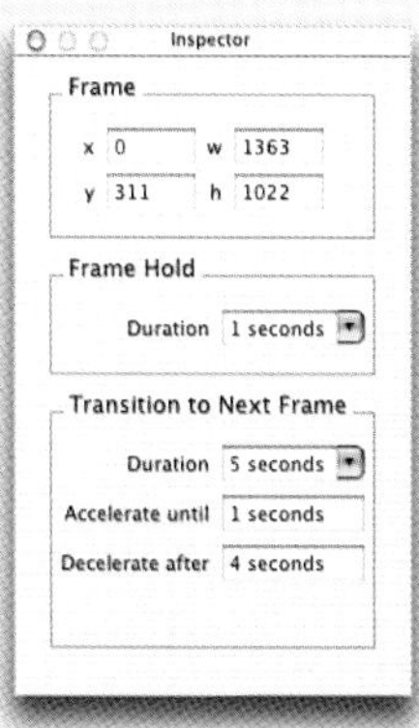

SlickMotion. This simple program is included with GeeThree's Slick Transitions and Effects Volume 4, an extensive library of iMovie effects. SlickMotion also supports ease-in/ease-out, and adds the ability to rotate images.

Virtix Zoom & Pan. This program is an effect plug-in that runs directly within iMovie. It also supports image rotation.

Adding Audio to Movies

In movie making, sound is at least as important as the picture. An audience will forgive hand-held camera shots and poor lighting—*The Blair Witch Project* proved that. But give them a noisy, inaudible soundtrack, and they'll run for the aspirin.

Poor quality audio is a common flaw of home video and amateur movies. One problem is that most camcorders don't have very good microphones—their built-in mikes are often located on the top of the camera where they pick up sound from the camera's motors. What's more, the microphone is usually far from the subject, resulting in too much background noise. And if you're shooting outdoors on a windy day, your scenes end up sounding like an outtake from *Twister*.

If your camcorder provides a jack for an external microphone, you can get much better sound by using one. Clip-on and wireless mikes work well for video. Get the mike up close to your subject.

If you've already shot your video or you can't use an external mike, there is another solution: don't use the audio you recorded. Instead, create an audio *bed* consisting of music and, if appropriate, narration or sound effects.

iMovie provides several features that you can use to sweeten your soundtracks. Take advantage of them.

Importing Music from an Audio CD

Click the Audio button.

Simply insert the CD. If your Mac is connected to the Internet, iMovie will access CDDB (described on page 21) to retrieve the disc and track names.

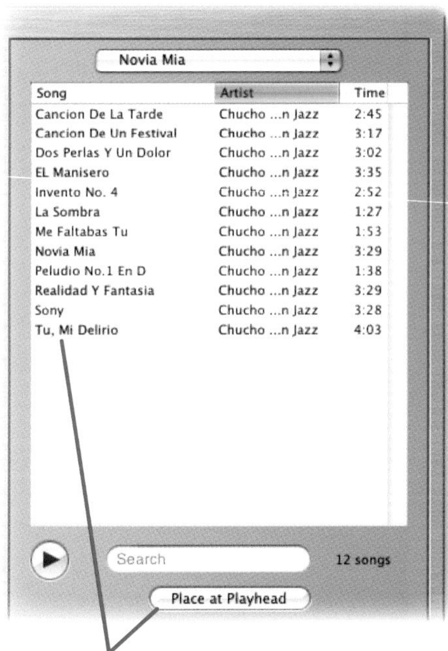

To add a track, select it and click Place at Playhead, or simply drag the track to one of the timeline's audio tracks.

Note: Depending on how you've set up your iTunes preferences, your Mac may also start iTunes when you insert the audio CD. If that happens, simply click the iMovie icon in the dock or click anywhere in the iMovie window to make iMovie the active program again.

See how to import music from an iTunes library.
Importing a Music Track

Importing Music from Your iTunes Library

Use the iTunes browser to bring in music from your iTunes library.

Step 1.

Position the playhead where you want the music to begin playing.

Step 2.

Click the Audio button.

Step 3.

Locate the song you want to import.

You can choose a specific playlist from this pop-up menu.

You can sort the list of songs by clicking on a column heading. Drag columns left and right to move them. Resize columns by dragging the vertical line between their headings.

Use the Search box to quickly locate a song based on its name or its artist's name.

To play a song, select it and click this button, or simply double-click the song's name.

To add a song to the movie, click Place at Playhead.

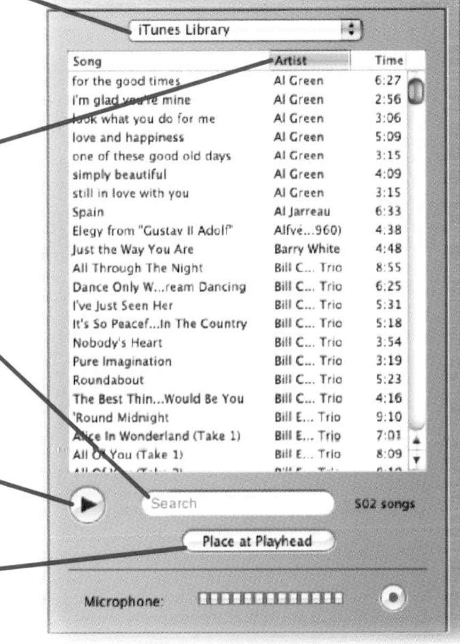

Step 4.

Click the Place at Playhead button.

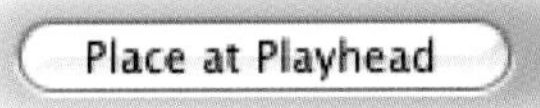

iMovie adds the music to the timeline's second audio track.

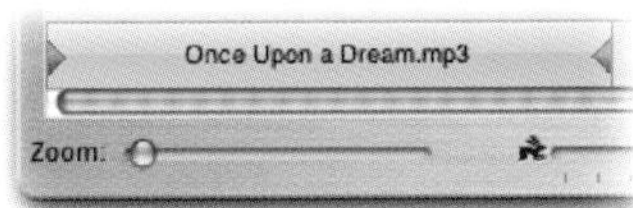

Tip: As an alternative to clicking Place at Playhead, you can also click and drag a song to any location on the timeline.

Recording an Audio Narration

If you connect a microphone to your Mac, you can record narration directly within iMovie.

To begin recording, click the red button next to the volume meter in iMovie's Audio pane.

As you record, iMovie adds your narration to the first audio track, positioning it at the playhead's location and giving it the name *Voice 01*.

Tip: For the best sound, you want to record loud but not too loud. At its loudest, your voice should illuminate the yellow portion of iMovie's volume meter. If you illuminate the red portions, your sound will be distorted.

Good

Bad

Also, position the mike carefully to avoid the "popping p" syndrome—bursts of breath noise. Record the phrase "pretty poppies" as a test, and back off if the results sound like a hurricane.

Audio Insights: Working with Sound

Adjusting the volume of an audio track is a common task. And when you combine audio in any way—mixing music, sound effects, dialog, and background sounds—you almost always need to adjust the relative levels of each sound to create a pleasing mix.

iMovie provides several ways to work with sound levels. You can reduce the volume of an entire sound clip. You might do this if you're mixing music with the sound of the surf, and don't want the waves to drown out the music. You can also vary a track's volume level over time.

When combining music and narration, you might want the music to start at full volume, fade when the narrator talks, then return to full volume when she stops. The timeline viewer provides several controls for adjusting volume levels.

Adjusting the Volume of a Clip

To adjust the volume of an entire audio clip, select the clip and then drag the volume slider located below the timeline.

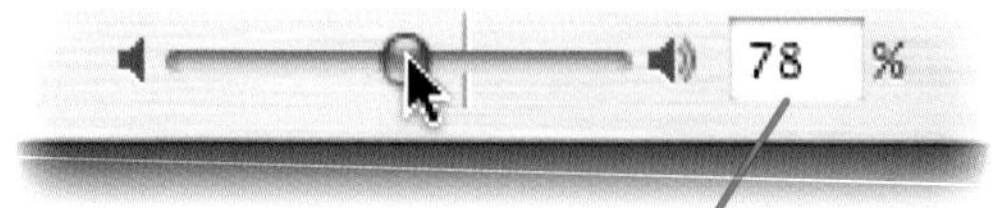

You can also type a value in the text box.

To Fade In or Fade Out

Each volume marker has a tiny twin, a smaller marker that appears to its left. To create an audio fade-in, drag the smaller of the two markers all the way down to the bottom of the clip. To specify the duration of the fade, drag the two markers further apart or closer together.

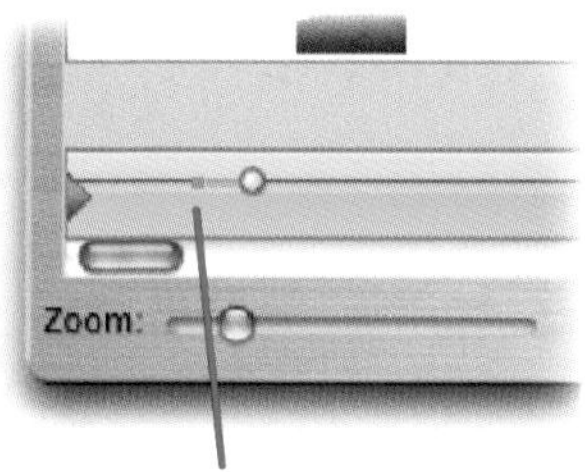

Before: Drag the tiny marker down; drag it left and right to adjust the duration of the fade.

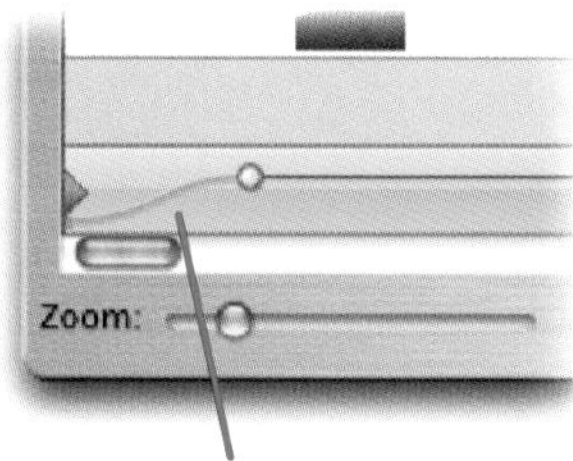

After: The completed fade-in.

Similarly, to create a fade-out, drag the larger of the two markers all the way down.

See techniques for working with sound.
Creating an Audio Bed
Adjusting the Volume of a Clip
Fine-Tuning Volume Levels
GO TO DVD

Adjusting Volume Over Time

Adjusting the volume of a clip over time involves creating volume markers, then dragging them as necessary.

Step 1.

Click the Edit Volume check box below the timeline.

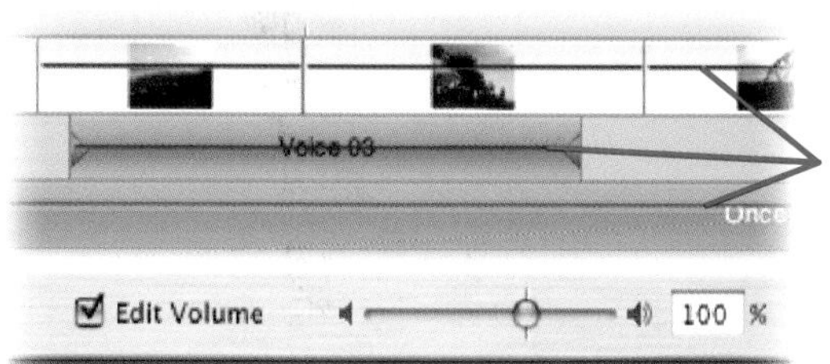

When the Edit Volume box is checked, iMovie displays a volume level bar on each track.

Step 2.

Click on the audio track's volume level bar at the point where you want to adjust the volume. A volume marker appears.

Step 3.

To lower the volume, drag the marker down. To increase the volume, drag the marker up. To move the point at which the volume changes, drag the marker left or right.

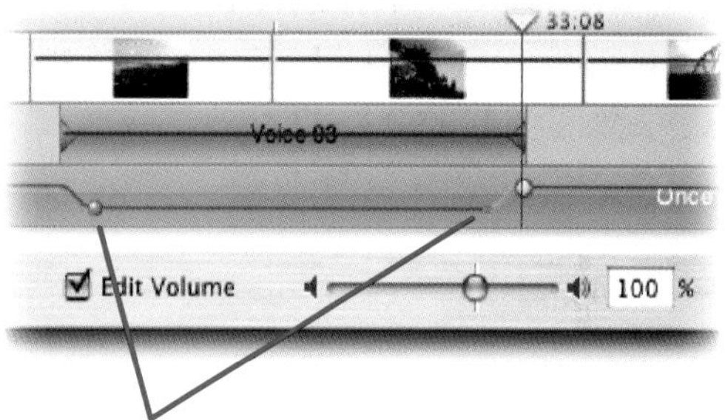

Here, the volume of a music track has been tweaked so that the music gets softer during a narration passage.

To delete a marker, select it and press the Delete key.

Step 4.

When you've finished tweaking volume levels, uncheck the Edit Volume box.

More Sound Advice

Extracting Audio

You may want to use only the audio portion of a clip. For example, you're making a documentary about your grandmother's childhood and you'd like to show old photographs as she talks.

To do this, drag the video clip to the timeline, then select the clip and choose Extract Audio (⌘-J) from the Advanced menu. iMovie copies the audio, places it in Audio Track 1, and mutes the audio in the video clip.

Next, select the video clip in the timeline and press the Delete key. The video vanishes but its audio lingers on, and you can now position still images and other clips in the video's place.

See this technique in action in the iMovie segment of the DVD.

Repeating Sound Effects

You might want some sound effects to play for a long period of time. For example, iMovie's Hard Rain sound effect is less than 10 seconds long, but maybe you need 30 seconds of rain sounds for a particular movie.

For cases like these, simply repeat the sound effect by dragging it from the Audio pane to the timeline as many times as needed. If the sound effect fades out (as Hard Rain does), overlap each copy to hide the fade.

You can build magnificently rich sound effect tracks by overlapping sounds. To create a thunderstorm, for example, drag the Thunder sound effect so that it overlaps Hard Rain. Add the Cold Wind sound while you're at it. And don't forget to use iMovie's audio controls to fine-tune the relative levels of each effect.

Overlapping Audio in the Timeline

iMovie may provide just two audio tracks, but that doesn't mean you're limited to two simultaneous sounds. You can overlap multiple audio clips in the timeline's audio tracks: simply drag one audio clip on top of another.

Cropping Audio

To crop an audio clip, go to the timeline viewer and drag the triangles at the beginning and end of the clip. You can remove the unwanted audio by choosing Crop from the Edit menu, but you don't have to—iMovie will mute audio outside the crop markers.

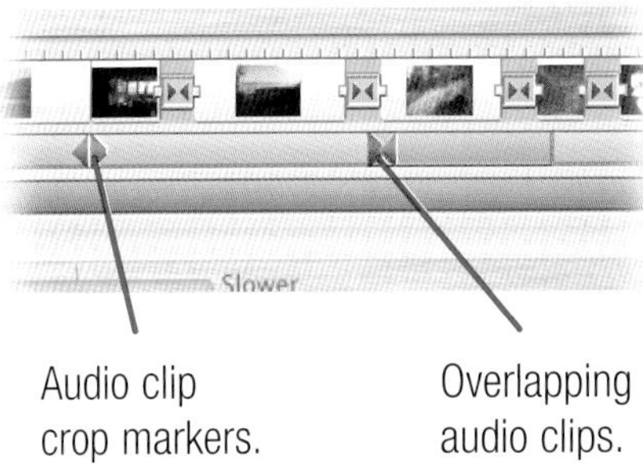

Audio clip crop markers.

Overlapping audio clips.

Get links to sources of sound effects and music.
www.macilife.com/imovie

GO TO WEB

Muting an Audio Track

You can mute an audio track entirely by unchecking the box to its right in the timeline viewer. If you uncheck the box next to the video track, iMovie mutes the video's sound. This can be handy when you're replacing the audio in a series of clips with an audio bed—a segment of background audio that will play across multiple clips—as I do on the DVD.

Splitting Audio Clips

You can divide an audio clip into two or more separate clips whose position and volume you can adjust independently. First, select the audio clip you want to split. Next, position the playhead where you want to split the clip. Finally, choose Split Selected Audio Clip at Playhead from the Edit menu or press ⌘-T.

Sources for Sound Effects and Music

Sound Effects

iMovie's library of built-in sound effects, accessed through the Audio pane, covers a lot of aural ground.

But there's always room for more sound, and the Internet is a rich repository of it. One of your first stops should be FindSounds, a Web search engine that lets you locate and download free sound effects by typing keywords, such as *chickadee*. SoundHunter is another impressive source of free sound effects and provides links to even more audio-related sites.

Most online sound effects are stored as WAV or AIFF files, two common sound formats. To import a WAV or AIFF file, use the File menu's Import command or simply drag the file directly to the desired location in the timeline viewer.

Managing Sound Effects

If you assemble a large library of sound effects, you might find yourself needing a program to help you keep track of them. You already have such a program: it's called iTunes. Simply drag your sound effects files into the iTunes window. Use the Get Info command to assign descriptive tags to them, and you can use iTunes' Search box to locate effects in a flash. You might even want to create a separate iTunes music library to store your sound effects.

Music Sources

As for music, if you're a .Mac subscriber, you'll find a symphony's worth of clips on your iDisk. Open the Software folder on your iDisk, then the Extras folder—there they are.

Plenty of royalty-free music is also available online from sites such as SoundDogs and KillerSound. These sites have powerful search features that enable you to locate music based on keywords, such as *acoustic* or *jazz*.

Loopasonic is another cool music site. It offers hundreds of music loops—repeating riffs—that you can assemble into unique music tracks.

And for building custom-length music tracks, you can't beat Sonic Desktop Software's Movie Maestro software. Movie Maestro provides an expandable library of songs, each of which is divided into blocks that the Music Maestro software can assemble to an exact length. It's very clever and it works beautifully.

Adding Transitions

Visual transitions and text titles add a professional touch to your project. Titles help set the stage by describing a place or scene, and they give credit where credit is due. And visual transitions, when used sparingly, can be appealing alternatives to jarring cuts.

Transitions also help tell a story. For example, a cross-dissolve—one clip fading out while another fades in—can imply the passage of time. Imagine slowly dissolving from a nighttime campfire scene to a campsite scene shot the following morning.

Similarly, iMovie's Push transition, where one clip pushes another out of the frame, is a visual way of saying "meanwhile..." Imagine using this transition between a scene of an expectant mother in the delivery room and a shot of her husband pacing in the waiting room, chain-smoking nervously. (Okay, so this is an old-fashioned maternity movie.)

And effects can add a special spice—again, when used sparingly. You can distort clips, adjust colors, turn color clips into black-and-white ones, and much more.

To create transitions, titles, and effects, you work in one of three panels. Each panel appears when you click its button below iMovie's Clips pane.

Adding Transitions

To add a transition between two clips, first click iMovie's Transitions button to display the Transitions pane.

Some transitions, such as Push, allow you to specify a direction (for example, to push from left to right or from top to bottom).

To preview the transition in iMovie's monitor, click Preview.

When you select a transition, a preview appears here.

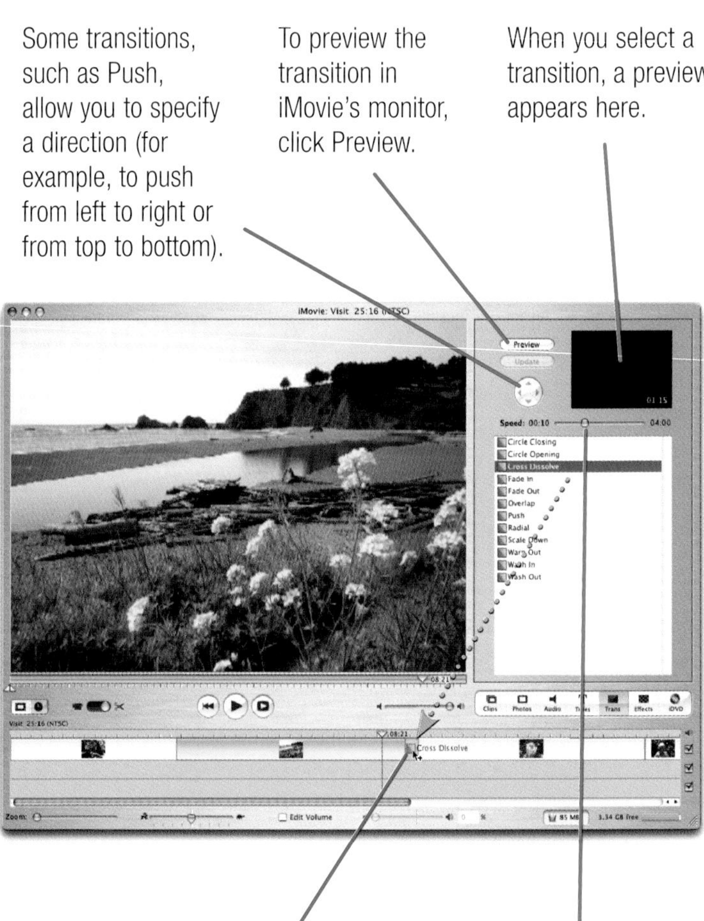

To add the transition, drag it between two clips.

To change the transition's duration, drag the Speed slider. The current duration appears in the lower-right corner of the preview box.

See techniques for working with transitions.
Adding Transitions

Testing the Transition

To see the finished transition, select it and press the spacebar.

If you aren't happy with the transition, you can delete it (press the Delete key) or choose Undo.

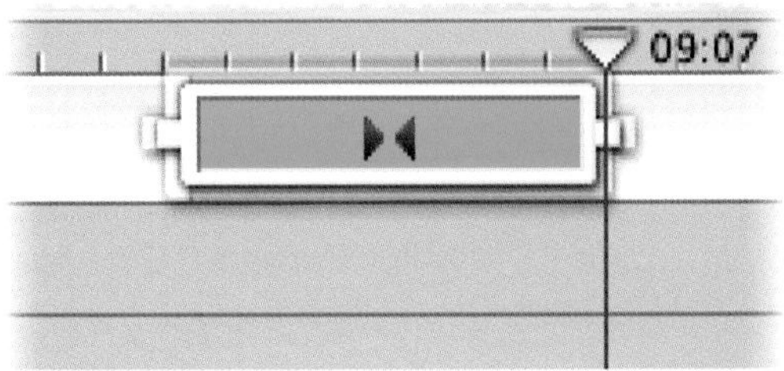

Inserting a Clip at a Transition

When you create a transition between two clips, you establish a connection between those clips.

If you need to insert a new clip between those two clips, you must first delete the transition: select it and hit Delete. Now you can insert the new clip.

Updating a Transition

Change your mind about using a particular transition style? To change an existing transition, first select it in the clip viewer or timeline viewer. Make the desired changes, and click the Update button in the Transitions pane.

Some Background on Rendering

When you create a transition, title, or effect, iMovie must create the video frames that represent your efforts. This rendering process takes time and memory; you'll notice iMovie slows down a bit during rendering.

You can continue to work while rendering takes place. You can even play back your movie, although you may notice stuttering playback when iMovie reaches areas it hasn't finished rendering.

Although you can work during rendering, you might want to avoid adding multiple transitions or titles in rapid-fire succession, as doing so slows iMovie to a crawl. To gauge how long rendering will take, look at the transitions, titles, or effects that you've added: a little red progress bar shows how far along rendering is.

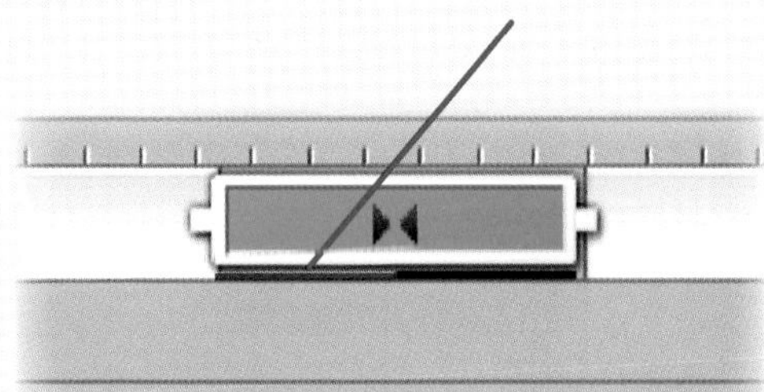

Creating Titles

What's a movie without titles? Incomplete. Almost any movie can benefit from text of some kind: opening and closing credits, the superimposed names of people and places, or simply the words "The End" at, well, the end.

iMovie's Titles pane is your ticket to text. You have more than 30 title styles from which to choose, with customizing opportunities aplenty.

Some of iMovie's title styles are animated, and it isn't difficult to transcend the bounds of good taste and enter the terrain of tackiness. Use restraint and lean toward classic title styles like Centered and Rolling.

Regardless of the style you choose, you'll get the best results with sturdy fonts that remain legible despite the limited resolution of television. For example, at small text sizes, Arial Black often works better than Times, which has ornamental serifs that can break up when viewed on a TV set.

To Create a Title

Creating a title involves choosing the title style, specifying title settings, and then dragging the completed title to the timeline.

Step 1.

Click the Titles button to display the Titles pane.

Step 2.

Choose the title style you want by clicking its name.

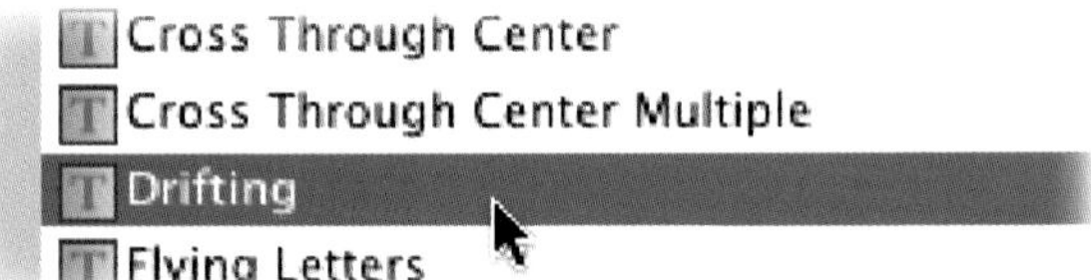

Step 3.

Specify the title settings.

See the opposite page for an overview of title settings.

Step 4.

Add the title by dragging it to the timeline.

Notes: To add a title to the middle of a clip, split the clip first. To superimpose title text over a specific clip, drag the title to the immediate left of that clip, as shown above.

Changing a Title

Need to change an existing title? In the timeline, select the title. Next, display the Titles pane and make your changes. Finally, click the Update button in the Titles pane.

See how to add titles to a movie.
Adding Titles

To edit an existing title, select it in the timeline, make your changes, and apply the changes by clicking the Update button.

With some title styles, you can specify text position and scrolling direction.

Normally, iMovie superimposes the title text over a clip. For a simple black background instead, check Over Black.

If you won't be viewing your movie on a TV—perhaps you'll be publishing it on a Web site—you can check this box to have iMovie position titles closer to the edges of the screen.

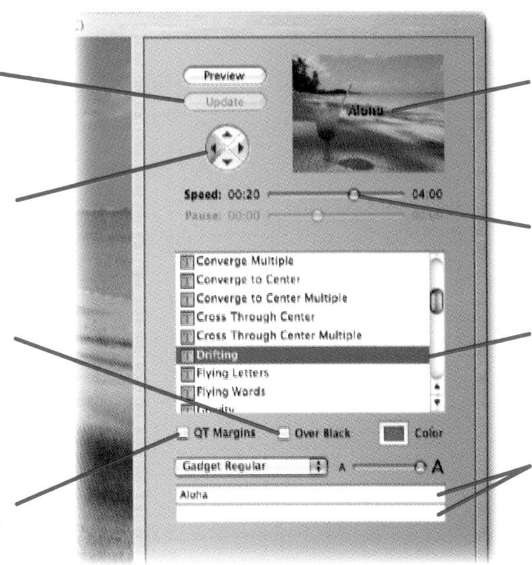

This is a preview of the title. To update it, click the current title style. To view a large preview in the monitor, click the Preview button.

Use this slider to adjust the title's duration. For some title styles, this slider adjusts scrolling speed.

To add the title, drag its name to the timeline viewer or clip viewer.

Type or paste the title's text here. In title styles that provide multiple text boxes, you can jump from one box to the next by pressing the Tab key.

Tips for Titling

Choosing Colors

You can choose the color for title text by clicking the Color button in the Titles pane. Click on the color palette to choose your hue. To match a color that appears in a clip, click the magnifying glass icon, position the pointer over the color you want to pick up, and then click.

When superimposing text over a clip, choose a text color that contrasts with the clip's contents. And lean toward larger font sizes—they'll be more legible.

Photoshop Titles

You can use Adobe Photoshop or Photoshop Elements to make gorgeous, full-screen titles. You can add photos, create color gradients, shadow effects, and more.

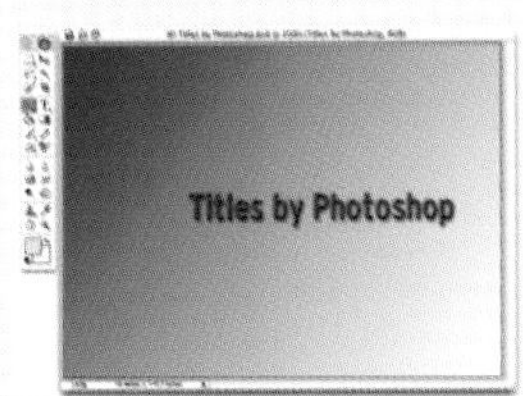

To create a title in Photoshop, specify an image size of 720 by 534. (This size is one of Photoshop's presets.) Create your title, and avoid putting any text in the outer ten percent of the screen. (It might get cut off when the title appears on a TV set.) And to avoid flicker, make the thickness of any horizontal lines an even number of pixels (for example, 2, 4, 6).

To add the title to your movie, first display the Photos pane and drag the Duration slider to specify how long the title should be. Next, drag the completed title's icon into iMovie's Clips pane. iMovie will complain that you won't be able to apply pan-zoom to the clip. Who cares? Click OK, and enjoy your title.

To be able to apply the Ken Burns effect to a Photoshop title, save the title in JPEG format, and drag the JPEG into iMovie.

You can combine Photoshop and iMovie's built-in titling to create titles whose text is superimposed over a moving textured background. Create the textured background in Photoshop and save it in JPEG format. Import the JPEG into iMovie and apply the Ken Burns effect as desired (a horizontal pan works nicely). Finally, superimpose a text title over the resulting clip.

Adding Effects

Special effects are the spice of the movie world. When used sparingly, they enhance a movie and add appeal. When overused, they can make your audience gag.

iMovie's Effects pane is the gateway to a full spice rack of special effects. The Aged Film effect makes a clip look like old movie film, complete with scratches and jitter. The Lens Flare effect simulates the glare of bright light entering a camera's lens. Fairy Dust gives you that Tinkerbell look, while Electricity creates *faux* lightning bolts. And the Earthquake effect creates a fast, back-and-forth blur that may tempt you to duck beneath a desk.

You can also apply speed effects to your clips. Slow a clip down to get slow motion, or speed it up for a chuckle.

Have fun with iMovie's effects. But remember: too much spice is worse than none at all.

To Add an Effect

Adding an effect involves choosing the desired effect, specifying its settings, and then applying the effect to a clip.

Step 1.

Select the clip to which you want to apply an effect.

Step 2.

Click the Effects button to display the Effects pane.

Step 3.

Choose the desired effect by clicking its name. iMovie displays a preview of the effect in the Effects pane.

Step 4.

Specify the desired settings for the effect.

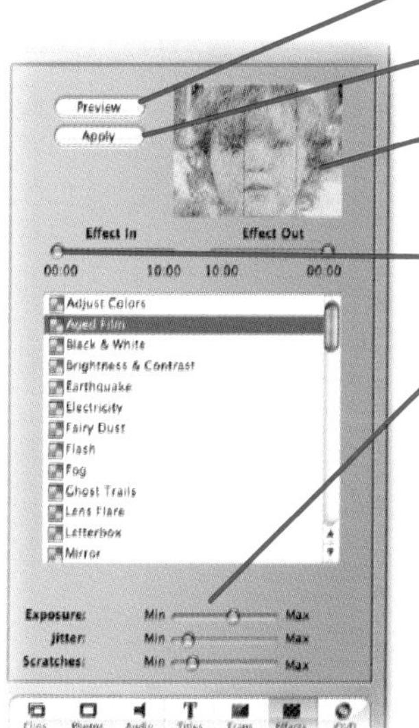

To preview the effect in the monitor, click Preview.

To apply the effect to the selected clip, click Apply.

The preview box shows the results of the current effect and its settings.

iMovie can apply or remove an effect over time; see "Effects Over Time" on the opposite page.

Each effect has its own controls; they appear in this area.

Step 5.

To apply the effect, click the Apply button.

iMovie renders the video frames required to create the effect.

See a sampling of iMovie's built-in effects.
A Sampling of Effects

Effects Over Time

Effects aren't an all-or-nothing proposition—iMovie can apply or remove an effect gradually. Apply the Black and White effect over time to make a clip start in black and white and turn into Technicolor. Animate the Soft Focus effect to make a clip start out blurry and come into focus, or vice versa.

To animate effects, use the Effects pane's Effect In and Effect Out sliders.

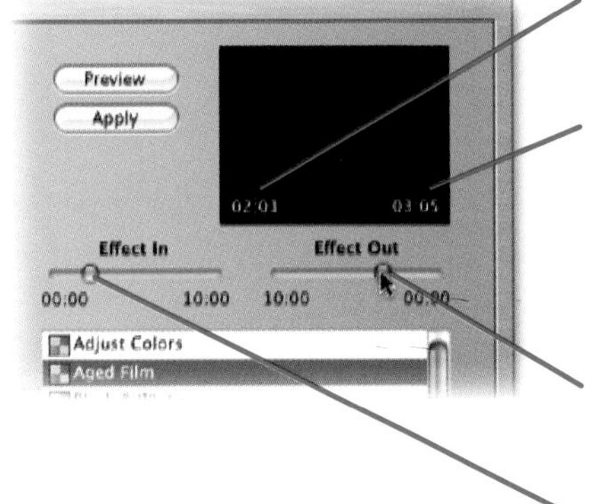

This value indicates how much time will elapse until the effect is fully visible.

This value shows when the effect will start to fade. The time is measured from the end of the clip—in this example, the effect will begin to fade 3 seconds and five frames from the end of the clip.

To make an effect go away over time, drag the Effect Out slider to the left.

To have the effect appear over time, drag the Effect In slider to the right.

Speed Effects

That video of Junior's winning soccer game could use some slow-motion instant replays. iMovie provides them. Just select a clip in the timeline, and adjust the clip speed slider at the bottom of the timeline viewer.

To speed up the clip, drag the slider toward the rabbit.

To slow down the clip, drag the slider toward the tortoise. (You know that, didn't you?)

Because slowing down or speeding up a clip alters its audio playback, you'll want to mute the audio of a clip when you change its playback speed: select the clip and drag its volume slider to its leftmost position.

Slowing down a clip can also be a nice way to smooth out jerky camera movement. If you had too much coffee before shooting that flower close-up, slow the shot down a bit.

When you export a project containing slowed clips, iMovie displays a dialog box advising you to render those clips for best quality and giving you the option to proceed with or without rendering. Choose the Render and Proceed option, and iMovie performs additional processing that blends adjacent frames to smooth out the slow motion.

It's a Wrap: Exporting to Tape

You've finished your epic—now what? You decide. With iMovie's Export command, you can record your movie back to videotape or save it as a QuickTime movie that you can burn to a CD or post on a Web site for all the world to see. With the tools in the iDVD pane, you can add DVD chapter markers and send your movie to iDVD.

If you don't have iDVD and a SuperDrive DVD burner, chances are you'll export most of your movies back to tape. Once you export a movie to tape, you can connect your camcorder to your TV and screen your efforts. Or, connect the camcorder to a videocassette recorder to make VHS cassette dubs of your movie.

Exporting to Camera

Connect your miniDV camcorder to your Mac's FireWire jack and put the camcorder in VTR mode. Be sure to put a blank tape in your camcorder, or fast-forward until you're at a blank spot in the tape. Don't make the mistake of recording over your original footage—you may need it again in the future.

Step 1.

Choose Export from the File menu (Shift-⌘-E).

Step 2.

In the Export dialog box, be sure To Camera appears in the Export pop-up menu.

Step 3.

Click Export; iMovie puts your camcorder in record mode and plays back your movie, sending its video and audio data over the FireWire cable to the camcorder.

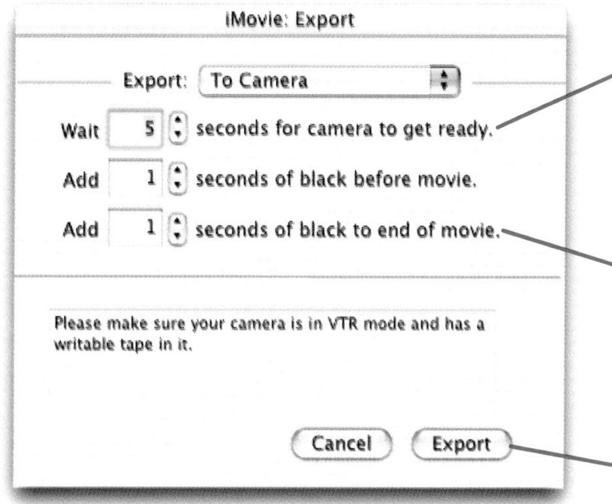

iMovie gives your camcorder five seconds to crank up and prepare to record. Feel free to lower this value—at least until you find you're cutting off the beginning of the movie.

iMovie will add some black footage before and after your movie, eliminating the jarring jump from and to the camcorder's blue standby screen. The preset values of one second probably won't be long enough—add a few seconds of black before the movie, and at least five to 10 seconds of black after it.

Be sure your camcorder is on and in VTR mode, then click Export.

Making VHS Dubs

To make a VHS dub of a movie, connect your camcorder's video and audio outputs to the video and audio inputs of a videocassette recorder.

Your camcorder included a cable that probably has a four-conductor plug on one end, and three RCA phono plugs on the other. Connect the four-conductor plug to the camcorder's output jack (it will be labeled A/V In/Out or something similar). Connect the yellow RCA plug to your VCR's video input jack, the red plug to the audio input jack for the right channel, and the white plug to the audio input jack for the left channel.

You may have to adjust a setting on the VCR to switch input from its tuner to its video and audio input jacks.

Once you've made the connection, put a blank tape in the VCR, press its Record button, and then play back your movie.

If your camcorder and VCR each provide S-video jacks, use them for the video signal. S-video provides a much sharper picture. If you use an S-video cable, use only the audio plugs of the camcorder's cable; just let the yellow one dangle behind the VCR.

Tip: If you'll be doing a lot of dubbing, look for a VCR that has front-panel audio and video input jacks, which eliminate the need to grope around the VCR's back panel.

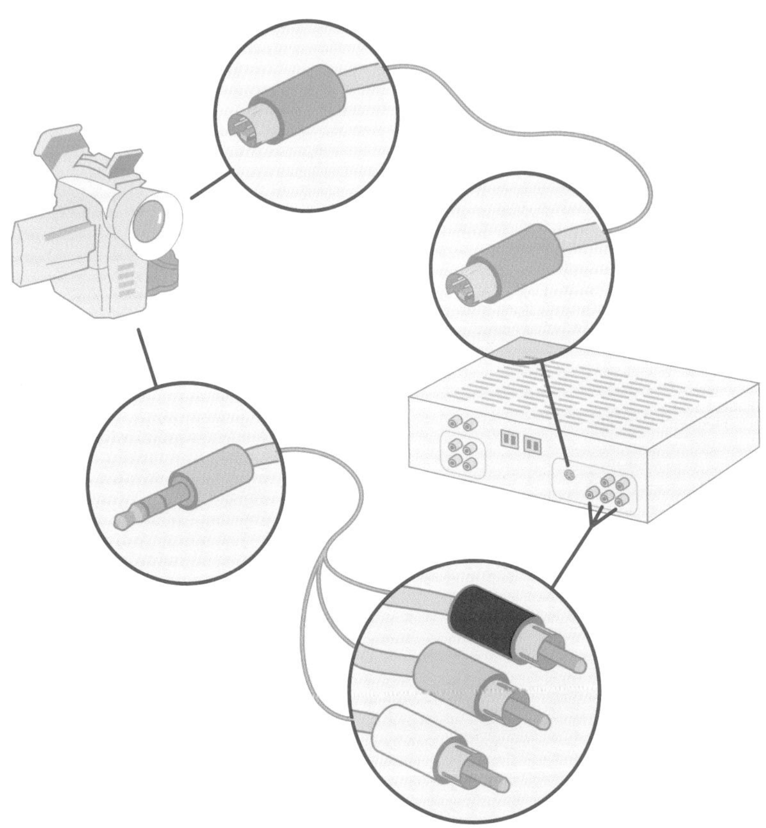

Creating Chapter Markers for iDVD

DVD chapters let you view video on your own terms. Whether you're watching a Hollywood blockbuster or the DVD that accompanied this book, you can use on-screen menus to instantly access scenes of interest. You can also use the Next and Previous keys on your DVD player's remote control to jump to the next chapter or to return to the beginning of a chapter and watch it again.

By adding chapter markers to your movies, you give your viewers this same freedom of movement and spare them the tedium of fast-forwarding and rewinding. Chapter markers are video bookmarks; you can create up to 36 markers in iMovie, and iDVD will create menus and buttons for them.

Even if you don't have a SuperDrive DVD burner, chapter markers can be handy. You can use them as bookmarks to enable you to quickly navigate through a lengthy movie: when you click a chapter in the iDVD pane, iMovie immediately moves the playhead to that location in the timeline.

You don't have to create chapter markers in sequential order. If you add a marker to a movie that already contains some markers, iMovie automatically renumbers any markers that are to its right.

Adding Chapter Markers

Step 1.

Position the playhead at the location where you want the chapter marker. Note that you can't have a chapter marker within the first one second of a movie.

You can drag the playhead there or use the keyboard shortcuts described in "The Keys to Precision" on page 119.

Step 2.

Click the iDVD button.

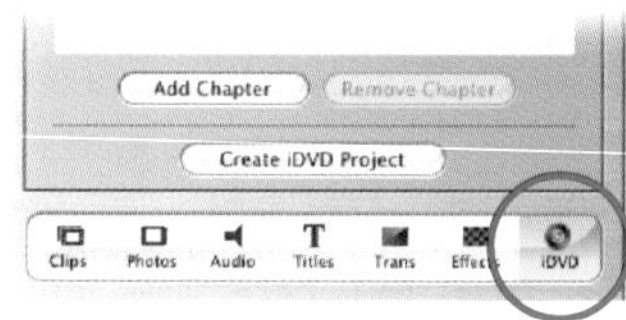

The iDVD pane appears.

Step 3.

Click the Add Chapter button.

Repeat these steps for each chapter marker you want to create.

In the timeline viewer, iMovie displays a small diamond at each chapter marker's location.

See how to create and work with chapter markers.
Creating Chapter Markers

Naming Chapters

For movies containing chapter markers, iDVD creates a "Scene Selection" menu button. When your DVD's viewers choose that button, they get an additional menu or set of menus that enable them to view each scene.

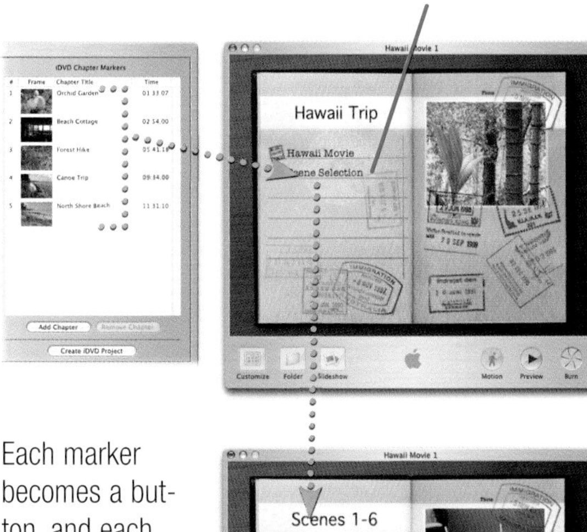

Each marker becomes a button, and each button's name corresponds to the chapter title. Notice that iMovie automatically creates a marker for the very beginning of the movie.

Tip: To quickly rename a series of chapters, select the first chapter you want to rename, type a name, and press Return. iMovie renames the marker and selects the name of the marker below it. Type the new name for that marker and press Return again. Repeat until you've renamed all the markers.

When you add a chapter marker, its name appears in the Chapter Title area of the iDVD pane. iMovie automatically names a chapter after the clip that appears at the marker's location. When you use that movie in an iDVD project, iDVD names buttons according to the chapter titles.

If you haven't named your clips as I recommend on page 118, you can wind up with meaningless chapter titles and button names, such as *Clip 03* or, for iPhoto images, *Roll 86-2*.

Even if you have named your clips, you might still want different button names. You can always edit button names in iDVD, but you can also edit chapter titles in iMovie: simply double-click on the chapter title and then type a new name.

Tips for Creating Chapters

How might you use DVD chapters? That depends on what's in your video. Here are some scenarios to give you ideas.

A wedding video
Create chapters for each of the day's main events: the bridesmaids beautifying the bride, the groom arriving at the church, the ceremony, the reception.

A kid's birthday party
Create chapters for each phase of the party: the arrival of the guests, the games, the opening of presents, the fighting, the crying.

A vacation video
Create chapters for each day or for each destination you visited.

A documentary
Create chapters for each of the main subjects or periods of time that you're documenting.

A training video
Create chapters for each subject or set of instructions.

Exporting to QuickTime

To email a movie, burn it on a CD, or publish it on a Web site, choose the To QuickTime option in the Export dialog box.

When you choose To QuickTime and then select the email or Web options, iMovie compresses the movie heavily and, in the process, introduces you to The Three Musketeers of Internet video: jerky, grainy, and chunky. The movie will have a lower frame rate, so motion may appear jerky. The movie's dimensions will also be much smaller—as small as 160 by 120 pixels, or roughly the size of a matchbook.

A movie that you compress for email or Web delivery will take less disk space and transfer more quickly over the Internet. You're still likely to end up with a large file, though, and you'll probably be disappointed with the movie's appearance. If your movies are more than a couple of minutes long, think twice—maybe even three times—before using the Internet to distribute them, unless you and your recipients have fast connections.

Understanding QuickTime Settings

The Formats pop-up menu contains several options, each aimed at a particular application. The menu also contains an Expert option that enables you to specify compression settings.

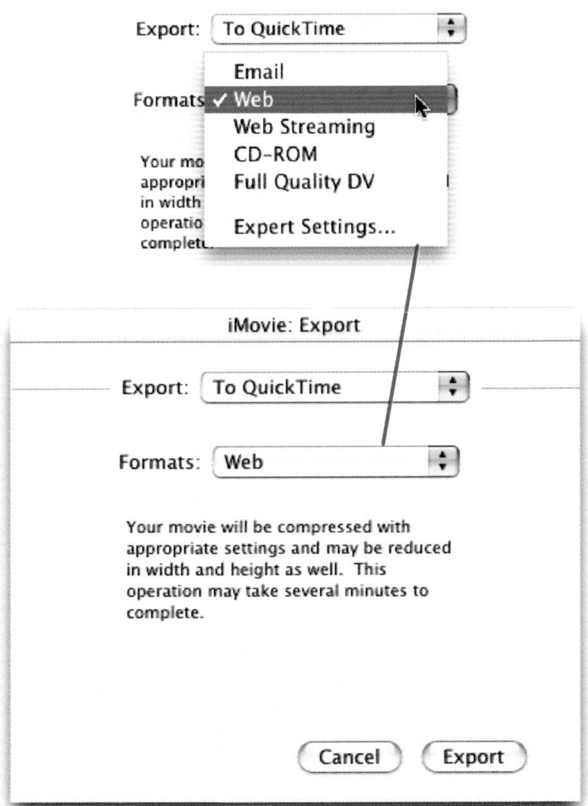

To export your efforts as a QuickTime movie, choose Export from the File menu. Next, choose To QuickTime from the Export pop-up menu. Finally, use the Formats pop-up menu to choose the desired degree of compression.

Learn more about QuickTime compression and Video CDs.
www.macilife.com/imovie

GO TO WEB

Publishing a Movie on Your .Mac HomePage

Just as you can publish an iPhoto album on your .Mac HomePage, you can also publish a QuickTime movie. After exporting the movie in QuickTime format, copy it to the Movies folder of your iDisk. (This is a "virtual disk" included with your .Mac membership. It's also where you'll find hundreds of royalty-free music clips you can use in your movies, as described on page 135.)

After you copy the movie to your iDisk, sign on to .Mac and use the HomePage options to choose a style for the movie page.

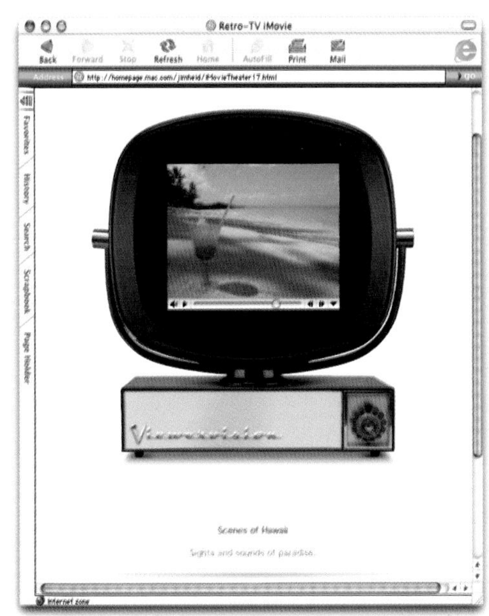

Burning Movies to CD and Video CD

If your Mac has a CD burner, you might want to burn your exported movie to a CD to share it with others. In the Export dialog box, choose the CD-ROM option. Then, insert a blank CD into your Mac's optical drive and copy the movie to the CD. The resulting CD will play on any Mac or Windows computer that has QuickTime installed.

If you have Roxio's Toast Titanium software, you can also create a *Video CD*. This video format is very popular in Asia and somewhat obscure everywhere else. But most stand-alone DVD players can play Video CDs, as can all current personal computers. (To play Video CDs on a Mac, use Mireth Technology's MacVCD software, available at www.mireth.com.)

All you need to burn a Video CD are a CD burner and Toast Titanium. Toast includes a compression plug-in for QuickTime that enables iMovie to export movies for a Video CD.

Video on a Video CD is compressed in MPEG-1 format. The image quality is a far cry from that of the MPEG-2 format used on DVDs; Video CD image quality is more akin to that of VHS videotape. One reason is because the video frame size is smaller—352 by 240 pixels instead of DVD's 720 by 480. Another is that the video itself is compressed more heavily—about 90:1, compared to roughly 30:1 for MPEG-2. But on the plus side, a Video CD can shoehorn about 70 minutes of video onto a CD-R disc. Yes, Video CD is a second-best alternative to DVDs, but if you don't have a SuperDrive, any alternative is better than none. For background on the Video CD format, see www.vcdhelp.com.

iMovie Tips

Here's a montage of tips for getting more out of iMovie.

Moving Clips from the Timeline

On occasion, you may want to remove a clip from the movie but keep it on iMovie's Clips pane to use later. If you're working in the clip viewer, this is easy: simply drag the clip back to the Clips pane.

But the more powerful timeline viewer, where you're likely to be doing most of your work, doesn't let you drag clips back to the Clips pane. Here's a workaround: In the timeline, select the clip you want to move to the Clips pane, and choose Cut from the Edit menu. Then select any clip on the Clips pane and choose Paste from the Edit menu.

Copying and Pasting Clips

Speaking of the Edit menu, it's worth noting that you can make additional copies of a clip by copying it to the Clipboard and pasting it into the Clips pane or the timeline. If you want to experiment with different effects or cropping schemes, select the clip and choose Copy. Next, select another clip on the Clips pane and choose Paste. iMovie makes a copy of the clip and puts it on the Clips pane for you.

You aren't consuming vast amounts of disk space with this technique—rather than duplicating the actual clip's footage, iMovie simply creates a reference to it.

Moving Clips Faster

If you need to move a clip a significant distance—say, from the end of a project to the beginning—you could just drag it and let the clip viewer scroll automatically. But there's a faster way. Drag the clip from the clip viewer into any empty box on the Clips pane. Scroll through the clip viewer to the new destination, and then drag the clip from the Clips pane back into the clip viewer.

Hacking iMovie's Preferences

iMovie relies on a *preferences file* whose entries govern numerous aspects of iMovie's operation. By editing this preferences file, you can customize iMovie.

The useful modification you might make is to put Ken Burns out of work. If you'll be importing several photos and don't want to apply the Ken Burns effect to each one, you can turn the effect off by editing the preferences file.

For iMovie 3, the preferences file is named com.apple.iMovie3.plist. To locate it, first quit iMovie, then go to your Home folder. Open the Library folder, then open the Preferences folder.

Before making any modifications to the preferences file, make a backup of it: select the file and choose Duplicate from the Finder's File menu. Stash the duplicate someplace safe, such as in your Documents folder.

Open the preferences file using a text editor such as TextEdit, included with Mac OS X. To disable Ken Burns, use TextEdit's Find command to locate the following entry:

```
<key>Option autoApplyPanZoomToImportedStills: %d
</key>
<true/>
```

Change the word *true* to *false*. Save the file, and start iMovie again. Test your work by dragging a photo to the timeline.

If you edit the preferences file incorrectly and cause iMovie to start misbehaving, either replace it with the duplicate you made or simply throw it away. The next time you start up iMovie, it will create a new file.

Get links to iMovie add-ons.
www.macilife.com/imovie

Adding On to iMovie

Several companies sell inexpensive add-ons that expand iMovie's repertoire of effects, transitions, or both.

Companies offering iMovie add-ons include Virtix, GeeThree, and Stupendous Software. Each of these companies also offers some free iMovie effect plug-ins. Many companies also offer sound effects and royalty-free music that you can use in your projects.

Importing Other QuickTime Movies

Your kid dressed up as Darth Vader for Halloween—so why not include a snippet of the *Star Wars* trailer in your Halloween video? (Just don't try to sell the resulting movie, lest some copyright lawyers come trick or treating.)

To add an existing QuickTime movie to an iMovie project, simply drag the movie into the iMovie Clips pane or use the File menu's Import command.

Editing Like the Pros: Making the TV Connection

What a difference a check box makes. Activate iMovie's Play Video Through to Camera option (in the Preferences dialog box), and anything you play—a single video clip, a title or transition, or your entire project—plays back not only on the Mac's screen, but also on your camcorder.

What's so hot about that? Simply this: the video iMovie outputs to your camcorder plays at full resolution and full motion—it isn't the jittery, preview-quality video iMovie displays on the Mac. Pop out your DV camcorder's LCD monitor, and you can use it to get a far more accurate assessment of the video.

But don't stop there—connect your camcorder's video output to a TV to view your work on a large screen. This is how video professionals edit, and once you try it you'll never settle for iMovie's preview-quality playback.

First, connect your DV camcorder to the Mac with a FireWire cable as usual.

Next, connect your camcorder's video output to the video input of a TV set. If your TV and your camcorder each have S-Video connections, you should use them for the best video quality. If your TV lacks S-Video but has a composite video input (an RCA jack), use it. If your TV lacks video inputs, add an RF modulator between the camcorder and the TV set. You can buy the modulator at Radio Shack for about $30.

Once you've made the connections, choose Preferences from the iMovie menu and click the Play Video Through to Camera check box.

When this option is selected, your project's audio will not play back through your Mac's speakers. You can rely on your camcorder's tiny, built-in speaker for sound playback, but you might want to connect your camcorder's audio outputs to your TV's audio inputs, if it provides them; to a stereo system; or to a pair of external amplified speakers.

To make VHS dubs of your projects, connect a videocassette recorder between the camcorder and TV: connect the camcorder's outputs to the VCR's inputs, and the VCR's outputs to the TV's inputs.

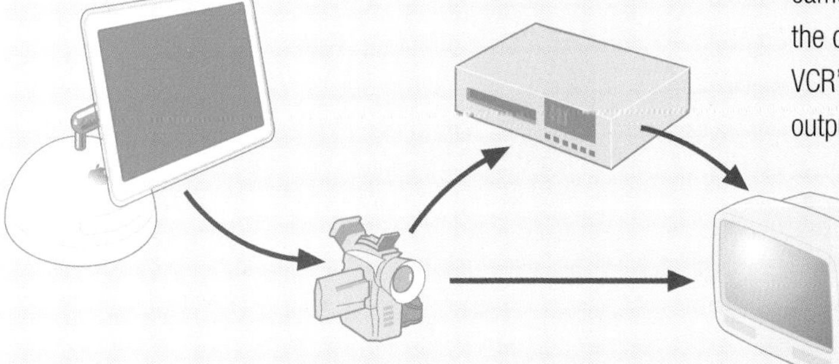

Tips for Making Better Movies

Editing takes more than software. You also need the right raw material. Advance planning will help ensure that you have the shots you need, and following some basic videography techniques will make for better results.

Plan Ahead

Planning a movie involves developing an outline—in Hollywood parlance, a *storyboard*—that lists the shots you'll need to tell your tale. Professional movie makers storyboard every scene and camera angle. You don't have to go that far, but you will tell a better story if you plan at least some shots.

Consider starting with an *establishing shot* that clues viewers in on where your story takes place—for example, the backyard swimming pool. To show the big picture, zoom out to your camcorder's wide-angle setting.

From there, you might cut to a medium shot that introduces your movie's subject: little Bobby preparing to belly flop off the diving board. Next, you might cut away to Mary tossing a beach ball. Cut back to Bobby struggling to stay afloat, and then finish with a long shot of the entire scene.

Keep in mind that you don't have to shoot scenes in chronological order—sequencing your shots is what iMovie is for. For example, get the shot of Mary's throw any time you like and edit it into the proper sequence using iMovie.

Steady Your Camera

Nausea-inducing camera work is a common flaw of amateur videos. Too many people mistake a video camera for a fire hose: they sweep across a scene, panning left and right and then back again. Or they ceaselessly zoom in and out, making viewers wonder whether they're coming or going.

A better practice is to stop recording, move to a different location or change your zoom setting, and then resume. Varying camera angles and zoom settings makes for a more interesting video. If you must pan—perhaps to capture a dramatic vista—do so slowly and steadily.

And, unless you're making an earthquake epic, hold the camera as steady as you can. If your camera has an image-stabilizing feature, use it. Better still, use a tripod or a monopod, or brace the camera against a rigid surface. Keeping the camera steady is especially critical for movies destined for the Internet—because of the way these videos are compressed, minimizing extraneous motion will yield sharper results.

Compose Carefully

The photographic composition tips on pages 108-109 apply to movie making, too. Compose your shots carefully, paying close attention to the background. Get up close now and then—don't just shoot wide shots.

Editing to Music

If you're using music in your movie, consider editing so that your scene cuts are in rhythm with the music—at the start of each verse, for example, or any time the music changes significantly.

The timecode readout that appears alongside iMovie's playhead is a valuable tool for editing to music. Use it to determine how long a clip should be in order to fill a particular passage of music. For example, if the timecode readout displays 01:10:04 when a music passage begins and 01:22:06 when that passage ends, you need a clip about 12 seconds long to fill that passage.

Record Some Ambient Sound

Try to shoot a couple of minutes of uninterrupted background sound: the waves on a beach, the birds in the forest, the revelers at a party. As I mention on the DVD, you can extract the sound from this footage and use it as an audio bed behind a series of shots. It doesn't matter what the camera is pointing at while you're shooting—you won't use the video anyway.

After importing the footage, use the Extract Audio command described on page 134 to separate the audio.

See and hear techniques for stretching the truth with sound.
Creating an Audio Bed
GO TO DVD

Be Prepared, Be Careful

Be sure your camcorder's batteries are charged; consider buying a second battery so you'll have a backup, and take along your charger and power adapter, too. Bring plenty of blank tape, and label your tapes immediately after ejecting them. To protect a tape against accidental reuse, slide the little locking tab on its spine.

Vary Shot Lengths

Your movie will be more visually engaging if you vary the length of your shots. Use longer shots for complex scenes, such as a wide shot of a city street, and shorter shots for close-ups or reaction shots.

Don't Skimp on Tape

Don't just get one version of a shot, get several. If you just shot a left-to-right pan across a scene, for example, shoot a right-to-left pan next. The more raw material you have to work with, the better.

Converting Analog Video and Movies

Somewhere in your closet is a full-sized VHS camcorder—the kind that rested on your shoulder like a rocket launcher. You have a FireWire-equipped Mac, and you want to get some of that old VHS video into it.

If you've since upgraded your artillery to a miniDV-format camcorder, connect it to your VHS camcorder or to a VCR and then record your VHS footage on DV tapes. Connect the video and audio output jacks on the VHS deck to your DV camcorder's video and audio input jacks. If your VHS deck and camcorder each provide S-video jacks, use them to get the best picture quality. After you've made your DV dubs, connect your DV camera to the Mac and use iMovie to import the video.

An Analog-DV Converter

A faster way to get analog video into your Mac is through a converter, such as those sold by Formac Electronics, Dazzle Multimedia, Sony, and others. These devices eliminate the time-consuming process of dubbing VHS tapes to DV format. Connect a converter to your Mac's FireWire jack, then connect your old VHS rocket launcher to the converter's video and audio inputs. Then, launch iMovie and use its import features to bring in VHS video. Using iMovie's Export command, you can also blast edited video through the converter back to the VHS camcorder.

When importing VHS video, you may notice a thin band of flickering pixels at the bottom of the image. Don't worry: these artifacts won't appear when you view your finished video on a TV screen.

Converting Films

As for those old Super 8 film-based flicks, you'll need to send them to a lab that does film-to-video transfers. Many camera stores can handle this for you. The lab will clean your films, fix bad splices, and return them along with videotapes whose contents you can bring into the Mac. If you have a DV camcorder, be sure to use a lab that will supply your converted movies on DV cassettes—you'll get much better image quality than VHS provides. Some labs also offer optional background music and titles, but you can add these yourself once you've brought the converted video into the Mac.

iDVD: Putting it All Together

The Macintosh
iLife

iDVD at a Glance

With Apple's SuperDrive DVD burner and iDVD software, you can go from being a viewer to a producer. iDVD lets you burn movies and photos to DVD-R and DVD-RW media, complete with menus you can fully customize.

Designers and photographers can use iDVD to assemble digital portfolios that they can hand out like brochures. Filmmakers and advertising professionals can distribute rough cuts of movie scenes and commercials to clients and colleagues. Businesspeople can create in-house training discs and video archives of corporate meetings. Videographers can offer DVDs of weddings and other events. And home-movie buffs can preserve and share family videos and photographs.

Creating a DVD involves choosing and customizing a menu theme and adding the movies and photos you want to include on the DVD. You can perform these steps in any order and preview your work along the way. When you've finished, you can burn the final product to DVD-R media.

You can narrow down the list of themes displayed.

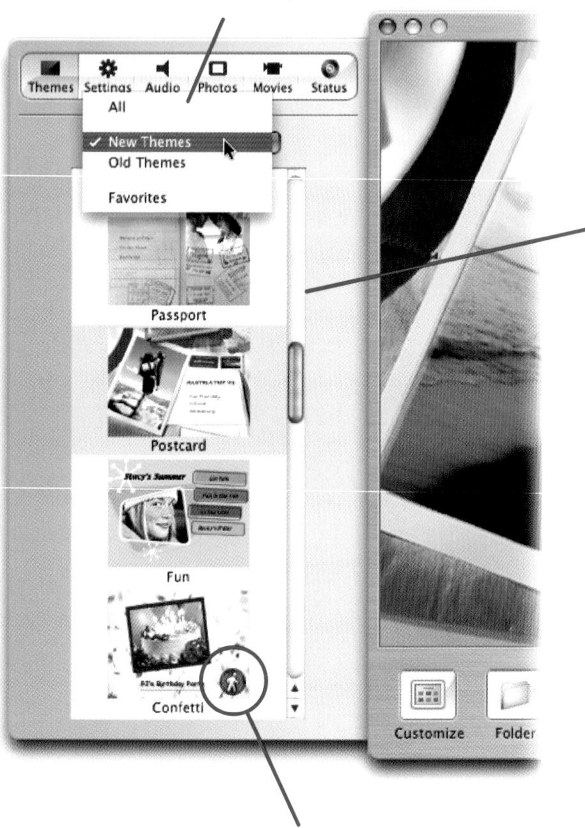

Themes with motion menus are indicated by the motion icon.

A Short Glossary of DVD Terms

authoring The process of creating menus and adding movies and images to a DVD.

button A clickable area that plays a movie or slide show, or takes the user to another menu.

DVD-R The blank media that you'll use most often when burning DVDs. A DVD-R blank can be burned just once.

DVD-RW A type of DVD media that you can erase and reuse.

menu A screen containing clickable buttons that enable users to access a DVD's contents.

motion menu A menu whose background image is an animation or movie, a menu that plays background audio, or both.

MPEG-2 The compression format used for video on a DVD. MPEG stands for *Moving Picture Experts Group*.

See the iDVD authoring process.
iDVD: Putting it All Together

As you work in iDVD, the program compresses movies you've added into MPEG-2 format. You can monitor the status of this process here.

iDVD provides several predesigned menu templates, called *themes*, some of which provide motion menus and audio.

To create a custom menu background, drag an image from iPhoto or another program to the iDVD window (page 165).

Many themes have drop zones, special areas into which you can drag photos or a movie (page 157).

Each menu on your DVD has a title, whose position and formatting you can customize (page 164).

To add a movie to your DVD, drag it into iDVD's window. iDVD creates a button, whose appearance you can customize (page 158).

After you've customized a theme, you can save it for future use (page 170).

To show or hide the Customize drawer, click Customize.

A DVD can have multiple menus; to create an additional menu, click Folder (page 167).

You can create slide shows containing images from iPhoto and background music from iTunes (pages 160–163).

To preview and burn menus containing motion or background audio, click Motion.

To try out your DVD before burning it, click Preview (page 158).

To burn your finished DVD, click Burn (page 168).

Choosing and Customizing Themes

A big part of creating a DVD involves choosing which menu theme you want. iDVD includes menu themes for many types of occasions and subjects: weddings, parties, vacations, kids, and more. Many of these themes have motion menus containing beautiful animations and, with some themes, background music or sound effects.

Your design options don't end once you've chosen a theme. Many of iDVD's themes provide *drop zones*, special areas of the menu background into which you can drag photos or movies. Drop zones make it easy to customize a theme with your own imagery.

Most drop zones have special effects that iDVD applies to the photos or movies that you add to them. For example, the Moving Bars theme has a drop zone that adds abstract, animated vertical bars to your imagery. The Projector theme creates an old-movie appearance, complete with scratches. The Theater drop zone adds animated curtains—and if you look closely, you'll see the curtains even cast shadows on your imagery.

Some extremely sophisticated software engineering lies behind themes and drop zones. But who cares? What matters is that they let you create gorgeous DVD menus with a few mouse clicks.

Choosing a Theme

Step 1.

Click the Customize button to open the Customize drawer.

Step 2.

If the list of themes isn't visible, click the Themes button.

Step 3.

Choose the theme you want by clicking it.

Note: In order to see a theme's motion, you must have motion turned on. To turn motion on or off, click the Motion button. As you work on your DVD, you'll probably want to turn motion off since iDVD runs faster this way. Just remember to turn motion back on before burning your DVD.

Motion

Take a tour of iDVD's themes, and see how to customize them.
Touring iDVD's Themes
Adding Items to a Drop Zone

Adding Items to a Drop Zone

Step 1.

If you want to add one or more photos to the drop zone, click the Photos button in the Customize drawer. To add a movie, click the Movies button.

Step 2.

In the iPhoto or iMovie media browser, select the item or items you want to add.

You can select multiple photos or an entire album. If you add multiple photos to a drop zone, iDVD displays them successively as the menu is displayed. You can add up to 30 photos to a drop zone. You can add only one movie to a drop zone.

Step 3.

Drag the selected items into the drop zone.

As you drag into a drop zone, a dotted line indicates the drop zone's boundaries.

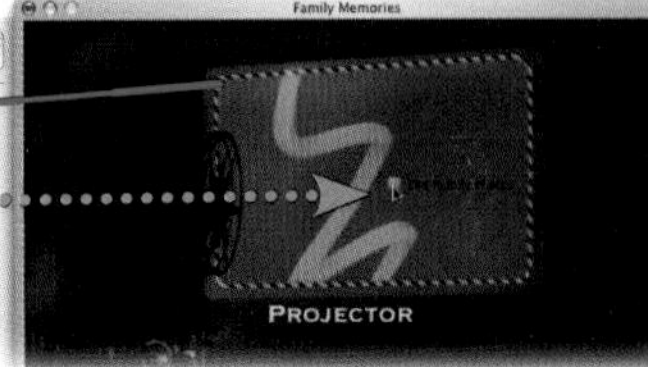

Step 4.

To fine-tune an item's position within the drop zone, drag it using the hand pointer.

Tips for Working with Drop Zones

Drop Zones Aren't Buttons

It's important to understand the difference between drop zones and buttons. A drop zone is merely an area of imagery within a DVD menu—it isn't a clickable button that your DVD's viewers can use to watch your DVD. A drop zone is a piece of eye candy; a button is a navigation control that plays a movie or slide show or jumps to another menu.

How to Tell the Difference

As you drag items into the menu area, how can you tell whether you're dragging into a drop zone or creating a button? Easy: When you're dragging into a drop zone, a dotted-line pattern appears around the edges of the drop zone, as shown above. If you don't see this pattern, you aren't in the drop zone, and you'll end up creating a button.

Other Ways to Add Items

You can also add items to a drop zone by dragging them from the Finder: simply drag the items' icons into the drop zone. And you can drag photos from iPhoto directly into a drop zone.

If you don't like dragging and dropping, here's one more way to add items: Control-click within a drop zone, and choose the Import command from the pop-up shortcut menu that appears.

Removing Items

To remove the contents of a drop zone, drag the item out of the drop zone. When you release the mouse button, the item disappears in a puff of smoke. As an alternative to dragging, you can also Control-click within the drop zone and choose Clear from the shortcut menu.

Adding Movies to Your DVD

iDVD's job is to integrate and present assets created in other programs. The assets you're most likely to add to your DVDs are movies you've created in iMovie or another video-editing program, such as Apple's Final Cut Express or Final Cut Pro.

You can add movies to your DVDs using a couple of techniques. Use the movie browser to access movies stored in specific locations on your hard drive. Or, simply drag a movie directly into the iDVD window.

As you add movies and other assets, remember that you can preview your DVD-in-progress at any time by clicking the Preview button.

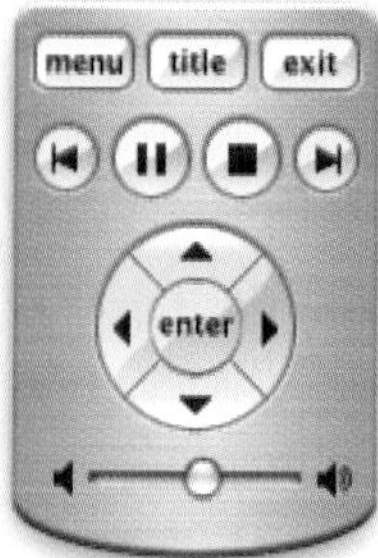

When previewing, use the remote control to test your DVD.

Adding a Movie Using the Movie Browser

Step 1.

Click the Customize button to open the Customize drawer.

Step 2.

Click the Movies button to open the movie browser.

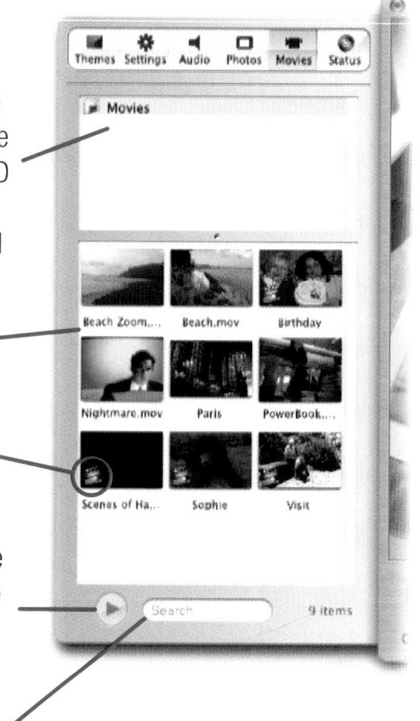

iDVD lists movies contained in your Movies folder. To have iDVD list movies located elsewhere on your hard drive, choose Preferences from the iDVD menu, click the Movies button, and add additional folders to the list.

Available movies appear here.

Movies created using iMovie contain a small iMovie icon.

To preview a movie in the movie browser, select the movie and click this play button, or simply double-click the movie.

Use the Search box to locate a movie in the browser.

See how to add movies.
Adding a Movie
GO TO DVD

Step 3.

Drag the desired movie into your DVD's menu area.

iDVD adds the movie to your DVD and creates a menu button for it.

Tip: Be sure you don't drag the movie into a drop zone; see "Tips for Working with Drop Zones" on page 157.

If the movie contains DVD chapter markers, iDVD creates two buttons: one named Play Movie and another named Scene Selection. If the movie lacks DVD chapters, iDVD simply creates one button, giving it the same name as the movie itself. To rename any button, select it and edit the name.

Other Ways to Add a Movie

You can also add a movie by dragging its icon from the Finder into the iDVD window.

And finally, you can add a movie by choosing the Video command from the File menu's Import submenu.

Tips for DVD Movies

Length Matters

iDVD can burn a DVD containing a total of 90 minutes of video. However, to get the best video quality, restrict the total amount of video on your DVD to a maximum of 60 minutes. If your DVD contains more than 60 minutes of video, iDVD compresses the video more, reducing its quality.

Technically speaking, on DVDs containing less than 60 minutes of video, iDVD compresses at a data rate of 8 megabits per second (Mbps); if you have a total of more than 60 minutes, iDVD compresses at 5Mbps. And just as with MP3 audio, the lower the bit rate, the higher the compression—and the more quality suffers.

Whether that higher compression is acceptable depends on your content. Scenes with lots of motion—a sporting event shot with a hand-held camera, for example—may exhibit chunky compression artifacts at 5Mbps. On the other hand, relatively static scenes—talking heads photographed with a tripod-mounted camera—will probably look acceptable.

Burning Old Movies

You can burn nearly any kind of QuickTime movie onto a DVD, including movie trailers downloaded from the Web or old QuickTime movies from CD-ROMs. If a movie is smaller than the DVD standard of 720 by 480 pixels, iDVD enlarges it to fill the screen. This results in a loss of sharpness, but many enlarged movies will still look surprisingly good when viewed on a TV.

Using Movies from Final Cut

iDVD can also accommodate movies created in Final Cut Pro or Final Cut Express. Export the movie by choosing the Final Cut Pro Movie command from the File menu's Export submenu. (In Final Cut Express, this command reads Final Cut Movie.) If your movie contains chapter markers, be sure to choose the Chapter Markers option from the Include pop-up menu in the Save dialog box.

Creating DVD Slide Shows

You might want to create slide shows to present a series of photos. iDVD slide shows are a great way to share images. Even low-resolution photos look spectacular on a television screen, and they can't easily be copied and redistributed—a plus for photographers creating portfolio discs. (You can, however, opt to include the originals on the disc, as described in "The DVD-ROM Zone" on page 173.)

iDVD provides a few ways to create a slide show. You can use iDVD's iPhoto browser to drag an entire photo album into the iDVD window. You can also use the iDVD button in iPhoto to send an album or a selection of photos to iDVD. And you can manually drag photos from iPhoto (or anywhere else) into iDVD's slide show editor.

You can give your slide shows background music from your iTunes library and fine-tune other aspects of their appearance. The one thing iDVD slide shows don't provide is a cross-dissolve transition between each image. This limitation is due to the way slide shows are stored on a DVD. If you want a cross-dissolve between images, create the slide show in iPhoto and export it as a QuickTime movie (see page 98). Or use iMovie, and add the Ken Burns effect to your photos.

A slide show can contain up to 99 images. Each image can be any size and orientation; however, vertically oriented images will have a black band on their left and right sides.

Creating a Slide Show Using the iPhoto Browser

Step 1.

In iPhoto, create an album containing the photos you want in the slide show, sequenced in the order you want them to appear (see page 76).

Step 2.

In iDVD, click the Customize button to open the Customize drawer.

Step 3.

Click the Photos button.

The iPhoto browser appears.

Your iPhoto library and its albums appear here. To display more photos or more albums, drag the horizontal separator below the album list up or down.

The photos in your library or a selected album appear here.

To search for a photo based on its title, type part or all of its title here.

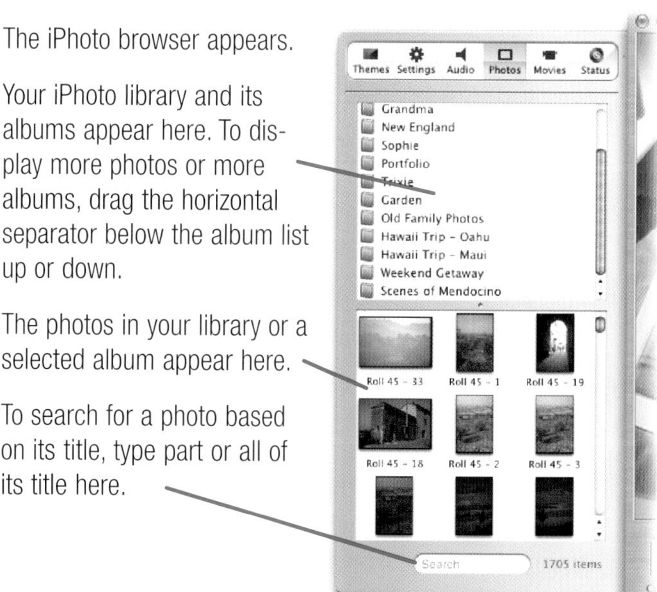

GO TO DVD

See techniques for creating DVD slide shows.
Creating a Slide Show
Using iPhoto's iDVD Button
Adding Music to a Slide Show

Step 4.

Locate the desired album and drag it into the iDVD menu area.

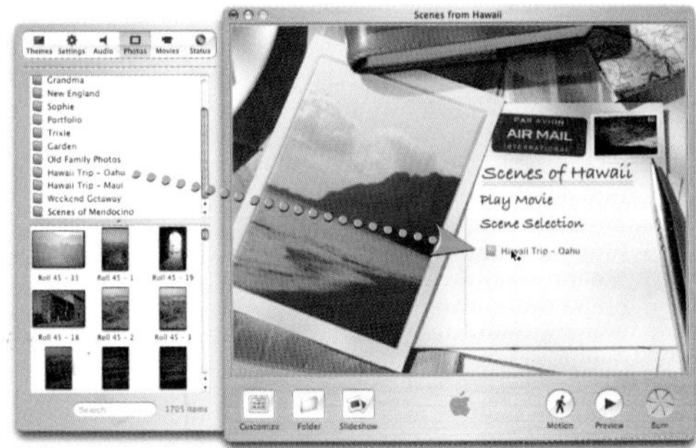

Tip: Be sure you don't drag the album into a drop zone; see "Tips for Working with Drop Zones" on page 157.

iDVD creates the slide show as well as a menu button for displaying it. iDVD gives the button the same name as the album, but you can rename it to anything you like.

Creating a Slide Show Within iPhoto

When you're working in iPhoto, you can send an album or a selection of photos directly to iDVD, where they become a slide show.

Step 1.

Select the photos you want to include in the DVD slide show. To include an entire album or roll, select the album name or the roll name.

Step 2.

Click the iDVD button in iPhoto's Organize pane.

iPhoto sends the photos to iDVD, which creates a new slide show for them.

Creating a Slide Show from Scratch

You can also create a blank slide show and then manually add photos to it. You might use this technique to add photos that aren't stored in your iPhoto library.

Step 1.

Click iDVD's Slideshow button.

iDVD adds a button named My Slideshow to the currently displayed menu. Rename this button as desired.

Step 2.

Double-click on the button that iDVD just created.

The slide show editor appears.

Step 3.

Drag photos (or a folder containing photos) into the slide show editor.

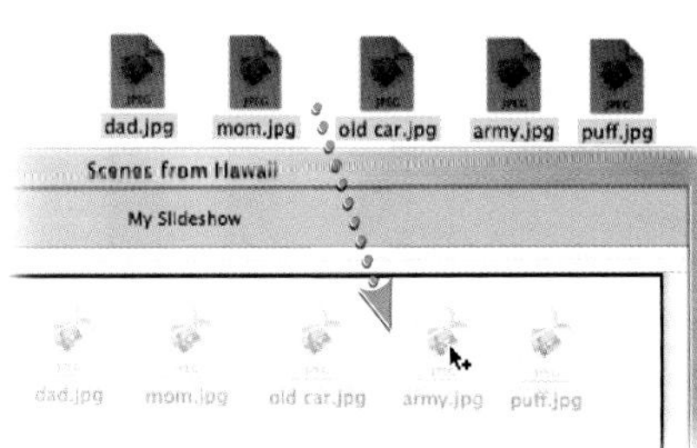

Refining a Slide Show

Regardless of how you create a slide show, you can fine-tune it by using the slide show editor. To display the editor, double-click on the menu button that corresponds to the slide show you want to edit.

The slide show's images play back in top-to-bottom order. You can change their playback order and perform other tweaks.

To change playback order, drag images up or down. You can select multiple images by Shift-clicking and ⌘-clicking.

To add background audio to the slide show, drag an MP3 file or QuickTime movie to this area, called the Audio well.

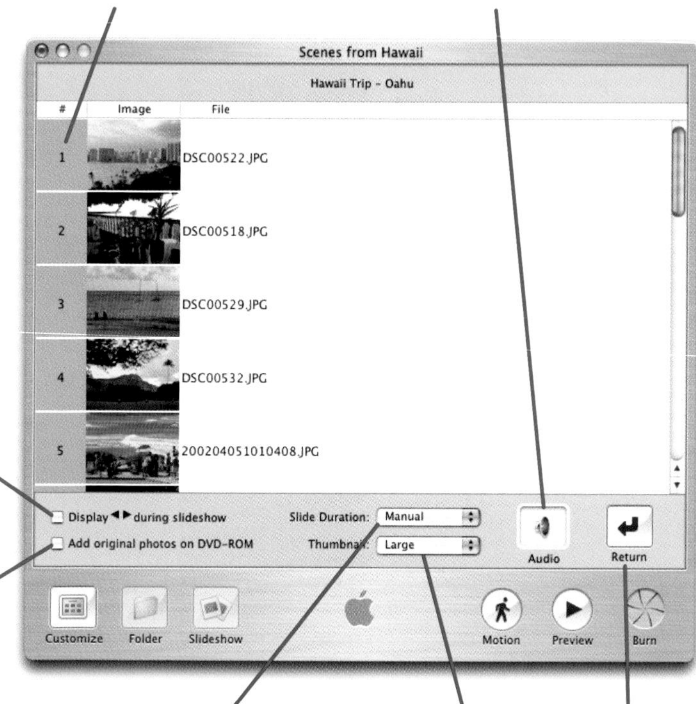

When checked, this box superimposes arrows over the images as a hint to viewers that they can move back and forth in the slide show using their DVD remote controls.

To have iDVD store the original images on the DVD, check this box. (For details, see "The DVD-ROM Zone" on page 173.)

You can specify a duration for each image, or have the slide show timed to match its background audio. If the slide show has background audio, the Manual option isn't available.

To display large thumbnails in the editor, choose Large. To see more images at once, choose Small.

Click to return to the menu that will lead to this slide show.

See techniques for refining a slide show.
Including Original Images
Refining a Slide Show

Adding Music to Slide Shows

You can add a music track to a slide show. One way to add music is by using the iTunes browser in iDVD. Open the Customize drawer and click the Audio button. Use the iTunes browser to find the song you want, then drag the song to the Audio well of iDVD's slide show editor.

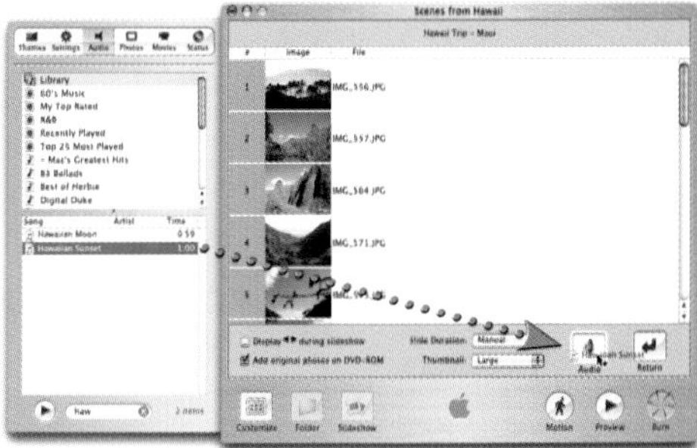

You can also drag a song directly from the iTunes window or, for that matter, from any folder on your hard drive. And you don't even have to drag an audio file: if you drag a QuickTime movie to the Audio well, iDVD will assign its audio to your slide show.

If you create a slide show by clicking the iDVD button in iPhoto, the slide show will retain whatever song was assigned to it in iPhoto. (For details on assigning songs to albums, see page 97.)

How iDVD matches your soundtrack to your slides depends on the option you choose from the Slide Duration pop-up menu. If you choose a specific duration, such as five seconds per slide, iDVD repeats your soundtrack if its duration is shorter than the slide show's total duration. If the soundtrack is longer than the slide show, iDVD simply stops playing the soundtrack after the last slide displays. And if you choose the Fit to Audio option, iDVD times the interval between image changes to match the soundtrack's duration.

To remove a slide show's background music, drag the icon out of the Audio well. When you release the mouse button, the icon vanishes in a puff of smoke.

TV-Safe Slide Shows

Normally, when you view a slide show on a TV screen, you don't see the outer edges of each photo. This is because TV screens typically crop off the outer edges of an image. If you want to see your images in their full, uncropped glory, choose iDVD's Preferences command, click the Slideshow button, and check the box labeled Always Scale Slides to TV-Safe Area. When this option is active, iDVD sizes images so they don't completely fill the frame—thus eliminating cropping.

Customizing Your DVD's Interface

The design themes built into iDVD look great and, in some cases, sound great, too. But you might prefer to not use off-the-rack designs for your DVDs.

Maybe you'd like to have a custom background screen containing your company logo or a favorite vacation photo. You might like the background image of a particular iDVD theme, but not its music or its buttons' shape or typeface. Or maybe you'd just like to have the title of the menu at the left of the screen instead of centered.

You can customize nearly every aspect of your DVD's menus and navigation buttons. With the Settings pane of the Customize drawer, you can modify buttons, add and remove background audio, change a menu's background image, and more.

Customizing Button Positions

Normally, iDVD positions buttons on a fixed grid. This keeps them lined up nicely, but there are times when you might want to manually specify a button's location—perhaps to line it up with a custom background image.

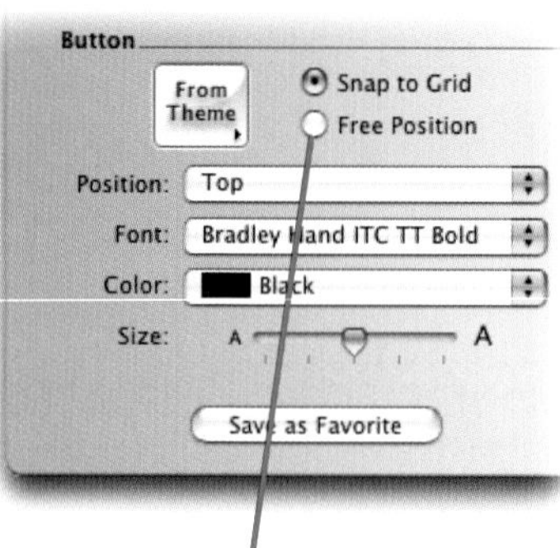

To manually control button position, select the Free Position option in the Button area of the Settings pane. Now you can drag buttons wherever you like.

Kill the Watermark

iDVD displays the Apple logo watermark on each menu screen. To get rid of it, choose Preferences from the iDVD menu, click the General button, and then uncheck the Show Apple Logo Watermark box.

Inserting a Line Break

You may want to create a button or title whose text spans more than one line. You can't simply press Return to start a new line—instead, type your multi-line title in a text editor such as TextEdit or Word. Then copy it, switch back to iDVD, select the button's existing text, and paste.

Staying TV-Safe

TV sets omit the outer edges of a video frame—a phenomenon called *overscan*. To make sure buttons and other menu elements will be visible on TV sets, choose the Show TV Safe Area command in the Advanced menu and be sure to keep buttons and other elements well away from the shaded border.

See techniques for customizing a menu.
Customizing a Menu
Removing the Apple Watermark
Staying in the TV Safe Area

Changing the Background Image

To change the background image of an iDVD menu, simply drag an image into the iDVD window. For the best results, be sure to use a photo whose proportions match the 4:3 aspect ratio of television. You can ensure these proportions when cropping in iPhoto: from the Constrain pop-up menu, choose 4 x 3 (Book, DVD).

Tip: Some photos make better backgrounds if you reduce their brightness and contrast so the image doesn't overwhelm the buttons. In iPhoto, duplicate the image and then adjust the brightness and contrast of the duplicate.

If your project contains several menus (as discussed on page 167), you can apply the new background image to all the menus in your project by choosing Apply Theme to Folders from the Advanced menu. Conversely, if you applied a background image to a folder menu and want to apply the same image to the project's other menus, choose Apply Theme to Project.

And, if you decide you'd rather just have the theme's original background, simply drag the custom background's image thumbnail out of the Image/Movie well in the Settings pane.

Customizing Button Shapes

iDVD's design themes not only specify things such as background image and audio, they also determine the shape of each menu button. To change the shape of a menu's buttons, choose an option from the pop-up menu in the Button area.

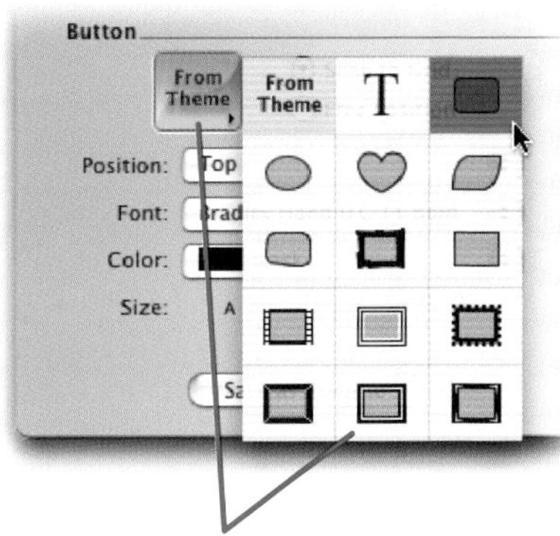

To use the button shape from the current theme, choose From Theme. For a text-only button, choose the T option.

Each button style has its own style of highlight, which appears when a user selects the button. To see the highlights for a button style, click iDVD's Preview button.

Changing Button Text Labels

You can change where a button's text labels appear in relation to the button's thumbnail image. You can also get rid of the thumbnail image and just have text buttons, or you can get rid of the text and just have button images.

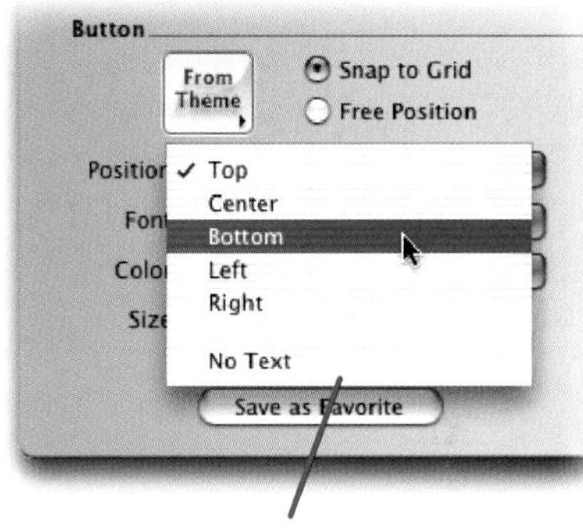

To customize button labels, choose an option from the Position pop-up menu.

You can also change the font, font color, and type size for button text and for the menu's title. If you don't like the results, choose the Undo command as many times as needed to get back to where you started.

Menu and Interface Design Tips

When creating a DVD, you're also designing a user interface. If your DVD contains a couple of movies and a slide show, the interface will be simple: just one menu containing a few buttons.

But if your DVD will contain a dozen movies and another half-dozen slide shows, you'll need to think about how to structure a menu scheme that is logical and easy to navigate.

Another aspect of interface design involves motion. It's tempting to use visually slick motion menus and motion buttons, but all that movement can be distracting. Don't give your viewers motion sickness—avoid the temptation to junk up the DVD's menus with so much motion that viewers have trouble navigating.

The same cautions apply to background music in menus, which can get tiresome when a user has heard it for the tenth time.

The watchword is restraint. Serve up eye and ear candy in moderation.

Planning Your DVD

If your DVD will be presenting a large number of movies or slide shows, you need to plan how you will make that content available to the DVD's user. How many menus will you need? How will you categorize the content in each menu? This process is often called *information design*, and it involves mapping out the way you want to categorize and present your content.

A good way to map out a DVD's flow is to create a tree diagram depicting the organization of menus—much as a company's organizational chart depicts the pecking order of its management.

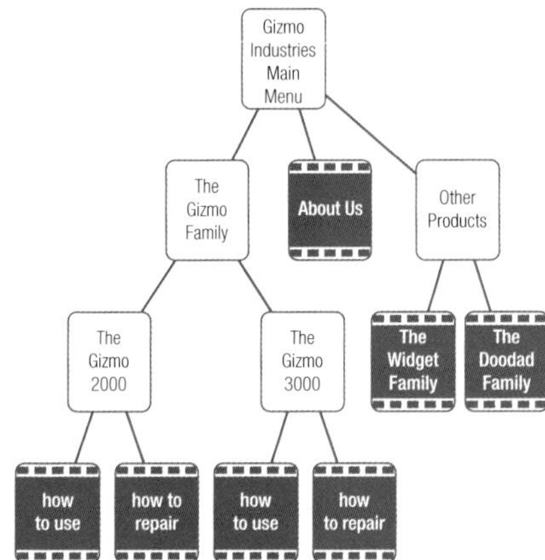

The chart shown here depicts the flow of a DVD a company might create to promote its new Gizmo product line. A main menu contains three buttons: two lead to other submenus, while the third plays a promotional movie about the company.

The submenu "The Gizmo Family" leads to two additional submenus, one for each Gizmo model. The "Other Products" submenu leads to two movies that promote other fine products.

See how to replace menu audio and turn off a motion button.
Turning Off a Motion Button
Replacing a Menu's Audio

Creating Additional Menus

iDVD calls submenus *folders*. To create a folder, click the Folder button.

To design the new menu and add content to it, double-click its button. You can customize the look of each submenu independently of other menus.

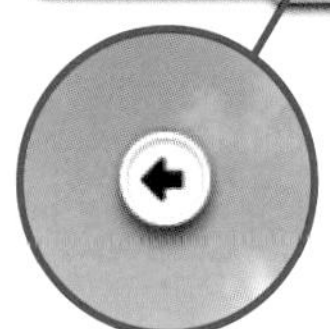

Each submenu has a return button that, when clicked, returns the user to the menu that led to the submenu.

Silencing Motion Menus

You might like the look of a motion menu, but maybe you don't want any music to play—a motion menu in iDVD can't be more than 30 seconds long, and those canned riffs can get tiresome when they repeat every half-minute.

To remove a motion menu's music, drag the icon out of the Audio well in the Settings pane. It disappears in a puff of smoke, and your motion menu will be blissfully silent.

Stopping the Motion

Conversely, maybe you want some background audio to play, but you don't want motion in your menus. First, choose a theme that lacks motion, or replace an existing motion theme's background with a static image.

Next, drag an audio file or QuickTime movie into the Settings pane's Audio well. Remember that you must click iDVD's Motion button in order to hear (and burn) your menu's background audio.

Motion Menus and Motion Buttons

iDVD also applies motion to your movie buttons: small, thumbnail versions of the movies play back when the menu is displayed. You can even specify which portion of the movie plays: just select its button and then drag the slider that appears above the movie.

There are times when you might not want a movie's button to be a thumbnail movie. Maybe the movie is dark, and its thumbnail version is illegible. Or maybe you feel that the movie thumbnail distracts from the motion menu's background. In any case, simply select the movie's button and then uncheck the Movie checkbox that appears above it. You can now use the slider to choose a static thumbnail image for the movie.

Creating a Custom Motion Menu

You aren't limited to the motion menus that accompany iDVD. You can make any QuickTime movie a motion menu background: just press the ⌘ key while dragging the movie into iDVD. You don't even have to start out with a motion menu theme—you can also ⌘-drag a movie into a static theme, such as Brushed Metal.

If your motion menu movie is smaller than full-screen, iDVD scales it to fit. For the best video quality, make the movie's dimensions 640 by 480 pixels—those are the dimensions of iDVD's existing motion menu movies.

Because motion menus loop continuously, you'll want to design them so that they aren't visually jarring when they repeat. For some tips, see "Making Motion" on page 172.

Burning Your DVD

You've massaged your media and made your menus. What's next? Burning the final product onto a DVD-R blank. Simply double-click iDVD's Burn button and insert a blank disc. But before you burn, read the following tips.

Preview First

Before you insert that pricey blank DVD-R, preview your work by clicking iDVD's Preview button. Use the iDVD remote control to step through your menus and spot-check your video and slide shows. If your DVD contains motion menus or background menu audio, be sure to click the Motion button before previewing.

Run Lean When Burning

When burning a DVD, avoid running complex programs that put a lot of demands on your system. Also, consider turning off file sharing and quitting any disk-intensive programs.

Plus or Minus?

When shopping for blank DVD-R and -RW media, you're likely to see DVD+R and DVD+RW blanks, too. Avoid them—they use a different recording standard than most SuperDrives, and they won't work in them.

You can learn about the different standards that exist for DVD burning by reading Jim Taylor's superb DVD FAQ (www.dvddemystified.com).

Burning to DVD-RW Media

Apple doesn't publicize it, but the SuperDrive can read from—and write to—rewritable DVD media, called DVD-RW. A DVD-RW blank costs considerably more than a DVD-R blank, but you can erase and reuse it about a thousand times.

You can use RW media to test your project before committing it to a write-once DVD-R blank—but you have to trick iDVD. Here's how. Double-click the Burn button as you normally would, and insert a DVD-R blank when iDVD tells you to. Next, when you see iDVD's "Preparing" status message, press your keyboard's Eject key and replace the DVD-R with an erased DVD-RW. (To erase a DVD-RW, use Mac OS X's Disk Utility program.) iDVD will never know the difference.

But the DVD player in your living room probably will; currently, relatively few consumer DVD players can play DVD-RW media. If you're shopping for a new DVD player, do some tests at what DVD developers jokingly call Circuit City Labs: take a burned RW disc to your local electronics megastore and, with the permission of a salesperson, test it in a variety of players. (Several Web sites also contain lists of compatible players; you'll find links at www.dvddemystified.com/.)

After the Burn

If you're running low on disk space, you can reclaim a few gigabytes after burning your DVD. In the General area of iDVD's Preferences dialog box, check the box labeled Delete Rendered Files After Closing a Project. When you quit iDVD or open a different project, iDVD deletes the MPEG-2 movie files that it created from your original videos. But note that if you want to burn another copy of the disc, iDVD will have to encode its video all over again.

You can burn multiple copies of a DVD using iDVD, but you might find the job easier with Roxio's Toast Titanium, which provides disc-duplication features. Insert the DVD you burned and then copy its Video_TS and Audio_TS folders to your hard drive. You can burn additional copies of the disc by dragging these folders into Toast.

Toasting Slowly

If you do use Toast to burn additional copies of your DVD, consider burning at a slow speed, such as 1x or 2x. Burning at a slow speed can yield discs that play more reliably, particularly on set-top DVD players.

Watch the DVD burning process.
Burning a DVD

MPEG: Compressing Space and Time

One of the jobs iDVD performs is to compress your movies into MPEG format, the standard method of storing video on DVD-Video discs. Like JPEG image compression and MP3 audio compression, MPEG is a lossy format: the final product lacks some of the quality of the original. But as with JPEG and MP3, the amount of quality loss depends on the degree to which the original material is compressed.

Like JPEG, MPEG performs *spatial* compression that reduces the storage requirements of individual images. But video adds the dimension of time, and MPEG takes this into account by also performing *temporal* compression.

The key to temporal compression is to describe only those details that have changed since the previous video frame. In an MPEG video stream, some video frames contain the entire image; these are called *I-frames*. There are usually two I-frames per second.

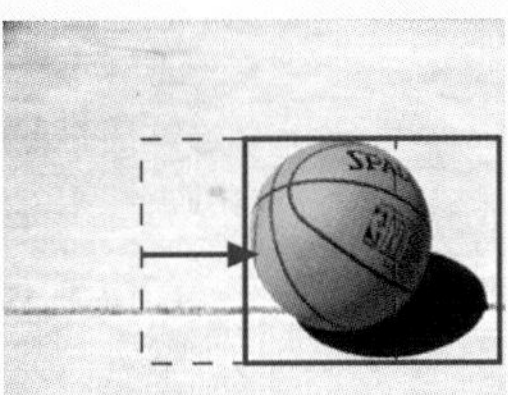

An I-frame describes an entire scene: "There's a basketball on a concrete driveway."

Sandwiched between those I-frames are much smaller frames that don't contain the entire image, but rather contain only those pixels that have changed since the previous frame.

"It's rolling toward the street."

To perform temporal compression, the video frame is divided into a grid of blocks, and each square is examined to see if anything has changed. Areas that haven't changed—such as the stationary background in this example—are simply repeated in the next frame.

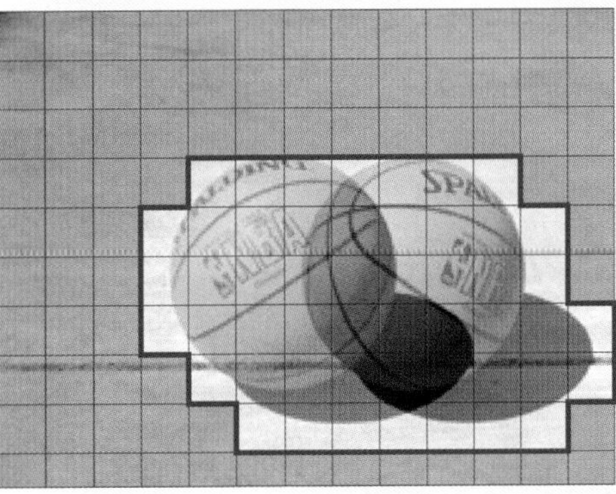

iDVD Tips

DVD Player Compatibility

You've polished your DVD interface until it glitters, burned it to a DVD-R disc, and have just inserted the final DVD in your boss's player. You press the play button—and nothing happens.

Welcome to The Incompatibility Zone. The sad fact is, some DVD players and personal computer DVD drives are unable to read DVD-R or DVD-RW media. Generally, older DVD players and drives are most likely to have this problem, but you may encounter it in newer players, too.

It's estimated that roughly 85 percent of DVD players can read DVD-R discs and that about 65 percent can read DVD-RW discs. Those are encouraging numbers, although they won't be of much solace if your player—or your boss's—is in the minority.

The bottom line is that if you're shopping for a new DVD player, be sure to verify compatibility with DVD-R (and, if you plan to use rewritable media, DVD-RW). And diplomatically inform your friends, family, and business colleagues that if they have problems playing your DVD, the fault lies with their players, not with your DVD.

Commercial Replication

If you need to have more than a few copies of a disc—for example, 2,000 training DVDs for a large company—you'll want to work with a replicator. Most replicators will now accept a burned DVD-R as a master, as well as the more traditional digital linear tape (DLT). Prices vary widely and, as you might expect, go down as the quantity you order goes up. For a run of about 2,000 discs, expect to pay a few dollars per DVD, a price that generally includes printing on the DVD from artwork that you supply.

Reverting Your Project

You've made some modifications that you don't like. Many programs have a Revert command that lets you get back to the last version you saved. iDVD lacks a Revert command, but you can simulate one: just reopen the project by choosing its name from the Open Recent submenu in the File menu. Click Don't Save when iDVD asks you if you want to save changes before reopening the project.

Saving a Customized Theme

You can save a customized theme as a "favorite" and apply it to future projects with one mouse click.

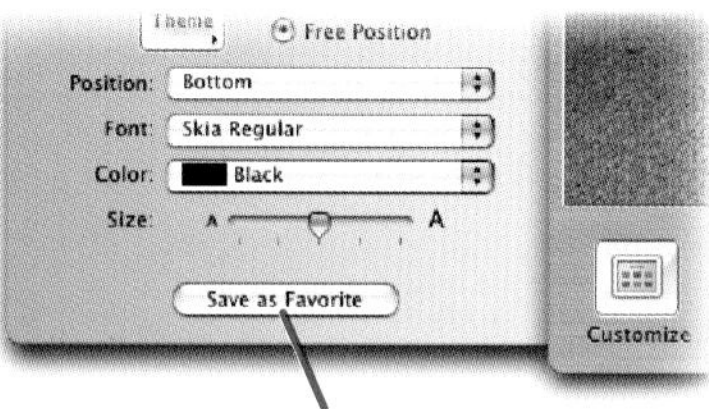

To save your design as a favorite, click the Save as Favorite button at the bottom of the Customize panel.

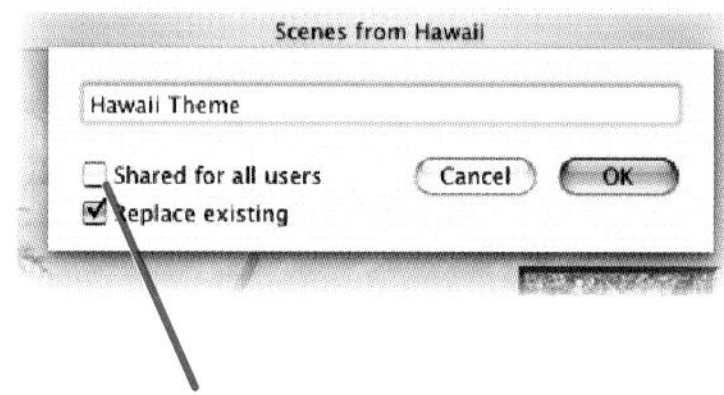

If you have multiple user accounts on your computer, you can check this box to make the custom theme available to all users.

The new theme appears in the Themes panel.

Project Management Tips

When you add a movie or set of images to iDVD, the program doesn't actually add those files to your project file. Rather, iDVD simply links to the existing files on your hard drive.

If you think you might be moving your project from one Mac to another, create a folder for the project and store all its assets in that folder.

If you opt for this authoring approach, you won't be able to use iDVD's media browsers to add content to your DVD. That's because these browsers simply create links to content that is stored elsewhere on your hard drive—in your Movies folder, for example, and your iPhoto library. Instead, copy the assets you'll be using into your project's folder, and then drag them into iDVD.

Broken link icon appears for missing assets.

If you copy just the project file—or if you delete an asset that you added to the project—iDVD displays broken-link icons for buttons whose assets are missing.

When you open a project containing broken links, iDVD gives you the opportunity to locate the missing assets. But you can avoid the hassle by keeping a project's assets in one folder and not moving them after adding them to iDVD.

To get the big picture of a project, choose Project Info from the Project menu.

You can change the DVD's name here. This doesn't change the name of your project file; rather, it changes the name of the final DVD. Because the DVD specification doesn't permit disc names to have spaces in them, iDVD will replace any spaces you type with underscores, as in Hawaii_Scenes.

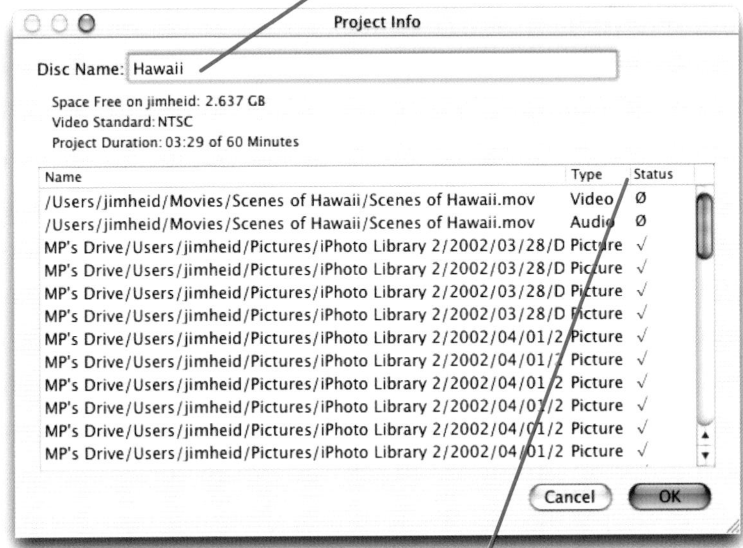

The Project Info window displays a list of the project's assets; its Status column indicates if any assets are missing.

More iDVD Tips

Customizing Watermarks and More

You can customize iDVD to have your own watermark graphic. Indeed, if you're adventuresome, you can customize many aspects of iDVD, including the size and shape of buttons, the motion movies of iDVD's themes, and more.

The iDVD application icon is a *package*, a kind of sophisticated folder that stores iDVD's program code and other resources. Modifying iDVD involves editing some of the resources in the iDVD package.

To open the package, Control-click on the iDVD application icon and choose Show Package Contents from the pop-up contextual menu. The Finder displays a directory window showing the contents of the iDVD package.

Double-click on the Contents folder, and then on the Resources folder. Within the Resources folder, locate the file named watermark.tif. Drag a copy of it to another folder so you'll have a backup. Now use the image editor of your choice to create your watermark graphic, and save it as a TIFF file under the name watermark.tif. Stash the graphic in the Resources folder, and it will appear on your DVD menus whenever the Show Watermark box is checked.

As you explore the Resources folder, you'll find that it also stores iDVD's themes. Each theme is a package, too. You can explore and modify its contents using the techniques I've just described. But take care to not throw away or alter any resources whose purpose you don't understand, lest you have to reinstall iDVD.

Making Motion

Subtle use of motion can make your menus more attractive and engaging.

In a DVD, a motion menu replays continuously, or loops, until the viewer makes a choice from the menu. Between each repetition, there's a momentary pause in the video and audio.

One way professional DVD developers work around this pause is to create lengthy motion menus—if a motion menu's movie is, say, five minutes long, only those few viewers who stare at the menu for five minutes will see the pause between loops.

iDVD doesn't permit this work-around—it limits motion menus to a maximum of 30 seconds. That means two things. First, design the menu's movie with looping in mind. If you plan the movie so that its last frame is identical to its first frame, each loop point will be harder to notice. Apple's designers did this in iDVD's motion menus. In the Global theme, for example, the globe rotates exactly once, and when the movie loops, its rotation is seamless—except, of course, for that unavoidable momentary pause.

As for actually creating the movies, you can use any video-editing program—iMovie, Final Cut Pro, Adobe Premiere. If you want the layered look visible in iDVD's Family theme, you'll need a program with compositing features, such as Final Cut Pro or Adobe After Effects.

You can also buy royalty-free libraries of animated backgrounds that you can use as motion menus. For links to sources of background animations, visit this book's companion Web site.

iDVD and AppleScript

iDVD provides thorough support for AppleScript, the automation technology that's built into the Mac OS. iDVD's AppleScript support enables you to create scripts that automate the creation and layout of DVDs.

The ultimate example of iDVD's autopilot features is a free utility that Apple has created called iDVD Companion.

Get links to background animations and other iDVD add-ons.
www.macilife.com/idvd

iDVD Companion is a program that runs alongside iDVD, adding a window containing three tabs that let you nudge buttons in single-pixel increments, align multiple buttons, and specify the exact pixel location of a menu's title—all things that iDVD alone can't do.

iDVD Companion also provides its own menus, and their commands do things iDVD can't do by itself. For example, iDVD Companion's Select Back Button selects the arrow-shaped back button that iDVD uses in menus and slide shows. Once that button is selected, you can use iDVD Companion's nudge features to change its position.

Other commands streamline the process of using iTunes songs as background music, importing iPhoto albums, and much more.

To download iDVD Companion and other iDVD scripts, visit www.apple.com/applescript/idvd.

The DVD-ROM Zone

A DVD can hold more than video and slide shows; it can also hold "computer files"—Microsoft Word documents, Acrobat PDF files, JPEG images, and so on. You might take advantage of this to distribute files that relate to your DVD's content. For example, if you've created an in-house training DVD for new employees, you might want to include a PDF of the employee handbook. Or, if you've created a DVD containing a couple of rough edits of a TV commercial, you might also want to include some PDFs that show the print versions of your ad campaign.

When a DVD-Video disc also contains "computer data," it's said to have a *DVD-ROM* portion. This ability to hold audio and video as well as computer files is one of the things that makes the DVD format so versatile. If users play the DVD in a living-room DVD player, those computer files are invisible. However, if they use that same DVD with a personal computer, they'll be able to access the files.

iDVD lets you exploit this versatility. As described on page 162, when creating DVDs containing slide shows, you can have iDVD copy the original images to the DVD-ROM portion. Simply check the box labeled Add Original Photos to DVD-ROM.

This option is ideal for photographers who want to distribute high-resolution versions of their images along with slide shows. You might also find it a useful way to back up a set of digital photos. The slide shows serve as a handy way to view the images, while the original, high resolution files are archived in the DVD-ROM portion of the disc.

The Status pane of the Customize drawer contains a pop-up menu labeled DVD-ROM Contents. Choose this option, and you can add computer files to the DVD by dragging and dropping them from the Finder.

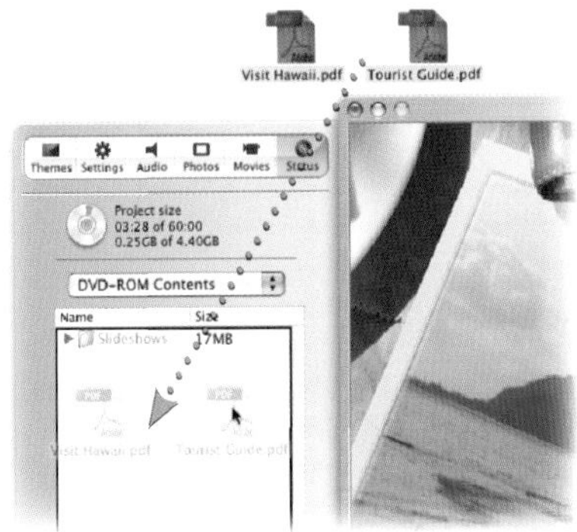

Setting the DVD-ROM Preference

If you always want to include a slide show's original images on your DVD, choose Preferences from the iDVD menu, click the Slideshow button, and check the box labeled Always Add Original Slideshow Photos to DVD-ROM.

Index

Index

F

G

H

I

Index

M

N

O

P

U

V

W

X

Y

Z